Tubelo's Gre

Mythos, Ethos, Female, Male & Priestly

Mysteries of the Clan of Tubal Cain

By Shani Oates

"Green fire is the sign of the new body
my love and yours engenders in the bed of dawn.
green fire licks all pride from the skull
soaks each trembling cell with heaven." Rumi

Mandrake of Oxford

Published by
Mandrake of Oxford
PO Box 250
OXFORD
OX1 1AP (UK)

ISBN 978-1-906958-07-7

Foreword

"A 'driving thirst for knowledge' is the forerunner of wisdom. Knowledge is a state that all organic life possesses; wisdom is the reward of the spirit, gained in the search for knowledge."

Robert Cochrane

It is often said that every picture tells a story, but the grandest narratives are excited by the symbols envisaged by creative use of the written language. The purpose of this book is to convey, in principle, the Word. And the Word conveys 'Revelation.' The onus is upon every wordsmith to engineer such within the mind of the reader. To work thus from the heart and with inspiration under the weight of age and expectation evokes the spirit of elation. But this elation, when yoked by tradition or convention strives relentlessly until it morphs consciousness into that happy liminality where poetic insight resolves all dichotomies. Here, the Word becomes a vision, a journey of transportation to the source of Truth. Hidden within the text, patterns and formulae arouse the reader to new levels of perception and discernment in alignment with the mystery of the Word.

A good teacher shies from informing you what to think, but nurtures instead the ability to intuit that for yourself and where and how to apply it. Clues are given, scattered among the text like treasure awaiting discovery. The more artful the teacher, the more varied and diverse the sources exploited in this purpose. Robert Cochrane declared his belief in the value of *"poetic inference, by thinking along lines that belong to the world of dreams and images."* In this long cherished tradition and in honour of two consummate artisans [both past Magisters of the Clan of Tubal Cain], the author structures her purpose in total accord with their principles. Our mentor, the late Evan John Jones was quite fond of reminding me to "keep it simple." By this he meant that in order to understand and express the mysteries proper, we must first release all desire and pretention to do so for its own sake.

Obvious as this may be, it first becomes essential to deconstruct our misconceptions or even pre-conceptions. This is achieved best by immersion in complexity – this serves to distract the ego sufficiently for that Zen moment to occur, allowing the revelation to percolate into a marvellous act of reductionism, leading effortlessly thereafter into acts of utter simplicity. Illumination strikes in release, we have to learn all to let it go. Within the following pages, the text subtly weaves the premise by which this may be achieved, presenting an emotive and magical journey in the truest sense of the Word.

Robin-the-Dart,
Magister of the Clan of Tubal Cain

MAY THE WORD PROTECT YOU FROM THE LIE

Michaelmas, 2009

Contents

Illustrations

Front Cover - 'The Fortunate Isle' © Nigel A. Jackson

Frontispiece 'Lux Mundi' - © Liza Miskievicz

Illustrations 1-7 - © Liza Miskievicz

Acknowledgments

This book is dedicated to all those who aspire to tread the path of One; to those who seek to answer the riddles within the works of Robert Cochrane [1931-1966]; to the Clan for their unstinting support and encouragement; To Nigel A. Jackson for his enigmatic rendition of the Mysteries within his beautiful cover design 'The Fortunate Isle'; to Liza Miskievicz for her profound realisation of my vision through her insightful and beautiful illustrations, and most especially to John [E.J. Jones 1937-2003] who brought new light to my Craft.

Benizens one and all!

Preface

The 'People of Goda, of The Clan of Tubal Cain' is an imperious title for a Tradition over which much speculation has been vocalised spanning some four decades. Numerous debates have questioned the many issues surrounding Robert Cochrane's astonishing life and tragic death. Most of all, his authenticity and seemingly natural abilities are called to task. These questions become purely academic when we consider that any magical system stands or falls on its intrinsic ability to produce results. The energy, power and exultation of 'the rush' experienced during ritual are the only accountable testimonies to authenticity required.

There exists between 'being' and 'source' a symbiosis, which throughout millennia, many have sought to rationalise and ultimately to control. Of those, too few realise that to abuse it, is to abuse ourselves. Sadly, many gifted pioneers in the esoteric and occult sciences are no longer here to guide us in our quest for knowledge and salvation. Blindly we grope around in the dark, trying to make sense of the legacies left to us, many of which are incomplete.

Correspondences between Cochrane and others over the last few years of his life, created the teaching foundation from which this book is principally inspired. It is hoped this work will reflect those intentions to serve as a fitting tribute to a man whose Tradition will always remain an enigma. Having studied his numerous letters, I may confirm that clues are there for those who choose to unravel Cochrane's profound philosophies. Yet, so dark is the veil surrounding him, that even intimate knowledge shared by former members of the Clan, or privileged insights awarded to those initiated into his magical stream, reveal very little; only through the work and its magics both within and without the Clan is it possible to truly comprehend the man behind the myth, and the myth behind the man.

For those who devise rituals based upon his works, be prepared to experience something very deep, raw and primal. Requiring no elaboration, the power lies within its simplicity. Subtle it is not. Of the many modern traditions, revived or otherwise, 'The Clan of Tubal Cain' bears little resemblance to Paganism, remaining true to its Craft roots. Indeed, Cochrane postulated that certain ideals and practices inherent within his teachings separated Witchcraft from Paganism. For him, the Mysteries of life, death and beyond generated the pursuit and enrichment of his Craft, with a zealous and unrelenting passion. This legacy continues.

As the seasons unfold, the Mysteries enjoined do more than celebrate the transitional cycle of life through death and where rituals rely more on the focussed power of the mind to work in altered states rather than subscribing to an overt show of pomp and circumstance. Conversely, it requires that we recognise our humanity in deference to our 'divinity;' moreover, it is a totally humbling experience to realise our puerility in the presence of such immense and all encompassing numinosity. Contained within its eclectic praxes are many fundamental truths, keys that have inspired magical consciousness for countless generations. These are not works for the feint-hearted. Out on the moors, in Moons both dark and full, elemental forces enthral and captivate inducing a sense of 'otherness' that pervades every nuance of being. Experienced at close quarters, the primal virtue imbued by the 'Wild Hunt' contrasts sharply with the ethereal and mystical beauty of the over arching Truth revealed.

Rites that clearly echo all forms of ancestor reverence honour the Clan family, both past and present. All spatial and temporal boundaries disintegrate as the true historical legacy unfurls, transcending the notoriety of its promulgator, Robert Cochrane. Either directly or indirectly, both Robert Cochrane and his successor Evan John Jones have been vehicles for the continuity of religious-historical practices claiming to reach back to the resurgence of craft activities and other occultisms in the wake of the call for reason in the 18th century. It preserves many elements of 19th century cunning and folk magics, centuries of Gypsy-lore, Medieval demonology, Middle Eastern mysticism and Anglo-Saxon Witchcraft. Speculatively, via tenuous threads, aspects of Bronze-Age animism are suggested, though these are by no means continuous or self-aware.

My mentor and further inspiration for the works recorded within this anthology, the late Evan John Jones, had, since the tragic death of Robert Cochrane in 1966, kept alive the magic and spirit of one of the 20th century's most enigmatic and gifted exponents of the Craft. Yet Cochrane's genius was such that it often eluded even those closest to him. When Evan John Jones invested me as Maid and Virtue holder for The Clan of Tubal Cain, it became my singular duty to hold in trust a sacred legacy that is rightly an esteemed historical tradition. This volume of work is testament to the inspiration generated by my connection to this vital stream. The charge to myself was great, to take what I was given, to hold it, but also to feed it and offer it back in service, as did my predecessor, the wife of Robert Cochrane and previous Maid to his Clan, over four decades ago. May the culmination of all that Time and knowledge serve you well, as we the People of Goda continue to serve The Covenant of The Clan of Tubal Cain.

My purpose in compiling selected articles to form this anthology is manifold, though primarily it provides a cohesive construct through which something of the nature of my path may unfurl. These works formulate duty to a public legacy serving as a useful tool of reference and catalyst for exploration of the Mysteries through a diverse heritage of folk custom, myth and legend in prose and verse. They present explicit and implicit characteristics of allegory and metaphor, highlighting the significance of poetic inference, of lateral thinking and of honouring gifts shared by those who cross our path. Shadows, strangers, symbients; mentors, masters, magi - all of whom are drawn along the web to shape our wyrd.

From conception to execution, the structure of this book is defined by the praxes articulated by Robert Cochrane, past Magister and founder of the Clan of Tubal Cain, who determined a three-fold gate to the Mysteries. To his model, I have set the context by which they may be perceived and comprehended, en-fleshing the iron bones of his craft therein. Finally, the means of illumination are exampled such that the reader may recognise the source of gnosis on all levels in all media through the art of legominism. Seemingly disparate subject matter is fused into a cogitative pattern, preparing the ground for further contemplation. Truth reveals itself, through the gnosis of realisation, from word and deed, from vision and dream.

May these words fuel yours.....................

Mythos

'Qayin - the Bone Smith'

14

1 Mythopoesis:

"I am a child of Earth and Starry Heaven; but my race is of Heaven alone." (Orphic Mysteries)

Through the poetic beauty of enigma, this statement succinctly expresses the core tenet of our Faith; it is the true history of the 'fall,' not of man but of 'angelic beings,' who as non-corporeal forms energised a potent symbiosis with an infant mankind, teaching and tutoring him selectively through manifest avatars, both spiritually and physically, perfecting and elevating our perceptions of true divinity. Annual narratives relating legend, myth and folk history are dramatized still, in which unfold themes of creation, existence and evolution in sync with the motion of the starry canopy above and of the seasons below it. They are *living* myths, in remembrance of our heritage and lineage as created beings and are in accord with ancient tradition, preserving and continuing our role in the evolution of that legacy.

Myth preserves the magic of creation, of life and the Mystery of death. Magic has been man's greatest tool because it employs the greatest force - that of his own Will! When this force is combined with Gnosis we are able to transcend the spirals of existence and achieve our true purpose. This is the greatest gift of all, and yet many have sought it and not prevailed. Over Time, the Craft has become the natural repository of myth, knowledge and magical practice as such things declined usage within society, either through suppression, ignorance or ambivalence. Sadly, much exists only in fragmentary forms within folklore or as superstitions. Other arcane wisdoms have been preserved in more discernable forms within certain branches of the Traditional Craft.

Myth celebrates cyclical Time; against this, annual celebrations of recurrence, suspended in the dreamtime of the eternal present, indelibly preserve the relationship between man, his environment, and the Universe. It is important to assert here the distinction between cycles of the year and of Time itself. Repetitive seasonal progression simply provides an appropriate vehicle by which the genus of myth unfolds. Cain rises, fecunds the Earth, the harvest is reaped, Cain dies. But this myth is not a story of the sowing and harvesting of grain associated with an agricultural deity, but that of the concept of Cain as the original and eternal progenitor. It relates to palingenesis - the cosmic cycle where deification of an old 'father' God occurs in his death as the new God, his son or younger version of himself is reborn. It is one of sacrifice, dispersal and re-union of itself.

These myths are again linked to celestial and cosmological micro-macrocosmic relationships of the Earth and Heavens, giving rise to our calendar, both esoterically and exoterically. Against this symbiosis, the unconscious mind utilises specific symbols that alert the conscious mind of its origins and purpose within this eternal cycle of life that removes any fear of death as a finality. History satisfies the conscious mind, myth satisfies the unconscious mind. In speculating the Nature of deity Philo said: *'true knowledge is to recognise our ignorance - all that we know of God is that we do not know him at all."* All we can do is make relative statements. If we accept that deity is both immanent and transcendent, that is both within and without both spirit and matter, we have to finally concede an absence of dualism or polarity. Instead, we have unity; no more, no less - the final Mystery, a revelation of the hidden. This dark light within the light is the ultimate paradox, a Truth beyond all comprehension.

As a devoted student of this revered arte and member of the Faith, I present here, a brief and subjective synopsis, a tentative and exploratory excursion into the written word, in the tradition of Raziel (noted scribe and record keeper) to the 'Great Higher Council of Seven,' the forebears and progenitors of all esoterica and magical neumenon within the Craft. And so remembering that we as seekers exist simultaneously in all three marked Time zones – the past in memory, the present in the moment, and the future in our expectations, we thus experience the artes of Philosophy, Hermetism and Mysticism, respectively. In expressing this unfurling history, myth fuses with history to project our perceptions of reality.

Ante-deluvian cuneiform texts, discovered in Middle Eastern regions once known as Sumer and Akkad (Mesopotamia) suggest an intriguing origin for mankind. From translations presented from these clay tablets, many have posited the possibility of advanced proto-'Shamanic' beings named *'Apkallu'* who may be considered synonymous with the *'Elohim'* (plural and of both genders). As great ethereal guardians, the 'Shining Ones' were bearers of deep knowledge and wisdom, who through their shared exalted status accelerated humanity's development beyond his natural evolutionary capacity. Speculative sexual impregnation by these beings producing a hybrid race is very probably the most popular and enduring legend.[1] Certainly, this belief is recorded in the distant myths of all peoples of the world, from China throughout Europe, its sub-continents and into Britain. Analysis of all extant creation myths conceal praxes fundamental to this premise; of superior beings in spirit or flesh becoming the benefactors of mankind, introducing animal husbandry, agriculture, smith-craft and the arts, both aesthetic and spiritual. Commonly these beings are attributed with 'God-like' status.

Given as seven in number, with an overall leader, they may total eight (a magical number of completion and a symbol of infinity). Known in ancient Egypt as the 'Ogdoad,' these were the 'Neter' Gods (natural primal forces) of *'Zep Tepi'* or the first 'primal' Time (Chaos). In Sumer (Shumer), one writer records them as the 'Shem-ur,' or people of the 'shining/fire-stone' (meteorite?). [2] Their magics thrive still in the rites of the Yakut shamans of Siberia, the Yezidis of Kurdistan and some forms of Traditional Craft, all drawn from the rich and varied mythologies and religious practises of Persia (Bounteous Immortals), Iraq (Mesopotamian deities) and Israel (Angels and the true Qabbalah), the recorded legends of the Mayan and Inca peoples, the Knights Templar, Cathars, Freemasons and Rosicrucians, whose ophidic doctrines gestate the entire opus of belief.

The Mythos of the 'People of Goda,' of The 'Clan of Tubal Cain' thus recognises an archaic spiritual heritage - of 'Sangraal' Mysteries, of sacred priest kings, aligned to the serpent or 'Dragon line of Divine Kingship,' a unique symbience that evolved from mankind's interaction with these enigmatic benefactors. It is this (spiritual) ancestral legacy that we celebrate, honour and revere within our rites and ceremonies. Traditional Craft draws heavily from the knowledge and wisdom imparted by these otherworld avatars, allowing us to fully explore the darker, deeper (hidden, secret) aspects of magical experience upon the souls' journey towards fulfilment. Robert Cochrane freely embraced 'Luciferian' Gnosis within the philosophy taught and practiced within his own group in the 1960s before a tragic and early death left much of his insightful legacy undeveloped. His research and understanding of the 'left hand path' (Vama Marg) lives on through the current incarnation of 'The Clan of Tubal Cain' by virtue of the 'Rites of Transmission.' This direct inheritance is awarded and experienced through disciplined and sacred rites of kingship and kinship. It is essential to be aware that the 'sinister' (Latin for) left-hand path contains none of the modern connotations frequently associated with this term, which is in fact harmonised with those dexter elements drawn from the right side. In this fashion, the body similarly reflects and emulates the divine harmonic of apparent duality. The right side is deemed positive and male; the left side is deemed negative and female. Thus the right hand is used for beneficent acts of blessing, invocation and invitation/ greeting. Conversely, the left hand exalts baneful acts of cursing/evocation and banishing. Yet both partake of the One vital essence, both banish intrusive energies, both attract protection, and both express the will and intent of the practitioner. For clarification of this arcane principle, a selection of worthy occultists, comment positively upon the Nature of Lucifer:

"This Serpent Satan, is not the enemy of Man, but he who made Gods of our race, knowing Good and Evil; he bade them, know thyself! And taught Initiation..."

Aleister Crowley

"Lucifer is the angelic entity presiding over the light of Truth as over the day of light. He is in us, as our mind, our tempter and redeemer, our intelligence and saviour from pure animalism..."

Madame Blavatsky

"Darkness adopted illumination in order to make itself visible..."

Robert Fludd –
17th century Alchemist and Hermeticist

"The Camaraderies that existed between Freemasons and Witches derived from their common allegiance to Lucifer, the Lightbearer. Lucifer was deemed to be the indwelling spirit within the human mechanism. The fall of the angels, was correctly understood to represent the incarnation of divinity in carnal flesh. ..."

W. E. Liddell –
20th century occultist, historian and traditional Witch

"Hermetic doctrine implies that the Cosmic Creator, the Supreme Being, God of Gods is not responsible for the creation of the world. This was the task of the demi-urge, or 'son of God,' and the seven governors...Within the Corpus Hermetica, Adam is more than human, he is divine and belongs to the race of star demons, the divinely created governors…he is even said to be the brother of the creative word, demi-urge, son of God, the second God who moves the stars…"

Prof. Yates – 20th century academic of Theology

From these examples, it is clear that insightful views over recent centuries assert that Lucifer, the Lightbearer, is wholly unrelated to the dualistic personification of moral evil named Satan by the Church. Rather, he is a composite form, an archetypal figure of pre and non-Christian prominence based on an amalgam of Middle Eastern myths and beliefs concerning the 'fallen' angels, the Watchers and their progeny, later absorbed by the expanding philosophies of Greek and Roman cultures and subsequently bound into Grail myths of many diverse cultures.

In historical legend, Grail Kings are reputed to carry the ancient bloodline of the 'House of the Dragon' (Welsh/Celtic Pendragons), a Greek term for serpent, and the ultimate symbol of sovereignty. These amorphous creatures have more in common with the actual forms of snakes (both land and sea) and the crocodile than the fire-breathing creatures of popular myth. Egyptian pharaohs were in fact, anointed with the fat of the Nile crocodile before the placement of the 'wadjet' crown, the sacred serpent (cobra), symbolic of the wisdom and divinity of kings upon his brow. [3]

The keys to mankind's ancestry lay in Egypt and the Middle East during the ninth millennia BCE., manifesting later during the establishment of dynastic Egypt and Sumer, a Time they record as 'when kingship came down from the heavens.' Here, the first order of priest kings were granted sovereignty over their own kingdoms, authorised by their obeisance and loyalty to the Elder Gods (Ogdoad and Anannage, respectively), the 'Shining Ones' referred to in all Egyptian and Middle Eastern texts and written forms. Several thousand years later, Hebrew redactors and compilers of the Pentateuch (five books of Moses) would record these beings first as the 'Elohim,' then later as 'Angels.' Their deeds, subject to distortions of Time and purpose would precipitate the 'fall,' the grossly misunderstood and misinterpreted record of the advancement of the race of man (of Earth) by the interaction of the race of ethereal beings (of the stars and other dimensions) known eponymously as the 'Shining Ones.'

Throughout ensuing years, confused mythologies placed the original 'Nephilim/ Elohim,' the lofty ones of heaven, as the morally corrupt 'fallen angels.' Eventually subservient to Satan, the ultimate fallen angel and leader of their host they are consigned to apocryphal annals, myths and fairy tales. It is not without irony that the Church chose to immortalize these beings as serpents, preserving a key to their true form.

Fascinating figurines from Sumer (Middle East) circa 5000BCE. exhibit curious serpentine features very similar to those of Carpathian and Transylvanian origin. A script discovered in Transylvania over 1000 years older than those found in Sumer, mentions key figures of particular relevance to the unfolding cosmologies of much of the known world; Enki, Anu and the city of Ur. Royal graves unearthed at Ur contain Gold mined from the Black Sea; this is especially significant as the 'Watchers' were recorded in legend as a mining community. The Carpathian Tribal Warriors were known as the Pict-sidhe (pixies), and the seven foot mummified remains of their Chiefs are far better preserved than anything discovered in Egypt of much later dates.[4] From this region of the Black Sea, later confederate tribes of 'Celtic' speaking peoples migrated into Ireland and Scotland. It is especially noteworthy that the old Irish word for serpent is 'sumaire,' and the tradition of the 'Shining Ones' lived on in the legends of the *'Tuatha de Danaan'-* the 'People of Anu.' Serpents have always denoted archaic wisdom and sometimes forbidden knowledge, preserved among a selected few, protected from the profane, those outside the 'elect.'

Cuneiform tablets steeped in history, offer support to the many half-truths and anomalies previously alluded to within many tracts of esoteric lore. Translations of relative cosmological creation myths over the last few decades describe how inscrutable 'Angelic' forms became guardians of mankind but also the alleged cause of inter-racial wars and much destruction. Fragmentary though these records are, suggestions that strife between leading members of the 'Council' (of elders/judges) instigated a localised flood, help us to clarify how its survivors forged nebulous and mythical links of a continued interaction between the Gods and mankind.

Two central tanist deities, Enlil (Lord of Spirits/Air) and Enki (Lord of Earth and Sweet Waters) are described along with five other council members, one of whom is female. Partner to Enlil, this 'Lady' became known as the divine Mother, benefactress of man and epitome of 'wisdom.' The distant 'Anu,' the 'Most High,' became the supreme and ultimate authority, rarely concerning himself with the affairs of man. This history considers the testimony of the Sumerian King lists that stresses the import of *sceptre, throne, staff* and *sacred tiara*, the Royal Regalia presented to the first King and his heirs thereafter as symbols of their imbued divinity and right to rule – an early pre-cursor to the medieval feudal system. This era, when 'Kingship was lowered from Heaven,' witnessed the creation of a new social structure of city states, no longer ruled by Anunnaki/Anannage deities, but under evolving self rule - the 'Anu-oint-m-en-ted' carriers of the 'divine seed and holy blood' - the Sangraal. This indicates how the 'Priest-King' became empowered in legend to mentor his people spiritually and materially; martial empowerment came much later, and the sword was then included within the list of royal insignia as terms of office. As warriors, the Kings also became responsible for protection and therefore this role was subject to sacrifice, becoming true 'Fisher Kings' of legend.

Epic sagas of hoary age record sibling 'rivalries' between co-regents and brothers, but also of how for the most part, they remained loyal and committed to the advancement and development of the human race. Their immortality has since been secured as the model for all consequent 'opposing' factors within mainstream religions of the world, wherein, through the over pious and zealous priesthoods, they assumed a polarised duality.[5]

Ironically, the newly evolving city-states became increasingly subject to an over-arching, all enveloping perception of deity. The highest exemplar was Marduk, in whose glory many earlier texts were overwritten. It was said the old Gods became jealous; in fact myth recalls how the 'elder' son (Enlil) withdrew his protection from the people of Sumer. This 'action' expresses their belief in the causality that subsequently opened the gates to invasion by warring Akkadians (Semitic tribes of Amorites, Syrians and Elamites) allowing them to enter and conquer the vulnerable and exposed populace circa 1960BCE. One loyal, high-ranking dynastic family are recorded as fleeing Sumer to move northwards to Harran and into Canaan, where they were able to thrive. This lineage is of course that of the Biblical patriarchs, the family of Abraham and his progeny, known to be loyal followers of (Enlil) El Elyon, El Shaddai and ultimately formulated as the one God 'Jehovah' under established Hebrew kingship circa 1000BCE. Importantly, this deity was believed to have pledged a *'Covenant'* of Faith with his people (i.e. those of his Tribe or Clan), forever separating them from the remaining Middle East, dynastic Egypt and beyond. According to legend, Marduk remained triumphant in Sumer. Adopted by invading Akkadians under King Hammurabi, he became elevated to Supreme God, above even their own numerous deities.

The cuneiform tablets extol the adverse actions of the 'younger' brother, Enki as he nurtures Adam and Eve after their expulsion from Eden. Eventually he initiates the fabled Kingship through interaction with

Inanna, the divine feminine principle. Typical of all founding cosmologies, divine genetics raised and accelerated the evolution of mankind, advanced through Cain, firstborn son of Eve, mytopoetically fathered by Enki himself.

Remember that in the Enuma Elish and the epic of Gilgamesh, and indeed across much of the ancient world, in sacred texts other than the (sadly prejudiced) OT, along with Divine Kingship came ALL civilizing arts. A city by definition is the place of non-nomadic residence, ergo the cessation of a pastoral lifestyle. All cities are fed by agriculture. The two then are clearly synonymous with progress and evolution. The (still) nomadic Semites frowned upon this infringement and land appropriation condemning its proponents. But it is simple really: Cain and Abel are 'brothers,' not in our modern usage or terminology - only relatively (pun) as sons of God, His divine creation, and only one was deemed obedient (in their world view). The other desired change, innovation and evolution, thereby sought to act in apparent adversity to that (perceived) rule. Hence the role of liberator, opener of the ways etc is taken from 'Lucifer' through Cain and all his progeny. His 'punishment' or mission (a matter of perspective) was to wander across the world, bringing his innovation to all mankind. Paradoxically he became the 'wanderer' who brought foreclosure to the nomadic lifestyle.

Nonetheless, confused and contradictory histories record both brothers as man's benefactors, imparting agriculture and animal husbandry, providing man with a means to survive. Through the crafts variently imparted, they cultivated wisdoms, seemingly dissonant to each other, endowing spiritual advancement and esoteric experience via mentors and sages in the form of avatars. In this way, Enki 'opposed' Enlil, providing a plausible origin behind the label 'adversary' - the Satan (thereafter perceived as the perennial enemy of mankind.)

Curiously, *the 'Satan'* does not appear in mainstream Judaism, or any other ancient religion of the Middle East, only in Western Christendom, a post Jesus imperialist myth, a fabulous lie, a sad victim and necessity of incumbent socio-religious politics. Satans within the Old Testament are rarely mentioned, and then only as obedient servants of God; indeed, King David himself is referred to as *a 'satan'* (adversary) of the Philistines. In fact, nowhere in the Old Testament are *'satans'* meant in any way to imply anything malevolent or evil. These 'servants' of Jehovah within Judaic texts are named - *'bene-ha -Elohim,'* which simply translates as - sons of (male and female) Gods. Only later were these forms rendered as sinister beings, especially by later redactors of the New Testament. Heavily influenced by Persian dualism and confused Gnostic teachings (gleaned possibly from the Essenes), these scholars, in order to conceal their insecurities and inadequacies, firmly placed this adversarial personage in dialectic opposition to Yahweh as an expression and embodiment of ultimate evil.

Within the Old Testament lies an oft misquoted and misunderstood phrase from the prophet Isaiah (loyal to El Shaddai in the form of one 'brother' or Tutelary deity) concerning the fall of a 'corrupt' King of Babylon (loyal to the other): *"How you are fallen from Heaven, day star, son of the Dawn"* (Hel-el-ben Shahar). Hundreds of years later, when compiling theological instruction, 4th century Latin scribes working for the venerable Church fathers (Augustine and Jerome etc), interpreted this title, 'son of the Morning Star' (Venus) as 'Lightbearer' or 'Lucifer.' Sadly, this name has since been used to denote the negative Christian concept of an evil Satan, God's adversary. Subsequent redactors and teachers exemplified Lucifer's role as tempter and seducer of the faithful. This damaging fabrication has completely biased his role and position throughout history and is in absolute contra-distinction to all original constructs and composite characters from across the archaic Middle East. They are to be summarily dismissed and ignored; for our purposes, they are complete anathema.

Sumerian 'Tablets of Destiny,' inscribed with sacred symbols of God equate with the 'Tablets of Testimony' of Moses (*not* to be confused with the later composite Ten Commandments that had been influenced by Hammurabi's Law codes and those lifted from Pharaonic negative confessions within the 'Coming Forth by Day'). Through these oracular laws, instructions were given as to how man should live. According to the Gods, this moral code upheld the Laws of the Universe, of Fate and Destiny, what has always been and will always be. Later these tablets were to be represented in many magical traditions as 'The Zaddakim,' the two pillars that upheld the Earth, Mishpat and Zedek (Boaz and Joachim of Tubal Cain). Both Enlil and Enki as tanist deities are the first acknowledged guardians of these 'Tablets,' founding almost all subsequent twinnings throughout the following millennia of mythological associations. Solomon is reputed to have inherited this sacred text in the form of the (true) 'QBL,' the tradition of light and knowledge, known in some esoteric circles as the 'Book of Raziel.' He who possessed the (true) QBL (Qabbalah), possessed 'Ram,' the highest expression of cosmic knowingness.

It is noteworthy that many great men in the histories of Magical and

Mystery traditions have incorporated this term into their names including Avram (Abram/Abraham) and the Indian God Rama. Throughout India, Tibet, Egypt and the later 'Celtic' speaking world, which included the Druids, the word Ram indicated a high degree of universal aptitude. The QBL (Qabbalah) is not to be confused in any way with the KBL (Kabbalah), an entirely separate system meaning to twist or confuse; the two structures were quite distinct within early Judaism. While the KBL became the more widely accepted and known form, especially since the Middle Ages, the QBL, has remained an enigma, a closed Mystery School, where next to nothing other than its existence is known to outsiders.

With regret, it too is not free from considerable bias; it claims to teach that Enlil (assumed to have developed into the template for Yahweh) is in fact the deceiver, not Enki (who conversely assumes the role of Lucifer), whose deceptions began with Adam and Eve, continuing on through Time. This knowledge, once available to a privileged few, may even be the inspiring source that moved the great Magian prophet Zarathustra (Zoroaster) to elevate Ahura Mazda (meaning 'Shining Serpent Lord of Light' - Enki) as supreme authority, and to demote the great deceiver, 'the lie,' Ahriman (Enlil) as his almost eternal rival. Ironically, many hundreds of years later, Church authorities chose to translate these in contra-distinction, placing Yahweh/Jehovah as the Supreme power, with Satan/Lucifer as the great deceiver!

As a speculative summary of historical and mythological events, considerable revision would reasonably be required to replace it with one where all positive involvement with mankind, evolutionary deeds and gifts were rightfully attributed to either one figure or to both equally. Mythical versions of this cosmological truth are of course recorded within many Syrian, Assyrian, Egyptian, Sumerian, Babylonian and Persian texts and tablets. Some of these additionally record Inanna/Ishtar as the bride of God - the Shekinah, celebrated chiefly as 'Wisdom' and later represented by the Divine Sophia. Though the Bible is not an accurate transcript of history, it had been the only one available to the Western world for over 2000 years. Thankfully, we now have many other annals available to us, presenting an almost unanimous alternative to it.

Within some Craft history is held dear a Mythos encompassing a spiritual legacy and ancestry, relating a line of mythical descent, not from Seth, son of Adam, but of Cain, son of Enki/Lucifer, whose status has forever branded many with the 'Mark of Cain.' This invisible symbol of an inherited birth right is held within the etheric body upon the 'third eye,' the Ajna Chakra, seat of wisdom within the brain. This mark, a blessing and protection (not a curse) given to Cain, was a symbol of his sovereignty, a graphic representation of 'sacred kingship.' Revered and utilised by Phoenician/Canaanite peoples for many hundreds of years, it became later popularised by peoples known by the later 'Celtic' language groups and Anglo-Saxon people. Historically, this symbol is an equal-armed cross within a circle. Interestingly, the Akkadian word for kingdom/sovereignty is 'Malku,' and in true Qabbalistic tradition, all Mesopotamian Kings 'married' the 'Mother' of Creation in order to maintain the blood-line, the legacy of the aforementioned Dragon Queen (Tiamat), Mother of Enki. According to accounts given by the Church Fathers, worshippers of the Persian God Mithra were rumoured to receive a cogent sign upon the brow from the 'Devil' himself.

Accordingly, the ancient Egyptian Fraternity of the Royal Court of the Dragon re-established circa 2170BCE by Queen SobekNeferu (beautiful of the mighty crocodile, spirit of the 'messah q'ayin' - serpent ruler) incorporated this enigmatic insignia into her Royal Regalia.[6] The eternal serpent, the Ouroborous (circle), symbol of wisdom and wholeness (holiness), surrounds the cross of the four earthly elements, which when combined produce the 5th, the central point of focus. Similar to a Carpathian 'Sun' symbol, circa 3000BCE it maintains hesitant links to the Transylvanian (shamanic) hereditary priests of the 'blood.' This cross of the elements and Sun symbol curiously morphs into both the symbol for Venus and the Orb as part of the Royal Regalia of Kingship. In myth, this Regalia is passed in turn from divine rulers to mankind. So it is with many esoteric and sacred traditions, for only when something has been shared within the unity of spirit, can it truly represent the totality of the divine principle. Typically, this initiates a pre-dominantly Matrilinear descent reflected throughout varied esoteric traditions that practice or assert this maxim. The circle enfolding a cross symbolises the all seeing eye of divinity, associated commonly with Enki and Ra. It is the 'Ayin,' a Mystery of nothingness, the Void, a total blackness of light - hence, within the Qabbalah 'Ayin' is Absolute Nothing. It is cogently the alchemical symbol for gold and for Solar power. [7]

Metaphysically, the letter, Q (khu), developed from this profound and complex Venus symbol representing Q 'ayin-Queen. It denotes the ultimate Q 'ayin'ship of Venus, Isis, Kali and Nin-khursag - all 'black but beautiful,' the original gene source and Mother of mankind. The Hermetic symbol for the all Seeing Eye replaces the cross within the circle, with a

dot, (the central 'nux', the point of focus and energy). Thus it becomes
the 'Eye of Ra,' kamakala of Indian mystics, central point of all creation
within the totality of sacred space, the seed within the womb, and the fire
or generative spirit within a working 'circle' or sacred area.

Q'ayin also means kenning or knowing, an attribute gifted to man in
the form of smith-craft, a pre-requisite skill of the first priest kings. An
artificer of metals was a true ruler, a Q'ayin. The legendary smith and
Priest King of Kish, Mes-kalem-dug (Tubal-Cain), descendant and anointed
of Enki, is still revered as a Master craftsman by Freemasons today. Within
the tradition of The Clan of Tubal Cain, we especially acknowledge his
succession to the chief position of Atabba (Adama), as recorded in the
Sumerian clay tablets. Remember, that within the esoteric tradition of the
QBL, the first couple are often referred to as the 'Tree of Knowledge of
Good and Evil' and the Tree of Life, which are most probably one and the
same. Astonishingly, the verb to anoint can be etymologically traced to
the stem – *'messah'* and *'mu-hus'* (Sumerian forms), meaning serpent, and
anointed serpent/true lord of the blood, respectively.

The 'Cain' dynasty dominated various kingdoms from Ur, in southern
Mesopotamia, to Assur, in the North, all holding 'Malku[t]' heritage; this
sacred 'dragon' (serpent) - line was preserved in various Mesopotamian
sources outside the Bible, whose exponents promoted the distinct Sethian
line. From within this line descended the Hametic/Shemite/Semite lineage;
one of its claimants, the Pharaoh Raneb (c2890BCE) became famous for
his introduction of the worship of the legendary 'Goat of Mendes.'
Originally a 'Ram,' it later became associated with the goat of Capricorn,
the Goat of Azazel, whose symbol (of attainment) is the reversed
pentagram. The emerald jewel of illumination is placed between the horns
in this position; when upright, it becomes the sacred 'jewel' of the divine
feminine placed between the open 'legs' of the pentagram. Consequently
the Goat of Mendes is the true Sabbatic Goat with its Lunar ritual of
reflection and enlightenment, now synonymous with the cyclic, monthly
'Shabbat' feast. A possible origin for the word ritual is rooted within the
Sanskrit word 'ritu,' meaning the red-gold essence (but sometimes black).
Symbolic of the magical voice, the 'qoul' or 'call' refers to the womb, or
(Latin form) uterus, meaning utterer - the word or logos was the 'serpent,'
the holy spirit that created life.

Centuries later, Gnostic inheritors of this wisdom, the Cathars,
allegedly employed many of these symbols in their unorthodox practises,
leading to their frequent alliance to heresy (meaning free choice), an option

forbidden by the Church. Personal attainment had been replaced by the transference of grace via a priest, strictly controlled and monitored by Ecclesiastical authorities. The 'Goat of Mendes' became identified with the Devil and his alleged feasts; individual knowledge. Enlightenment or attainment of any spiritual Nature became actively discouraged by an unstable Medieval Church anxious to monitor our evolution whilst safe-guarding its own.

Lunar worship was instanced throughout much of the ancient Middle East as practised by early Israelites and more latterly by Mandeans, Sabbeans and Muslims. Variant forms of: Nanna, Min, Sin, Anu, Enlil/Yahweh etc, were qualified to carry the (Lunar) horns of kingship, conferring sovereignty through sacred priestesses as chalice 'bearers' of active 'kingship' to the next appointed King. In continuance of this, The Clan of Tubal Cain upholds the Horned (Horn King) God as 'Lord of Women' instanced where the Magister/Master holds keys to the Women's Mysteries, countered by the Maid who holds keys to the Male Mysteries.

Mercurial aspects within the writings of Hermes/Thoth, similarly connect him with the Moon (believed by some to be Ham, son of Cain, but Melchizadek by others), preserving many alchemical secrets commonly associated with the line of Cain. Unsurprisingly, the earliest Masonic teachings name Thoth as inheritor of the Wisdom of Lamech from Cain's line. Wisdoms inscribed upon sacred (two pillars or) tablets of destiny that speak of 'Anunnaki' sciences and lore, become later transcriptions by Thoth/Ham onto the legendary Emerald Tablet *('Tabula Smaragdina')*.

This jewel of illumination (the sacred eye) fallen from Lucifer's own brow, is popularly upheld as the 'true' holy grail. Eastern Masonic orders still maintain a Dragon (serpent) based doctrine where they travel the 'Path of the Serpent' in the 6th degree venerating the 'Lord of Light' and bearer of the Grail. Moreover, the 'Crux Ansata' (Ankh) developed from the Phallic Tau cross of Hermes/Thoth. It is also the last letter in many ancient languages, the Omega of the Chi-Rho (the Alpha - Omega) representing union of the Ouroborous with the Tau cross. As such it is a variation of the 'Orb' of sovereign regalia; together they symbolise unity and completeness of a divinity that brings forth everlasting life, fecundity and abundance. It is divinity carnate in flesh.[8]

Inheritors preserve this sacred legacy of spirit, of 'fire in the blood'; gifted from mythical Anunnaki progenitors. Reputedly it rests within several Royal Houses across the continent, selective historical religious sects including the Albi-gens (of elven blood), the Cathars (the pure), the

Templars, the Rosicrucians, Medieval Hermeticists, Freemasons and of course, last but not least, Hereditary and Traditional Craft families and Clans.

Aryan races from India to Ireland additionally maintain a belief in the powers of a 'divine' king, bearer of spirit infused blood from the Dragon Queen, the Mother of all and Fateful Sangraal. In quoting Robert Cochrane who said, *"In fate and the overcoming of fate, lies the true Grail,"* we realise that little has changed in several thousand years. 'Fate' in ancient Sumer was not deterministic; they believed, as do we, that apotropaic rites may influence the prevalence of Fate. Magical formulae used in both Egypt and Mesopotamia, may differ little in fact from our own, although the purpose for their execution may have. For exorcisms, quarter standards were raised, a circle of flour (cast with ash until the last century) delineated the 'sacred' area, which was often swept and sprinkled with water; incense made from juniper; cedar and myrrh were and are burned as offerings and purification.

Interaction with deity through amulatory and talismanic magic created alternative realities to those forecast; it was a symbiosis of astrology and magic that totally encompassed their lives. Like our ancient forebears, we too employ divination to learn our 'Wyrd' - the interplay of all possibilities. Though we may often find ourselves manipulated, our fate is not always insurmountable. Dawn was always favoured by our ancestors for acts of magic when Venus, the Morning Star was still visible in the soft light of the rising Sun. Solar worship prevalent throughout much of the World, especially in the Middle and Far East, Europe and India, enjoyed many revivals over Millennia, despite directives from the priests of Jehovah/Yahweh against it.

Angelic Forms:

Legendary 'bird-men' or 'shamen' are attributed with considerable magical powers; as winged beings of light their prowess resounds in myth and legend across the length and breadth of the globe we call Earth. Frequently described as feathered serpents, thunderbirds and angelic forms, myths enshroud their familiar interactions with sorcery, death, regeneration and healing. Often presented as androgynous beings, many of them denote perfection and completion. This may of course be symbolic, as we carry both genders, though rarely in 'perfect' balance or harmony.

We frequently work with forms deemed to be 'angelic' or 'fey' as they continue to instruct our progress towards individual and group Gnosis.

Sadducees, the original Hebrew priestly cast, believed that all divine emanations were aspects of ultimate divinity. Their word *'malakh,'* meaning 'Shadow of God,' more accurately expresses this concept than the later Greek - *'angelos,'* meaning messenger. The ultimate 'Shadow of God' is of course the Son behind the Sun: *'Lucifer,'* the hidden light and Gnostic principle of pleromic transformation. Thus it is that this brilliant light burns into our subconscious, searing and exposing all issues, forcing sub-summation. Working with this intense energy creates the constant facing of ONE's shadow self, like the Cathar 'perfects,' the drive towards wholeness is relentless; the pace is exacting and the road painful. Enki as Lord of the Earth and Sweet Waters was to the Sumerians, a bringer of culture and wisdom, never a preserver of the status quo.

Further back even than Lunar Cults, were those ascribed to Stellar virtue; evoked in high places, four (of the seven) royal stars named 'Watchers' (perceived as guardians and teaching benefactors of mankind) had dedicated symbols traced in the air with torches or ritual wands (symbolising air) to accompany the hallowing of their sacred names. As rulers of the elemental kingdoms they were awarded the following correspondences:

ALDEBARAN	SPRING	EAST	TAURUS	BULL
REGULUS	SUMMER	SOUTH	LEO	LION
ANTARES	AUTUMN	WEST	SCORPIO	EAGLE
FOMALHAUT	WINTER	NORTH	AQUARIUS	ANGEL/MAN

These sentinels eventually evolved into powers of the Cardinal Winds (perceived poetically in the Apocrypha as the 'Four Horsemen of the Apocalypse'), then latterly by Lunar and Solar cults who afforded them new, complex and varied correspondences evidenced as Archangels in Qabbalistic and other esoteric systems. It is pertinent here to recall the sanitization and concealment of many of these forms by the Church, for example: 'Mika-el,' originally a Kundalini Daka, fiery Archangel and Serpent of the Earth, became the sterile St Michael, slayer of serpents. The fiery 'Celtic' smith and Wisdom deity 'Bride' became St Bridget, the subjugated patron of 'womenkind.'

Angelic script partaking of the Angelic substance to which it subscribes, adopts its own divinity and power, becoming an organic and sentient link to the unseen world. Robert Cochrane understood this, stressing that sigils have universal significance, whose expression within the Craft supports the Mysteries stimulating magical comprehension.

"Symbols contain the seeds of their own revelation, the virtue (power) of which changes with each group/era using it." The 'Clan of Tubal Cain' utilises symbols both old and new including many forms of 'Angelic' script. He also expressed the Mysteries as a means by which man may *'perceive his own inherent divinity.'* He postulated that students of the Mysteries are seekers of truth and wisdom where magic is but a by product, a secondary device of little real consequence. For him, the Craft was a:

> "Mystical religion, a revealed philosophy, with strong affinities to many Christian beliefs. The Faith is concerned only with truth; that brings man into closer contact with the Gods and himself – the realisation of truth as opposed to illusion – fulfilled only by service."

He even described himself as a member of the 'people,' a simple 'Pellar,' not a 'Witch' and certainly not 'Pagan.' This is fairly typical of Traditional Craft who understand that it is not a remnant of a fertility religion, therefore does not practise seasonal rites per-se nor engage in Nature worship. It is a *priesthood* in the mold of the ancient Mystery Schools. Virtue here (accumulated/inherited spirit guide/s in the form of a Clan Egregore) is passed from male to female in accordance with ancient Law and Rites of Transmission. All Mystery teachings agree that within the Universe, many life-forms and intelligences exist outside the confines of matter, co-existing independently. Mystery stems from *'mysterion,'* which translates as 'sacred secret,' and originates in the verb - *'musteion,'* meaning 'to close the eyes or mouth,' a vital part of preserving the Mysteries, generally among initiates strictly confined to their own esoteric circles.

Men's and Women's Mysteries were traditionally separated, presided over by the Maid and Magister respectively. From the Maid the men of her Clan were taught law, truthfulness, bravery, smith-craft, commerce, and the arts, both visual and of civilisation (idealised during the Middle Ages as Courtly Love). According to Robert Cochrane, these find expression in the: spear, cockerel, pillar, flail, Sun, ladder, skull and crossed bones. From the Master or Magister, women learned about the cycle of death, of creation and destruction, of fertility and the feminine arts: wisdom, intuition, empathy, sensation and love. These are traditionally revealed through the vase, lantern, glove, rod, sword, scourge and shift/robe. Though taught separately, the two groups were brought together for the 'Nine Knots' (rituals) of the year. Access to these keys is facilitated in many ways, some of which utilise the four elements, generally represented symbolically or by cardinal spirits of the compass. The Mystery Schools have always provided training programmes to facilitate the joy, knowledge and awareness of Gnosis.

Within the Medieval period, for just a short Time, several artists appeared to have been divinely inspired, portraying the Tree of Life (Otz Chim), upside down, with its roots in the heavenly spheres and the branches tantalisingly poised within reach of man. It was thus his mission to clamber back up the tree (reminiscent of Jack and the Beanstalk) into heaven, to stand in the 'presence' of God. This became the goal of all mystics, more than a ladder, it shifts us from Earth to heaven, suggesting a Divine origin that is forever reaching down to us, inviting us 'up' to share and partake of its Divine essence. We are not therefore leaving nor negating the material plane, just acknowledging 'something other' on its own plane.

Even for theurgists, this means certain operative forms of thaumaturgy become requisite, for we must first 'draw down from heaven the mystic fire - the breath of the Shekinah' to enable us to ascend. We cannot complete the 'shift' without it. Ascent is impossible without a vehicle and the power to operate it. The Compass is such a tool and the 'Love under Will' of both God and man combined is the force to generate the shift. The wider implication of how that force descends from Kether to Malkuth along the central trunk of that great tree, is manifest within the Luciferian tenet of the **Lux Mundi**. We are mirror to that light, the personification of Himself as all creation. This is analogous too with the legend of Sophia, who desired to look, to know that reflection, and so she also 'fell.'

All light reflects, all shadows absorb - the angels/Sephiroth are both light and shadow, thus by default is man, as we are the reflex of the angel, the manifest cause. We yearn to re-trace that descent back to the All-Source: through experience we are led; through interaction we achieve understanding; through love are we refined; through will do we attain. We move through faith, belief, experience and truth. There we find the indwelling spirit, She who dwells within and without, the living breathing breath of life, the tree itself, whose body we climb, when all are redeemed so is She, the most precious Tree of all. Her arms embrace us within its folds. She is the spirit of the Tree, the Grace of All. Life is beautiful because of Her. Thus through the **Lux Mundi** and the **Anima Mundi** conjoined within ourselves do we become whole within the 'sight' and 'presence' of the All.

The writings of Robert Cochrane preserve a great many working praxes of 'The Clan of Tubal Cain.' Obviously, over Time, various disparate ideas have become grafted onto the original system, producing typically eclectic practices, common to mainstream Traditional Craft. While we accept this as a part of our cumulative heritage, we have endeavoured to seek out our roots, to acknowledge the ancient sources of our existence, and in so doing, learn to access a higher, deeper energy as our guide towards greater Gnosis.

Some of the many things to have influenced our and other Traditional Craft praxes are Eurasian Shamanism (Scythians, Thracians etc), the Iberian Cult of the Dead, Freemasonry (from phre -sun + mas - child = child of light), Middle Eastern Angelology, Medieval demonology, heretical forms of Christianity and indigenous faerie lore. From the Lunar Mysteries of 'Goddess' Cults we have inherited particular aspects of the Slain Gods Mythos, and from Solar Mysteries of European Cults we have preserved the concept of Divine Kingship. Accordingly, in all acts of ritual, The Master and Maid represent the Tutelary God (Devil) and a nebulous Goddess (Sovereign Consort) incarnate – 'The Old Lad and Lass.' The Teacher or Master is more commonly named Magister, but few use this term, opting instead for the folk or fey name - 'Robin.' Both Maid and Magister are typically assigned Tutelary names specific to their particular Clan or Family, having ancestral connotations. This relationship is quite distinct from that maintained within Wiccan practises, where many priests and priestesses enjoy autonomy and assignation to a variety of pantheons. Moreover, the 'Family' Tutelary God is honoured as an avatar of the 'universal spirit of enlightenment.' Though tools are not deemed essential, they are included to assist focus via intrinsic symbolism, implicit or explicit, especially where relative to ancestral contact within the tradition itself. Yet none are static items; some are given particular emphasis at different places relative to the rite, for example, fire can be central or in the east, the cauldron can be central or in the west, the Stang can be central or in the north.

The rites are performed as a solitary or group by simple adaptation. Rituals can be deceptively simple - they can be silent, they can be masked. In fact they can also be either calm or wildly ecstatic. Who would not admit that when working within a corporal or elemental 'ring' (best suited for work with *Genius Locii*) even meditation undertaken outside feels infinitely more invigorating than indoors - commune with all *sensational* forces here are experienced more directly, where they are not subject to diffusion, order or restraint. Rites are mainly performed robed. Nakedness though not excluded, is not a pre-requisite of Traditional Craft. Celebrations are Stellar, Lunar and Solar, achieved through nine seasonal rites, four additional inner rites performed by elders only, giving a total of 13 moons, or one full magical year. We work outdoors mostly, where the energy is organic, though not necessarily elemental, and ephemeral, where experience of pure sentience lifts the spirit from the elemental to the angelic realms.

The rites are more relaxed, yet paradoxically more intense, intrinsically primal; an archaic reaching out to experience the totally of being, a Mystery beyond comprehension....in simple acts of commune. Fate is embraced and gently manipulated in accord with mankind's birthright and destiny. To maintain a tradition does not mean to allow it to degenerate as it slips away from all relativity. It must evolve. In order to survive it must not stagnate; if it does, then it has no place in that society. The basic format and concurrent theme only are discussed briefly, but never rehearsed - the intuitive faculties are valued over ability to perform. Chanting, mantras, songs and incantations are commonly used for trance induction - these are naturally mesmeric and rhythmic, to induce a shift in consciousness - it either works or it doesn't. If the latter, then no matter how polished the performance, the impression will be flat! In this instance the *'hound has turned up his nose at the cake.'* This statement refers rather enigmatically to the idea of the 'energy' generated in the grinding of the Mill, where contact is sought and mediated, then transmuted into the pure gift, the sacrificial 'cake,' offered to the 'hound' or Guardian. Curiously, within the exposition of the Catholic Eucharist it was stipulated that no priest should *'give a dog that which is holy'* meaning that each person receiving it must first be confessed and absolved of 'sin.' In contra-distinction to this premise, we offer 'that which is holy' to our 'hound.'

We should pause again to remember that *"Symbols contain the seeds of their own revelation, the virtue (essence) of which changes with each group/era using it,"* which supports the precept that sigils have universal significance. Its expression within the Craft maintains the Mysteries and stimulates magical comprehension. *"The Mysteries are also a means by which man may perceive his own inherent divinity; that students of the Mysteries are seekers of truth and wisdom, with magic its by product, a secondary device of little real consequence."*

The Hearth is the altar stone, the place of indwelling spirit, a sojourn for deity – the Beth-El or God stone. As a covenanted medium to unseen forces it must retain contact with the Earth or lose its potency. Water and milk is poured over them as 'semen' to keep them active. Holy stones animated by spirit are a locus for divination and acts of magic. The Hearth stone must be activated by the Magister and the Stang by the Maid. Unlike the cup and knife that works on the direct *union* of embodied spirits between the Maid and Magister when they come together physically in their sexually alchemical roles, the Hearth stone as an upward extension of the Earth (perceived as female) is activated by the male spirit embodied within the Magister. Similarly, the Totemic Stang, Holy Barque (supreme spirit vehicle & Mask) as the Tree of Life (combined but expressed as male) is activated by the ophidian female spirit embodied within the Maid. The Maid and Magister in this way hold lineal contact with each deific force. This is reflected in the elemental polarity of: the Stang - Air/Spirit; Stone /Earth which oppose each other on our Compass.

The Working Tools (basic):

The Cord - contains 'not eight knots but five and three': five representing the round of life, the true Witch's pentagram – Birth, Love, Maternity/Maturity, Wisdom and Death; plus three more for the Triplicity of 'Fate,' of the past, present and future that she holds. The Creator, Preserver and Destroyer. Hence it is a noose, symbolic of death, and an umbilical cord, the instrument of life, and a measure – the work of one's life. It is a sign of subjection to the will of the weaver of Fate. Constraint, boundaries. The cord, usually red for neophytes has other colours for Officers, Maid and Magister. Looped at one end, and tasselled at the other it thus represents both male and female genitalia. When combined with the Knife, they become the two Pillars.

There is however, more than one meaning to a knotted cord, especially to the 'knotted ladder'.....usage varies according to principle being invoked or worked...taking the 'ladder' as an example it typifies how the many tools and symbols we refer to are far more flexible and fluid than we may at first imagine them to be. At its most basic level, a ladder may be described as that which enables us to move through various stages from one point to another, we begin at one end and complete that journey at the other; these stages/rungs/ knots need not be cumulative, but could be. They may also be separate but connected. They may be simple markers for whatever your purpose requires, from a reminder, memorial, of something (ie knot in a hanky) to storage or concentration of something (ie, 'wind' or other potency). They may thus bind/hold, count/register or preserve a 'thing,' or assist in movement towards a distant point, usually in 'ascent'.

In this way the ladder of the philosopher differs from that of the alchemist and to the basic ladder of the Witch. They may act as rosaries, symbolising principles ranging from the seasonal rites worked annually, to the more mystical perceptions of the cycle of life itself and the triune force behind it as in the 'not 8 but 5 and 3' knots of E. J. Jones. What this all highlights is the real need to move away from the rigidity of correspondences and symbology; so much is experiential, subjective, versatile and requisite of lateral thinking. Each 'thing' has many levels of meaning, and the ladder is a perfect way of expressing this, both literally and figuratively. We are constrained only by our imagination and its application.

Elements - To Man was bequeathed the power of Earth, Air and Fire; Woman holds Earth, Air and Water, she is the unbroken link to the racial line, her mitochondrial (DNA) gene carries the seed; but though Woman is all, Man alone holds Fire - Fire is the province of the Alder God of the Underworld, chthonic deities such as Lucifer, Bran and Tubal Cain, of smiths and metal workers: Masters of Craft, magic fertility and death and artifice/illusion. To be effective and work Divine magic, these elements are to be combined in balanced acts of love and worship. Fire (consciousness) and Water (un-consciousness), upward and downward pointing triangles; brought together they form the Hexagram, the six-pointed star, ultimate Solar symbol of the Divine Horned Child of the Sun, the *"star-crossed serpent."*

Knife - Male tool, representing Divine fiery seed and phallus. Substitute for lance/spear in creation of Eucharist. Unyielding, courage.

Cup - Female tool, representing Grail and womb of Goddess, who is occasionally referred to in later cross-quarter fire festivals as 'Hekate,' dark mistress of the cauldron, of magic and mother of the 'Fates'. In the earlier Solar, Stellar and Lunar rituals of the Equinoxes, she is Ishtar/Inanna, warrior Goddess of love, sex, fertility agriculture and sovereignty, and wisdom as the Shekinah.

Cauldron - Ultimate female tool, representing the true Grail, the Mystery of Divine inspiration activated by the priest (Magister/Master) thrusting his spear into it, an act of sacred marriage, of symbolic sex, where the symbol of life the spear, made of ash, the 'Mother' tree and steel, metal of

Khronos (Cosmic smith and Master of Time) is drawn to Earth in an act of sacrifice and love. Principally, this generates 'movement' within the Cauldron, hence creation and wisdom are gifts bestowed by it. The True Quest for the Grail lays in the Cauldron, in the overcoming of 'Fate,' of release from the endless cycle of life, death and rebirth, the attainment of pure wisdom- Gnosis (ayin soth). The Cauldron though forged by the great smith is a tool of the female Numen; it disperses ALL Gnosis achievable through inspiration. . . poetry and creativity are the gifts of the female muses, all forms of that ultimate Creatrix. . . as such they inspire the male to express the Mysteries, but these are actually revealed through the cumulative experience of all the other tools.

Broom - Often given as a female tool composed of all three female elements: Water (Willow); Air (Birch) and Earth (Ash) - the three Celtic mothers (death, birth and life/fate) that manifest into the world of form and consciousness. Metaphysically, the broom transmutes sexual energy via the *"turning without motion (riding), between three elements upon"* (the broom), hence its first principle is death - this is the substance of magic and mysticism.

Stang – Primarily the altar as significator of the point of union through the offering of one's true self. It is the gate, the guide, the horse, the psychopomp - Hermes, son of Saturn and Hekate, who guides us towards our mystical experiences. It is phallic and separates into three aspects as it rises. It is love, as the union of male and female Mysteries, and it is beauty, the child of this love - wisdom, the Horn Child. It is death and transformation. The 'horns' represent both masculine and feminine divinity, which conjoin to sublimate enlightenment. Even a portable stang may serve as an altar, which is technically and literally, the point of sacrifice (of self/surrender) hence, worship to and of one's deity anywhere. It is set within informal sacred space where no circle is denoted. It represents the Gate of Heaven and the Tree of Life; it is the ladder of the worlds for ascent or descent in all journeying. Finally, the Clan Stang is the totemic representation of its Tutelary deity and is therefore the standard of office. 'External' support.

NB. A Shrine however is not an altar. It is a place of dedication that indicates the presence of God.

Cloak - Humility, the concealment of Mystery, night - the hidder of light.

It is also poverty and charity, together equalling magical power. It should be black. The 'unseen' qualities, the invisible.

Sword - Male tool of power, summoning, justice and trial. On a mystical symbolic level, the 'Zayin' sword of Azazel denotes initiatic purification; this magic flaming sword is the epitome of alchemical lore, a metaphor of inner-fire, sexual force and transmutation - the thunderbolt of Gnostic wisdom, the ritual blade that seeds the cauldron, the lance point of the Grail. It is Caladvwlch/Excalibur, the sovereign sword of kingship and the 'bridge' between realms.

The Mill - Widdershins dance, often trodden in silence (though occasionally with a ritual chant or Mantra); where required a seven tone vowel chant invokes the vibration of the seven winds. These are as follows: ee ay ah I oh uu oo; when properly intoned as a round, this invokes 'EYER [I am] IO [God] and presages an apotheosis akin to that acclaimed by the Sufi mystic Halaj wherein the ego is totally subsumed. Designed to loosen the astral body and facilitate trance, on a practical level this opens up the chest and cardio/vascular system. Rhythm combined with exertion induces the body to eject the unconscious into the void. This where we 'grind' our Fate, where we traverse the maze towards the Castle to realise our destiny.

It is worth remembering that the Craft preserves (selective) elements of phallic cults and many maintain elements of Dionysian and Priapic celebrations; they also preserve Gnostic elements of the *'Love Agapae'*. These combine with ancestral reverence for the dead. Obeisance is offered to the 'Divil' (Lucifer), and when we dance the 'Mill,' we hope past adherents of the Mysteries will join us as we wind our way through the maze to the Castle. Blacksmiths engage phalli as amulets within their forges, even today. Solar worship is synonymous with the creative and phallic energy of the male principle, it is therefore possible that sexual induction into Clanships, could have evolved from the simple sacrifice of the first sex act to Priapus in more archaic cults, where the 'first fruits' of virginity were offered to the God via a stone phallus. In the archaic world the choicest portions of fruit, wine, grain and meat were always offered to the reigning deity within many cultures, and what more pleasurable thing could one offer the Gods than the sex act, in honour perhaps of the Time when the 'Gods' were believed in myth to have seeded humanity from their own sex act. As representatives of these archaic potencies, the Magister and Maid are obliged to exorcise this potent rite, entitled the 'Old Covenant' in gravid acts of transmission - *"like to like and blood to blood."*

The Compass:

Within the corporeal world, there are six cardinal directions: up, down, left, right, backwards and forwards; from any given point, a human being becomes a seventh point, the axis of the other six points, essentially the 'centre' of his/her world - the sacred omphalos, the 'Axis Mundi,' a temporal link to the Universe. Because we are portable, our 'sacred space' moves with us, presenting a radical argument that reflects the reality of Time and space existing anywhere and everywhere, both mythically and actually. A 360-degree horizon surrounds the epicentre where each of us represents the 'Qutub,' the sacred point. Convenience and practicalities dictate the need for visual markers, generally provided now by trees and stones etc. These merely serve to reflect the subjective phenomena of liminal Time and space, effectively creating a reference point for ordering the Earth, heavens and stars - a centralized focus of communication between spirits, Gods and ourselves, as determined by our position relative to them. Our presence alone delineates 'sacred space,' the focus of our meditations and work.

Furthermore, working areas contrary to popular belief, are not 'raised' to contain power, how could they? Nor are they designed or expected to provide protection. This is not the purpose of constructing a Compass at all. Corporeal, Earth based compasses of the eight fold wheel (of fate), provide for the group, an astral marker, which when seen from above, becomes, with the central fire, the 'Eye of Ra'- the 'Ayin' an astral beacon, or holy Mandala, drawing all into a space of becoming, at one with the 'son within the Sun.' This potency is absorbed directly into the Fire, the Cauldron, the Stang and ourselves as we move silently around the confined but not contained space. It is not static. Therefore, any protection, if desired, should come from within, either directly and/or supplemented via the use of personally charged talismans.

Typically, Witches and Pagans are depicted dancing or moving in circles. Traditionally of course, innumerable cultures continue to perform circular and serpentine dances *around* either a fire or deific icon! In folklore, faeries, with whom Witches were frequently associated after the 16th century, also danced in *rings*. Now as then, these are for celebration, prayer and acts of magic, denoting sacred space only. They offer no real protective value or purpose except in similar extreme circumstances to those employed in ancient times. A space is charged by intent. Actions are merely theatre for the mind. Remember too, many temples in the archaic world were formed from sacred theatres, whose circular buildings emulated the Divine celestial dome of the heavens. Note: historically, temples became places of corruption and material production, inspiring later Gnostic, Protestant and even later modern Wiccans to hold the disparaging view that none of it is necessary - *"where several people commune in my name"* - *"be free in your rites!"* This important directive and key principle proclaims that each rite must be open, spontaneous and free; they should not be rehearsed as scripted theatre. Rather, a rite should be engineered specifically for its advocates to experience the unfolding 'Mystery.' Squaring the circle is the Arcanum Arcanorum, the cross of the Sun, withholding the secret of the rose, the hexagram and the pentagram, where all become One in eternity, the rim of pearls, beyond the veil of the great sea - Marah.

Freedom of movement is granted in, out and around the working area - no barrier exists, indicating an acceptance of the presence of deific forces and otherworld spirits, deemed as omnipresent and omniscient within all fields...we are simply the lowest resonant manifestation, and cannot be placed 'beyond' its influence. Ergo, in ritual, we present ourselves to relevant potencies, in order to utilise those qualities; in awareness of them, we prepare ourselves for that shift. They are NOT summoned to us. Neither would we seek control or mastery over them, with the exception of certain acts of necromancy and sorcery if and when that should be desired. Areas used in modern Traditional Witchcraft often encompass more than one working area; movement between them is ardently encouraged. These include locations at caves, hilltops, forests, bridges, lakes - whatever is appropriate to the rite being performed: divination, spell-casting or communion. Significances once awarded to the four directions, are now 'marked' by the Solstices and Equinoxes, and do in fact register the Sun's most northerly and southerly setting points (south in Winter; north in Summer). The cardinal points cross these providing eight compass points in all.

To fully exploit the elements and energies, we endeavour to work preferably near running water (in the west, running north to south). In doing so, we are poetically reminded of the Grail Castle of Arianrhod, of *'Caer Ochren,'* where *Leukothea* or the Pale-faced Goddess resides over the meeting of souls, both carnate and dis-carnate. Many suppose this enchanted Castle that *'spins without motion'* lies within the Western regions, poetically poised above the watery horizon; others believe place it Northwards at the circumpolar stars - the *Coronae Borealis*. More probably, we perceive Her as the Moon, whose dark and light faces reveal and conceal themselves as they spin around the Earth without the motion of its own axis. Locked into the Earth's gravitational pull, the veil to Her dark side is never lifted or exposed. Cain resides there as guardian of the ancestral dead, guiding all souls through Her halls of re-birth.

Beyond Hyperborea, lies mythical Shambala, whose attendant legends place it ubiquitously wherever it is needed; this psychic refuge is visualised atop a high mountain, reached by a steep ascent up its stony outcrops. Surrounded by the river of Time and forgetfulness, the *'Lethe'* is breached only by Charon, ferryman to returning souls. Roses, symbolic of Luciferian Gnosis, the Sangraal and other Mysteries, entwine and circle the Castle walls and its three turrets. These are the five petalled 'dog' roses, red for Lucifer and white for Ishtar/Sophia.

Everyone should create their own Grail Castle for meditations and contemplation:

Prayer:	You telling God.
Contemplation:	God telling you.
Ecstatic Union:	God and You enjoying each other in sentient silence.

We should always seek knowledge rather than power; all life exists within the Source - not the other way around. Therefore, we must not hold onto the energy, to do so may cause overload and temporal breakdown. In every circumstance, Robert Cochrane unambiguously advocated that - *"All ritual must be prayer."*

In its highest form, the Compass becomes a 4th dimensional Merkavah, the supreme mystical vehicle of not just ascension or movement, but the phenomenal device that facilitates a noumenal 'connection'. We enter this spirit borne carriage, powered by the fiery winds, the four cardinal forces spinning in unison; the swastika is of course, a most ancient symbol of universal force and motion. The conjunction of inspiration with intuition, or fire and water expressed by the two triangles of the hexagram, generate the seventh and eighth manifest points (Daath and Malkut) articulating the basic structure of the Compass upon which all else is built.

In conclusion then, we may say that the inherent philosophy, the ancestry, the virtue, the vehicle...indeed the WHOLE thing, including the Clan Mythos itself becomes the embodied Compass. Declaimed poetically by Robin, the current Magister of the Clan as: *"the boatman, the ferry and the destination,"* and by Robert Cochrane's familiar expression *"the hunter, the hunted and the Roebuck in the thicket are all one"* it encompasses (pun intended) the Cosmology, Eschatology, and all experiential quantum mechanics. Most of all, if we imagine the whole descriptive media (of circles, domes, rings, wheels, rungs of a ladder, levels, planes, arcs and vaults) as expressions of a finely spun web or complex spherical matrix (metaphysically speaking, ritual or sacred space need not be round, but better serves the illusion of this sphere) wherein at any given moment, we as a single point, (Qutub) may trace our trajectory along that fine network of pathways thereto experience and utilise elements of the 'Source' as potencies or virtues assigned to all possible destinations. In truth, it is a four dimensional map of the Universe, embracing and articulating the Clan Mythos, cumulatively by the traveller along the one straight path that pauses only at these intersecting points of ingress and egress.

The Compass is therefore within and without; it is the micro/macrocosmic vehicle of being and of shifting one's awareness through all points traversed. The 'Ruach' or Shekinah, as primary wind, is therefore presented as the mystical breath of the Divine expirated across the primal sea, the waters of the Abzu. Marah, the void of being, which is not manifest 'water' at all, but the chasm of the Universe, is the atom, all land and the nothing. Beyond a mundane term for a 'tool' the Compass becomes everything from the air we breathe to the magic of realisation. It is as simple or as complicated as we allow it to be.

The Round Table may be another way of viewing the Compass, albeit on a more static level, suggesting again the twelve + one, the 'wheel' albeit a different configuration. The 13th seat or 'Siege Perilous' equates with the 'Mercy Seat' of the Kabbalah, that houses the Shekinah, whose 'presence' empowers it; through correct interaction of it, we may assume conjunction. Intriguingly, each seat is assigned particular qualities according to the virtue of the treasure associated with it.

The Nine Knots

"Our consciousness sustains the Gods; the older the Egregore, the more powerful it becomes. When a cult disappears, then the Egregore sleeps in the mists of the Astral dimensions, but it can be awakened again when worshippers recall its name and perform its rites..."

Robert Cochrane

The Clan of Tubal Cain celebrate nine special occasions throughout the year as follows: Yule, Twelfth Night (Wild Hunt), Candlemas, Lady Day, May's Eve (Roodmas), Midsummer, Feast of Hekate, Michaelmas and All Hallows (Martinmas), that honour ancestral traditions drawn from across Europe and the more ancient Middle East, particularly those celebrations coterminous with the Equinoxes. Evolved seasonal celebrations honour the 'Wheel of Fate' (quite differently to Pagan and Wiccan idioms), as a cosmological encryption regarding cycles of birth, death, fate within our unique heritage. Even so, we do acknowledge and incorporate a variety of relevant aspects preserved within extant 'folk festivals' throughout the British Isles.

Our Neolithic ancestors retained proto-shamanic links to certain priestly practises of the Middle East disseminated through several branches of the *'Anunnaki,'* notably, the *'Tuatha-de-Danaan,'* circa 1800-1500BCE. A bold testament perhaps to the many hundreds of megalithic monuments that scatter our landscape speculated to have once been aligned to the Solstices and Equinoxes. Pastoral celebrations of Nature, herding, social fairs, games and gatherings only many hundreds of years later acquired the magical significance now attributed to them. Conversely the Equinoxes and Solstices were always deeply revered as magical and devotional, a Time when Stellar, Lunar and Solar activity was coalesced synergistically.

Mystical currents were fully exploited by our ancestors and it is noteworthy that many Mystery religions including the Eleusinian and Orphic rites of Greece, and those of Egypt and Sumer were held at the Equinoxes. Agriculture as a much earlier phenomenon throughout the Middle East and Europe, appeared within the British Isles c1800BCE (our Bronze Age), taking precedence over the pastoral calendar as a seasonal marker. The Druids also revered and honoured the Solstices and Equinoxes.

Thereafter, celebrations held on these occasions masked their earlier significance, especially when only a few hundred years later, as we moved into the Iron Age our ancient megalithic monuments became neglected and abandoned. Migratory 'Celtic speaking peoples' popularised Samhain, the October fire festival in some parts of the British Isles as a major annual feast day. There is no evidence to support the erroneous belief they considered this to be their 'New Year,' and records do in fact confirm their accord with the official Roman New Year that began in January which was a calendrical convenience only, induced by the introduction of the Solar calendar. However, for purposes of law, commerce and religion, then as now, many countries continue to recognise March, rather than January as the 'advent' of the Year.

Ironically, these dates closely adhere to the Equinoxes and Solstices and are as follows:

Lady Day	March 25th
Midsummer's Day	June 24th
Michaelmas	September 29th
Christmas day	December 24th

Historically, records show that before the popular 'Wiccan' movement of the late fifties and early sixties, Imbolc and Lughnasadh, (the latter named after a Solar hero, Lugh) were celebrated in Ireland but nowhere in England; Beltane was celebrated all over Britain and Europe, by both farming and pastoral communities, some incorporating fire some not. All differed considerably in that there never was a definitive ritual for these events, nor a contextual chronology for them - this was a scholastic construction of the 18th and 19th century folklorists. Celtic language groups adopted some of the invading Norse and Saxon feast and holy days, grafting them onto an evolving eclectic Christian calendar.[9]

The (so called) 'Minor Sabbats' follow the more ancient Solar energies and are as follows:

Key words/themes for each season:
SPRING EQUINOX - SEEDTIME/NEW IDEAS
- Sun enters Aries, brings Fire

SUMMER SOLSTICE - CULTIVATION/NURTURE -
Sun enters Cancer, brings Water

AUTUMN EQUINOX - HARVEST/REWARD -
Sun enters Libra, brings Air

WINTER SOLSTICE - CLEARANCE/INTROSPECTION/HERMITAGE -
Sun enters Capricorn, brings Earth

Our Compass reflects these generic concepts, but preserve deeper aspects in trust to Officers of the Clan, taught as core Mysteries of the ethereal tides of Nature, used for otherworld magics through elemental (but non-corporeal) correspondences. Surrounding each festival are 'bridging' days, named 'Ember days' by the Anglo-Saxons whose influence within the Craft is considerable, especially regarding the Three Mysteries of hilltop, glade and cave which cumulatively explore triune threads of fate that bind them all.[10] These days of liminality refer to the instability and vulnerability of the three days that precede and follow the Solstices. As thresholds requiring safeguard, they are primary sources of magical current that should be fully exploited.

Clanship:

In anthropological terms, Clanships remain a core centred unit, existing either in isolation or among satellite groups. A Clan is a *social* unit (often within a *political* 'Tribal' unit), is frequently Matrilineal, considers kith and kin as 'blood' and binds its members under the auspices of an often mythic ancestor whose 'presence' is manifest through the Totemic Clan standard. [11] Many traditional and hereditary practitioners find security in systems that preserve the ethos of such cultural tribalism. Infused with folkloric beliefs, these uniquely subjective groups are as diverse as they are independent. Within The Clan of Tubal Cain, fealty is offered by everyone, including the Magister at regular intervals, usually of seven years, to a centralised familial base by those seeking protection under its hegemony. There is one titular head however, whose position is ascribed by the laws of Suzerainty rather than Sovereignty - an important distinction that affirms extant 'feudal' mechanisms. Numerous examples of this may be found in other accounts of the operative systems of Traditional Craft.[12]

Through the rite of the Old Covenant, the Magister acts as the 'son' of the Morning Star, aligning himself to the potencies of Lucifer as the Young Horn King, thereby assuming himself as 'Herald' of the Old Horn King. In this authoritative capacity, he holds 'tribal' symbols as visual and spiritual potencies, dispensing their largesse in matters temporal and cosmological to all descendants bound under its Law.[13] Prevalent throughout the ancient world, the 'Old Covenant' evokes a sacred compact, eloquently described as that which: *"binds its people within a kinship bestowed by Divine Grace through Time, beyond manifest form as a cohesive unit for its survival and continuity, rather than its dissemination and diaspora."* [14] For many schooled in modernity, this represents an abhorrence, contrasting as it does with Wiccan and Neo-Pagan independent and autonomous practices. Yet it is thus designed to eliminate or reduce factionalising corruptions and all the ensuing decimation that follows. Should fealty be refused or denied, severance from the Clan becomes an issue of eschatology, affecting all levels of being. Denial of access to the Clan Egregore in this manner is a privation at once intolerable and unbearable. Outcast from ancestral 'Lares,' this becomes an exile of the soul from that particular stream. Oaths are given before the ancestors; we make promises to the living and express discretion concerning all of consequence between. Secrets in this regard are therefore subjective and often unnecessary, requiring no oaths among brethren.

Where Clan oaths are taken, being fundamentally different to those taken to and by Wiccan High Priests and Priestesses, they serve an entirely contrasting cause and ethos. Those of the Clan are simple in principle and singular in purpose, binding each aspirant to the Tutelary deity:

The Law [Craft]
"Do not what you desire - do what is necessary.
Take all you are given - give all of yourself.
"What I have I hold!"
When all else is lost, and not until then, prepare to die with dignity."
                                 Robert Cochrane lived and died by this credo....

Unambiguously, this Law states that honour and duty to the highest faction is a commitment serviced by the Erinyes where transgressed. This exemplifies for us, the imperative of ancestral forces rather than elemental ones secured within many forms of Wicca. This is not to assert that either is in any way superior, rather it recognises intrinsic diversity. Even so, no one may 'own' the Mysteries; all any group holds, lineage based or otherwise, is their own experiences of ancestral pathways to them.

To transgress is considered an error of judgement based upon a choice between need and want. Want is the lure of the chase (Job's tempter for example), the Devil's advocate; but need becomes the catalyst for change. We must work through the adverse to retrieve the obverse. 'Choice' often takes us out of our comfort zone to a place where we are invited to analyse our needs and desires, to satisfy our deepest primal instincts, with or without the moral trappings of culture and our intrinsic humanity. This is why She is Severity upon the Tree; it is 'tough' Love indeed. On the other side is Unconditional Love or 'Mercy,' of Order, where choice is less catastrophic, more subtle and slower to effect. Here we need only agree to pre-ordained action, to make a choice that does not result in (obvious or immediate) change. She offers 'choice' rather than change, which can be to either continue upon the current path, or to choose between retreating or moving off on another tangent. Note the pathway that continues, requires us to move through Her!

Along the journey we each 'take' what is given, yet the giver also holds all that is theirs, without diminishment, that is until such Time as even that 'Will' is transmitted through 'Love.' Where dishonour or abuse of this tenet is manifest against another – the directive is clear.

Virtue:

Five artes were claimed by Robert Cochrane as Magister of the Clan, but four only were deeded by Evan John Jones to the current Magister (Robin the Dart), the fifth arte is a 'virtue' of the 'blood,' a potency of genealogical privilege composed of *personal* will, experience, empowerment and knowledge (commonly of practical matters, i.e. of certain charms). It is equally a debt and investment and so may be given up upon expiration or prior abdication by breath or passing of spirit familiars or charged possessions to direct kin exclusively.[15] Where thwarted, it remains a vital charge, borne even beyond the veil, whence Time is but a whisper within eternity. This *hereditary* right transfers *personal* virtue and remains distinct from that cumulative 'Egregoric' (*group*) Virtue assigned to the Tutelary spirit, mediated and transferred via an external source within the *appointed* Maid for the Clan. As such, Virtue is lineage specific and is cultivated by intense study of one-to-one mentoring.

Virtue, recognised by a show of omens, divination and other related phenomena is perceived as a descent of 'spirit,' alighting upon each successive heir, chosen in recognition of 'like to like.' Once embraced, it must be nurtured, distilled, reified and developed in accord with the sentience of the ancestral stream or Egregore or it will be lost; constriction equals stasis equals mortis. Held by the Maid in accord with converse micro/macrocosmic correspondence, the Magister through her is thus enabled to fulfil his role as 'sacrificial' king and true Master of the Compass. Past members of Robert Cochrane's group were able to verify this arcane principle. [16] As Shakti, she may receive and accede this primary force once only by breath, word and deed, from and to her preceding and succeeding Magisters. What is relinquished here is the authority to act as Titular head, the right to bear the regalia of office - the official standard and Clan Totem and with it, the care and tender of the Egregore, spirits guides, elementals etc. Without a Maid, a Clan Magister is said to act as 'caretaker,' maintaining the burden of the pact, acting from personal virtue only and not any ascribed to the Clan. Clearly, the imperative of her singular and pivotal role is herein emphasised. She receives, she holds, then passes on the Clan Virtue but *once*! Its operating system ground in an introvert and sentient Cosmology of experiential ancestral phenomena is again entirely distinct from the extrovert and static Cosmogony of Wicca. They brook no parallel whatsoever.

A Virtue holder is responsible for the evolving clarity and organic cohesion of the stream aligned to it. Through initiations into that stream, this potency is not diminished, as the Creatrix is not diminished by acts of creation. All those touched by this source begin to align themselves with the Egregoric force, acting in accord with it and the Will it represents.

The Clan Totem is seen as its familial guardian and is the symbol of mediation between carnate and discarnate ancestors - the symbol of the one 'flesh'- a magico-religious bond of a collective identity. Hostile or potentially negative members of the Clan are resolutely rejected by the Egregore through the sentience of the Totem.[17] Moving away from archaic sacrificial primitivisms, the Totem now invoked upon the Stang embodies the fateful element that binds the Magister in service to the sublime Creatrix, by Virtue of the Maid. Curiously, four such cycles evoke the Saturnian return and completion of duty to Hekate as Divine Providence and Fate.

Clan Deities:

Technically, the Clan is monolatrous, which maintains the elevation and focus of a Tutelary deity, while not denying the existence of other deific forms. 'Tubal Cain' as an avatar of Lucifer, is seen by some as the supreme deity of the Craft. Tracing the chronology and history of the 'Devil,' traditional Witch Master and 'Prince of this World' has revealed various esoteric Mysteries regarding his origins and variant roles. Amazingly, one of these places him as a legendary member of the Higher Council of Seven (The Anannage/Anunnaki or teachers) and son of Anu, the 'Most High,' a role and position without precedent. It is clear from early descriptions translated from cuneiform clay tablets of Sumer, that Enki, like Hermes articulates the qualities of an avatar of the Promethean Lucifer, *Lux Mundi* - Light of the World. Nonetheless, Robert Cochrane named three deities known for their requisite magical qualities as "close approximations," whose roles within the Mysteries were indicative of and synonymous with those of the Clan - A Supernal Triad, of Father, Son and Supreme Mother of All.

HERMES: Lord of Magic and Wisdom. **Lux Mundi**

DOMAIN: (between) Heaven and Earth.

SACRED NO: 40 (The Perfect Prayer!)

SYMBOL: Serpentine Caduceus

ANIMAL: Goat (fish is a sacred taboo creature).

ROLE: Patron of Artists, jewellers and Smiths, and all crafts of the wise. Patron and Creator of Mankind. Master Adept of Sorcery, Enchantment and Seduction.

SOLAR - Young Horn King (Hermes) - the Solar Child of Truth and Beauty.

LUX (Day/Light) LUX = Light within the Dark, born of NOX.

SATURN - Old Horn King (Pan/Anu), The Father of Time and Death and their cycles. The Egyptian God KhephRe, depicted as the Scarab, esoterically symbolises the backside of the Sun (the lesser light), which is the MOON.

HEKT/HEKATE: Goddess of Psycho/sexual magic,

The Mighty One of Enchantments. **Anima Mundi**

DOMAIN: Ubiquitous.

SACRED NO: 100 - the reproductive and creative force.

SYMBOL: Frog. Transformation from aquatic to terrestrial life, i.e. the waters of the primal abyss to the sacred mound. The 'leaper' between certain pathways, mystically and sexually. Symbol of the Qliphoth and Witchcraft.

ANIMAL: Dog.

ROLE: Mistress of Trivia (three ways), she is the power and force behind transformation. Mentioned in the Egyptian 'Book of the Dead' (Coming Forth by Day). Transformer of the dead into the ever living in the otherworld. Controller and Mistress of Time and Mother of Fate. The Creative productive force in gematria. LUNAR - Feminine Mysteries of Hekate... NOX (Night/Dark)

One of her common (though less known) titles in Ancient Greece was *'Phosphoros,'* meaning 'Lightbringer' in the form of the 'Morning Star'. Clearly, this links her esoterically to Lucifer, who shares these titles. Her origins lie in Egypt and Thrace, where her role as 'torchbearer' - guide to the Mysteries was engaged for many centuries before she became a Lunar force under Greek adoption. Like Hermes/Thoth, she is also known as the 'Gate.'

The Divine Feminine is invariably aspected as a Triune force, i.e. Triple Hekate, Three Gorgons, Three Harpies, Three Fates etc. All equate to the Dark or primal force of deity. But this is more than a passing whim of archaic Chauvinism; it is to equate Her with the Primal Void, the place of Creation and its Mysteries. As we return to that Void, She is also Mistress of the Mysteries of Death. As Primal Matter she is the force of Fate and guide in life and into death and beyond. Though common knowledge, such simplicity is often overlooked.

Beyond Hermes, Saturn and Hekate as wards of Fate, we hold the concept of a multi-faceted, multi-dimensional source, who in a very Monist sense, is the one, complete and whole; who by our existence and the existence of all other concepts of deity remains eternally unaltered, and who is 'ubiquitously' both immanent and transcendent. Cochrane's cosmology is resoundingly Orphic as this quote relates:

"At the beginning there was only Khaos (Air), Nyx (Night), dark Erebos (Darkness), and deep Tartaros (Hell's Pit). Ge (Earth), Aer (Air) [probably Aither the upper air] and Ouranos (Heaven) had no existence. Firstly, black-winged Nyx (Night) laid a germless egg in the bosom of the infinite deeps of Erebos (Darkness), and from this, after the revolution of long ages, sprang the graceful Eros [Himeros the elder Eros] with his glittering golden wings."[18]

Aristophanes, *Birds 685 ff (trans. O'Neill)*
(Greek comedy C5th to 4th B.C.)

The Gnostics prayed to 'Grace' as the Divine (wisdom) feminine principle - The '*Trimorphic Protennoia,*' the triple-formed Primal Thought, who bears more than a passing association with Hekate:

"I am Protennoia, the Thought that dwells in the Light.
I am the movement that dwells in the All,
She in whom the All takes its stand, the first-born among those who came to be,
She who exists before the All.
She (Protennoia) is called by three names,

49

Although she dwells alone, since she is perfect.
I am invisible within the Thought of the Invisible One.
I am revealed in the immeasurable, ineffable (things).
I am incomprehensible, dwelling in the incomprehensible.
I move in every creature."[19]

References:

1. Brien. O, C, & B, J, *'The Shining Ones'* Dianthus pub Ltd. p151 & UK Gardner. L, 2000 *'Genesis of the Grail Kings'* Bantam Books GB pp.76-77
2. Gardner. L, 2000 *'Genesis of the Grail Kings'* Bantam Books GB p.62
3. Gardner. L, 2000 *'Genesis of the Grail Kings'* Bantam Books GB pp.1-12
4. Gardner. L, 2000 *'Genesis of the Grail Kings'* Bantam Books GB pp.1-12
5. Brien. O, C, & B, J. *'The Shining Ones'* Dianthus pub Ltd. UK pp.186-190
6. Gardner. L, 2000 *'Genesis of the Grail Kings'* Bantam Books GB p.175
7. Gardner. L, 2000 *'Genesis of the Grail Kings'* Bantam Books GB p.179
8. Gardner. L, 2000 *'Genesis of the Grail Kings'* Bantam Books GB pp. 1-12
9. Hutton. R, 1999 *'Triumph of the Moon'* Ox. Uni Press. p.131
10. Jones. E, J. & Clifton. Chas 1997 *'Sacred Mask Sacred Dance'* Llewellyn. USA. p.138
11. Burne. Charlotte, S, 1996 *'The Handbook of Folklore'* Senate UK pp162-180
12. Liddell. W, E, & [ed] Howard M. 1994 *'The Pickingill Papers'* Capall Bann. UK pp.59-61 &111-113&119-122
13. Jones. E, J, & Howard. M, [ed] 2001 *'Roebuck in the Thicket'* Capall Bann UK p142
14. Levy. G.R. 1948 *'The Gate of Horn'* Faber & Faber Ltd. London p.197
15. Valiente, D. 1984 *'ABC of Witchcraft'* Robert Hale London p..203. Jones. E, J, & Howard. M, 2002 *'The Robert Cochrane Letters'* Capall Bann pp.153-5

16. Valiente. D, 1989 *'The Rebirth of Witchcraft'* Robert Hale London. p.129
17. Jones. E, J, & Valiente. D, 1999 *'Witchcraft, a Tradition Renewed'* Robert Hale USA p.39
18. www.theoi.com/Protogenos/Tartaros.html
19. www.Gnosis.org/naghamm/trimorph.html

2. 'Goda,' The Clan of Tubal Cain and Robert Cochrane

In 1914, Charlotte Burne[1] expressed 'Folklore' as: *"the learning of the people - a generic term under which the traditional beliefs, customs, stories, songs and sayings current among backward peoples or retained by the uncultured classes of more advanced peoples, are comprehended and included."* She records it as a belief about Nature, phenomenal and praeternatural, and mankind's interactions with it on all levels, permeating customs, rites, festivals etc. In fact she concludes it as an expression of the psychology of early man, recorded in habit and tradition. She notes especially, the cross-cultural similarities particularly amongst oral societies, ergo a commonality of humanity fundamental to all. Personal preference however, would express folklore as a composite conflagration of subjective facts and beliefs accrued eclectically over Time and space (subject to aeonic and demographic displacement) evolving within the (sometimes) fragile memories of generations of celebrants extant or otherwise. These 'traditions' are thus borne out, mystified and qualified by their exponents, against seasonal and calendrical perspectives whose significances are metered by the standards of industrial and economic values. This view shifts Ms Burnes' emphasis on the 'primitive' aspects of folklore, to its historical relevance, facilitating our understanding of it as an organic complexity of overlays, as opposed to a 'static' overview of atrophied traditions and customs. Why this is important, will hopefully, become clear as this essay progresses.

Gary St M Nottingham penned an interesting hypotheses entitled - *'Goda, The Regency and Robert Cochrane,'* (which appeared in White Dragon, #49). Briefly, it explores the legend of Eadric and his Faerie wife Godda drawn from a source commonly associated with Walter Map, courtier to Henry II. The *'De Nugis Curialium,'* is a book on trivia, anecdotes and gossip of the Time. Map firmly believed himself to be a descendant of the Faerie water sprite Melusine. Gary St M Nottingham plausibly speculates how Lady Godda within this tale could be a source for the Tutelary Goddess of 'The Clan of Tubal Cain' and not without good reason. However, while some support may be given to this as a legitimate theory (in a limited sense) in that together Eadric and Godda could represent the 'local' forms of the Horned God and his Consort, it is equally implausible in terms of perspective and application. This means quite simply that there are better reasons for accepting 'Goda' as having far greater significance than this. My esteemed colleague, Gary St M Nottingham has declared Ms Burnes'[2] review of the Faerie tale to be the finest, yet she cautions the over-zealous against jumping to conclusions, especially where religious or magical connotations are apparent. At heart, this is an aetiological story and therefore though indigenous in its nomenclature, has *universal* and significant parallels.

Burnes believed Eadric and Godda to be historical persons, onto whom the Germanic 'Wild Rade/Hunt' folktales, widespread during the 18th-19th centuries, were later grafted. Furthermore, Ms Burne shadows the tale with doubt of its authenticity, noting that many of the details related within the later 19th century tale seem 'tacked on'. Nonetheless, the Lady Godda has many important and relevant correlates, especially throughout Northern Europe. Namely, *'Frau Godden'* the Germanic Goddess of agriculture, abundance and prosperity, her many variants include *Gauden/Gaude and Gode, plus Holda/Hulda/Holle/Hertha and Bertha.*

Historically, Goda was a very popular Saxon name, especially for queens, nobility and (male) chieftains from the 9th century onwards, with variants such as *Godifu/Godgifu/Gondul and Godith.* Of note was Goda, the daughter of Aethelred the Unready, King of Wessex (968-1016CE) and Godgifu of Coventry in the 11th century. This was the assumed basis of the legend of Lady Godiva, wife of the historical Leofric, Earl of Mercia and who famously founded several monasteries across the Midlands. Derivatives of Goda can also be recognised within many family names such as Harold Godwinson, conferring his descent from Saxon chieftains. Odda/Oda additionally relate to Danish nobility of the 10th century.

Within the Anglo-Saxon Chronicles, 'Goda,' a Thane (Chieftain) of Devonshire is noted as slaughtered in 988 CE. In fact, several Eadrics are also listed, two of whom are relevant to our Time frame: Eadric 'Streaona,' a low-born man, raised to principal advisor to King Aethelred in 1006 and whom King Canute later executed for treachery in Mercia circa 1017, after playing both sides against the middle. Another Eadric 'Silvaticus,' a forester also known as 'Guilda the Wild,' was apparently the brother/nephew to Eadric 'Streaona,' a rebel who made his peace with William the Conqueror in 1067. The 'Faerie' tale is of course set in a 'forest,' which at that Time was no mere wooded area, but a Royal Park, complete with hunting grounds, managed woodland and agricultural field systems. Curiously then, both

10th and 11th centuries offer separate traditions of the known historical characters of Eadric and Godda. In fact it is not beyond the realms of possibility that Aethelred's daughter Goda/Godifu (by his Norman wife, Emma), could be the historical form of this legendary 'Faerie' wife of Eadric, the wild rebel and forester of the Welsh Marches. To further complicate matters, Aethelred also had a son named Eadric by his first (Mercian) wife Elfreda. This brief excursion into the permutations of a name or title as applied to known, historical persons, reveal how legends blur chronological and factual boundaries within the mists of Time, beguiling us with their enigmatic possibilities.

In Icelandic society of the 10th-11th centuries, hierarchical chiefdoms developed into political institutions around the local 'godar'. These chiefs were local religious leaders holding sway over their extended families, known as Clanships. Singularly known as the 'Godi,' he acted as judge, mediator, priest and leader, protecting his Clan and its fiefdoms. Godard meant chieftaincy, and the position of Godi could be bought, sold or inherited, the causal basis of many power struggles. By the 12-13th centuries, political evolution diminished the number of chieftains, leaving only a few families to monopolize huge areas of the land, becoming elite landowners, known as 'storgodar.' Within the Godiva legend are elements that suggest an original seasonal cultic procession of fertility. Coventry (Corfa's Tree - the boundary of a local chief?), within the 'Forest' of Arden could have easily retained these archaic practices. All this suggests a basic premise of Divine authority and origin within the male and female derivatives of 'Od,' which are not mutually exclusive, but in absolute accord. Therefore, Faerie Queens, and Priest-Kings alike share the qualitative positions of authority conferred within Clanships, becoming overlaid with Time, culture and geography, transcending their gender specifications. Moreover, the philological root of Goda is commonly associated with 'good' as in pure, or perfect (*catharii*) and latterly in the sense of the Divine authority of a hierarchical priest/chieftain.

According to the 'Brothers Grimm,' the Scandinavian Wood-Wife 'Huldra,' who may appear as an aging hag, though more commonly as a young and beautiful maid, could be heard singing dolefully in the forests carrying a milk pail. Milk is of course the famed drink of the Faeries, left out to placate or assuage their wrath. Irish legends tell of the trysting place of the 'Precious Pearl of Beauty,' Fand (the Goddess of healing and pleasure) and Manannan, the Sea God in the verdant forests. Scandinavian myth relates how it was believed that when Lucifer and his angels fell from Heaven, those who fell into the woodlands became sprites and genii of the forests.[3] Such relevant beliefs are popular throughout the mythologies of Eastern Europe and the Balkans.

As far-reaching as India, within the Shakti cult, Hindu legends tell of 'Shri Andal,' beatific devotee of Krishna (8th avatar of Vishnu). This flower-garlanded Nature sprite, and muse of poetry, renowned for her plaintive singing, beseeches her absent lover for re-union. 'Shri Andal' achieves rapture through Divine love (bhakti) after joining in the ecstatic dancing of the Gopis (who were also milkmaids). She is in fact a manifest incarnation of the Goda Devi, 'Mahalakshmi,' Goddess of Fecundity and Abundance (now sadly reduced to material wealth and financial prosperity). It is tempting to speculate a connection between the Goda Devi and Godiva, however tenuous, and yet Leland's criteria for forming an authentic link are worth considering. [4] Astonishingly, 'Mahalakshmi' is the spouse and consort of none other than Vishnu, a watery, redeemer God who was part fish, a correlate of the Irish Sea God, Manannan, and Enki, the Sumerian manifest saviour of mankind (whose spouse was also the Great Queen and Mother of the Gods). So delighted was Vishnu with Goda Devi, that he named her the 'Ruler' of the entire Universe! [5]

She rises from the milky waters of the cosmic ocean, radiant and beautiful; and like Aphrodite, she is a Goddess of not only beauty, devotion and creation but most interestingly, wisdom; ultimately representing Divine Love, Grace and Communion. One of three consorts to the Divine King, who severally embody the creative qualities of Will, Act and Energy; consequently the Universal Mother became referred to as the 'Three Queens.' This phrase was often used, coincidently, by Cochrane when referring to the Goddess in one of her numerous triune forms. Together they command the three planes of the three worlds. Goda therefore, as one facet of the Queen of Elfame is simply another representative of the Tutelary Goddess of Tubal Cain, aspected in earthly form, anthropomorphic and accessible, a familiar of the Faerie denizens.

Jeremy Harte[6] eloquently explains how this ethereal creature is restricted to the earthly realms, however liminal. However, when Thomas the Rhymer mistakes her for the Queen of Heaven (Mary), she answers negatively: *"No! I am the Queen of Elfland, come to visit ye!"* Harte explains how the belief in[7] Faeries as representatives of 'Old Gods' was culled from diverse cultural, racial and historical traditions, be they Pagan, supernatural or otherwise, concluding later[8] how names survive within folklore, 'often independent of their origins, transformed beyond recognition' by the overlay of culture, conquest and the march of Time. Harte [9] also reports the underlying social messages of taming free spirits fundamental to most Faerie marriages. Faerie traditions form the core of much occult lore, both ancient and current, across much of Europe and the Mediterranean. Etruscan *'Lasa'* evolved into exquisite ancestral spirits of divers localised Goddesses. Leland[10] opines a commonality among the animistic and elemental principles of Aryan, Teutonic, Italian and Asian myth and folklore relevant especially to both woodland and agriculture. Fate is another feature common to all.

Several members of Robert Cochrane's coven in the 1960s were avid folklorists and Faerie devotees, especially: Ronald White, George Winter and Norman Gills. It is unsurprising then that these three should pursue this passion extensively outside that group and throughout their personal lives, both during and after Cochrane's death. Doreen Valiente, also an ardent folklorist, was a curious, enquiring and erudite scholar, pursuing any legend however obscure, relative to all areas in which she visited, worked or intended to work magically. This engendered a wealth of lore with which she peppered her many books, letters and articles. As with any society, group or body of people drawn together by a common belief, need or focus, there remain points of digression both from the leaders of that group and amongst its adherents. This was no less typical of 'The Clan of Tubal Cain'.

More than a traditional 'Witch,' Robert Cochrane was a mystic; this allowed him to plunder the vast reservoir of folklore for allegories and analogical archetypes vital to his exploratory and innovative teaching methods, wheels within wheels, so to speak. His enquiring mind drove him to seek out all relevant symbols drawn from miscellaneous sources to express a narrative fundamental to his mystical and visionary Mythos. His overview was exceptionally ecumenical, at once enlightened and comprehensible. He would have been compelled to exploit all surviving examples/references of concepts of both his God and Goddess traceable within local legend. Analysis reveals a discernable origin for his views regarding Fate, drawn from Greece and Northern Europe; a Quaternary of Deity from the Judaic Qabbalah; a Triplicity of Queens from the archaic worlds of Egypt and Sumer; Angelic awareness from Platonic Gnosticism and finally, primal Imagery and Totemic symbolisms from the Near and Middle-East. Moreover, his absolute Goddess was Fate, the Creatrix and the Destroyer - giver of life, love, wisdom and finally death, the One in Seven Goddess, whose abode is *'Caer Ochren'* of the *'Prediue Annwn.'*

To Joe Wilson he explained that one may find the Goddess at liminal places where the veil is thin. His idiosyncratic view of the Traditional Craft and its inherent mysticism necessitated his adoption and adaptation of any and all means available to him to explore, experience and teach: *"We teach by poetic inference, by thinking along lines that belong to dreams and images."* More importantly, he refers to himself as a member of the 'People' throughout his writings; in one letter he refers to several groups of 'Witches' (in the Midlands) as 'People'. He elaborates how: *"The People are formed in Clans or families and they describe themselves by the local name of the Deity. I am a member of the People of Goda - of the Clan of Tubal Cain."* Here he is stating unequivocally how Tubal Cain is his deity; Goda is of the Clan i.e. Priest-King/Chieftain of that Clan ascribed to a particular deity, which in this case is Tubal Cain. His family are therefore the People aligned with or in service to that Priest-King/Chieftain, the *'hofgodi.'* In other words, he is here claiming descent from a long line of mystagogic teachers/leaders (Magisters), sworn to the worship and service of Tubal Cain. From this description, he clarifies beyond doubt, the true context and significance of 'Goda'.

Cochrane instructed Joe Wilson that 'Faith' too is the Mother of all Gods, that Christianity is part only of an even more ancient faith, that the 'People' are the direct descendants of those ancient priests and priestesses of their Mysteries. It could not be more lucid - Goda/Godi represents the priesthood, the Chieftains, the leaders of his Clan, and not the Goddess of it. Robert Cochrane states that 'The Clan of Tubal Cain' is of the 'Order of the Sun,' yet its people are children of the Moon, whose women hold the key to these Mysteries, advising all to seek supernatural manifestations of her in all her guises; this was axiomatic to his ethos- *she* is the presiding genius. A man, a priest, teaching the feminine Mysteries as explained by the Menhir of Brittany, leads the women of the Clan. Immanent and transcendent, this deity is not pantheistic but panentheistic.

He cautions Bill Gray in another letter not to underestimate any form of the Goddess, and to read the *Golden Ass*; above all, to understand the epiphanic, theurgical renditions rather than the frenetic, shamanistic, bacchanalian revelry, and the myths of the dark and light twins of the East, in particular, of Egypt and Persia. Eclectically, he speaks of the Shekinah, of Babylon and of Gilgamesh, also of Christ and of Thor. He believed emphatically that everything was linked symbolically with higher spiritual principles above and beyond the banal, the mundane and the obvious. Everywhere he sought her manifestations, in caves, woodlands, myth and poetry; anywhere local myth, lore or legend recorded her myriad guises.

In one of his many caving expeditions within the south of England, Wales and Shropshire, Cochrane was thrilled to have discovered what he believed to be a Neolithic 'temple'. He was of course inspired by the whole history of his Craft, and was able to incorporate its relevancies into the subtler methodologies of his teachings and Mythos: *"What do Witches call themselves? They call themselves by the names of their Gods, I am Od's (Woden's) man, since in me the spirit of Od lives, yet I am a child of Tubal Cain the Hairy One."* 'Truth' was also the absolute name for the Godhead, it being outside any religious affiliations or systems and therefore beyond even illusion. He asserted that each person's 'vision' represented individual subjective Truth.

He refers to the Queen of Spades as the 'Trump' (invocation of) - the Queen of Death, the Earth and the dark Goddess of Fate. Faeries, he names as elementals in a letter to Bill Gray, and rises indignantly to explain the use of elemental forces of Nature as a means to an end, a primitive and outmoded practice of little value to him, a lesser force within his tradition, not the greater. Asserting this, he declaimed: *"All mystical perception is based on the fact that we go to God, not that God comes to us. There are as many ways of seeing God as there are creations of God, and each individual is the Totality - the Hand that writes history as well as the writing. What is lacking is 'perception,' and that is what makes the path so long and bloody."*

When speaking of symbols he adds that man fashions his own interpretation according to his Time, viz. the 'Celts' were Goddess orientated, yet the Anglo-Saxons, being Father orientated, expounded male superiority. He shies from discussion of the Queen of Elfame, referring in general to his Goddess as Diana, or Hekate. In another letter to Bill Gray, he reveals a profound experience of a bright light within which he received a vision of a pale lady, naked upon a horse. He interprets this as a visionary representation of the supreme cosmic power - Truth; a vision of the inner-planes, wherein he was instructed by the Master to worship Her! This vision may suggest to some a superficial association with Rhiannon or Epona, but these images are merely subsidiary reflections of an even higher principle. Indeed, it is the Triune Hekate, Goddess of Life, Love and Death, the Pale-faced Goddess of the Castle, and Mistress of Fate, to whom he wistfully refers.

Finally, in a letter to Norman Gills he mentions the Alba (White/Pale) Guiden, a harsh mistress, a dark Muse whose third face is Terrible.

This dark Goddess is the enigmatic Pale-faced Lady in White, the beautiful and multi-faceted cosmic jewel and the pearl of wisdom. Metaphorically, as Queen of the Universe, she appears as the Lady (Virgin) astride or leading the *Unicorn*, the sacrificial Totemic emblem of the Master. Therefore, in saying that Godda, Faerie wife of Eadric, could indicate the Tutelary Goddess of Tubal Cain chosen by Cochrane, is to grossly underestimate the subtleties of a uni-sexual and universal term - Goda, and to limit the limitless qualities, form and existence of a nebulous and ineffable Creatrix. This is not to say that he was not aware and did not make use of all these forms both magically and psychologically, incorporating them within ritual and exploring them within meditations. As he states clearly in his letters: *"they were a means to an end, not the end."*

"I create the Father of the Universe on the summit of the worlds. My origin is within the cosmic waters, in the universal sea. From there I extend to all the worlds and touch the ridge of heaven. I blow like the Wind, setting in motion all the Universe. Far beyond heaven and far beyond this Earth extends my greatness."

Vak Ambhrini, Rig Veda X.125.7-8

References:

1. Charlotte Sophia Burne 1996 *'The Handbook of Folklore'* Senate Books. London. p1
2. Jennifer Westwood 1985 *'Albion, a Legendary Guide to Britain'* Book Club Ass. Gr. Britain. p249
3. Alexander Porteous 1996 *'The Lore of the Forest'* Senate Books. London. p84
4. T. Fisher Unwin 1892 *'Etruscan Roman Remains in Popular Tradition'* London. p80
5. Dr David Frawley 1997 *'Tantric Yoga and the Wisdom Goddesses'* Motilal Banarsidass pub. Delhi. pp146-9
6. Jeremy Harte 2004 *'Explore Fairy Traditions'* Heart of Albion Press p128-30

7. [*ibid.*] p23
8. [*ibid.*] p24
9. [*ibid.*] p58
10. C.G. Leland 1892 'Etruscan *Roman Remains in Popular Tradition*' T. Fisher Unwin. London. Intro.

Online Anglo-Saxon Chronicles.
My own copies of the Robert Cochrane letters

Previously published in: *White Dragon* #50 – November 06

Female Mysteries

4. Hekate - Dark Mistress of the Soul

"The Black Goddess is so far hardly more than a word of hope whispered among the few who have served their apprenticeship to the White Goddess - she will lead man back to that sure instinct of love he long ago forfeited by intellectual pride..."

Robert Graves

Who is this arresting presence and what force compels us to follow her? Both history and mythology demonstrate a discernable tradition of female initiatrix. A tenuous thread binds the Mysteries of ancient wisdom to Christian Medieval Europe, into the flowering of the Literary Renaissance. This domain of 12th century poets exalted the use of metaphor and allegory that prevailed esoteric erotica conjunct with orthodox Medieval media. Within the Gnostic Cult of the Black Virgin in Medieval Southern France, she is sometimes referred to as *'The Notre Dame de Lumiere.'* She is suggested by Peter Redgrove [1989:134] to be coterminous with the Black Goddess, Mary Lucifer the light giver - the Magdalene. Her symbol, the Rose, flower of Venus, exemplifies sacred/secret love, though it also represents esoteric wisdom within female Mysteries, both carnal and religious. 'Sub-rosa' information was thus 'revealed' only to initiates seeking enlightenment and Gnosis through those Mysteries.

Redgrove poetically reveals esoteric machinations disguised within the genre known as 'Courtly Love'; he describes how sexual energy radiated from the eyes of the beloved, fusing into the lover's subtle bodies, illuminating and elevating the spirit [*ibid.*]. Remembering how eyes are windows to the soul, this emanation of 'light,' the soul's 'psyche' power is further explained as follows: *"the invisible thus becomes sensible by the operation of spirits dependant upon the physiological workings of the body"* [*ibid.*]. Such intellectual foreplay induced radiating kalas erupting in miasmic waves of orgasmic pneuma, somatic secret-ions absorbed and transformed in acts of communion. Redgrove [1989:148] expresses this Dark Goddess force as the *"black light flexing as the loa, spinning her web around all within her grasp, she is the light of revelation within the darkness."* These powerfully evocative

'Hekate - Triadic Locus'

words suggest that she is cast in the role of 'Fate' whose 'maithunic' alchemical processes were actuated by women operating under the traditional role of hierodule or sexual initiatrix – but whom were they representing?

The Black Virgin was ever a symbol of the soul, a gateway into the supra-conscious or nodal crossroads of the senses. As whore and shadow Goddess she leads the Mysteries of death and rebirth, revealing her heretical knowledge of female menstruation and Kundalini magic; her serpent wisdom, explored in dreamscapes where revelatory experiences are to be marvelled [Redgrove, 1989:136-38]. Already, these images evince a far older, more ancient Goddess. The Black Madonna at Chartres is known as '*Notre Dame de Souterrain*' (our lady of the Underworld), [Picknett & Prince, 1997:151]. Our first hint perhaps of Hekate? Within allegory, Mary is often portrayed as a spinner, alluding to her role as Mistress of Fate – another role more traditionally attributed to Hekate.

Redgrove [1989:115-120] upholds the Black Goddess as primal woman, a primal Goddess, a Queen of Enchantments, of dark magics and all things occult; her hidden radiance the inspiration of poets and kings. Further, he posits this Black Goddess as cognate with the Holy Spirit, Wisdom - the Shulamite lover of Solomon: "*It was I who covered the Earth like a mist, Alone I made a circuit of the sky and traversed the depths of the abyss........whoever feeds on me will be hungry for more, and whoever drinks from me will thirst for more.......*" [*ibid.*]. Habitually expressed as a succubus, she haunts the nocturnal dreamscapes - the realms of Hekate, the sender of dreams. All aspects of the Goddess are explained by Redgrove [1989:117] as psycho-erotic, as multi-faceted, at once subliminal and physical.

Moreover as a form of wisdom, he sees the dark Goddess Hekate as the effulgent light - the dark flame, star maiden and gateway to other worlds [1989:138]. More interestingly, he distinguishes her as Mary-Lucifer, the '*lumen naturae,*' the illuminatrix of the soul [1989:156]. Is it possible though, to substantiate this phenomenal assumption? Certainly, historical mythologies do provide the relevant source material upon which the reader is encouraged to draw their own conclusions.

Within the Orphic Mysteries, Nyx, a black-winged spirit rose from the emptiness of the Void of Khaos to lay the silver cosmic egg containing the golden winged spirit of love - Eros, also known as Phanes the Revealer, whose radiant beauty illuminated the Earth. Nyx, primal Mother Night, within her dark starry realm also birthed the Fates, the Hesperides, the Furies and Nemesis [George, 1992:112-117].

As mythologies evolved, precedence became awarded to day and light; all things synonymous with the dark night became exiled to the chthonic (from *'khthonios'* - in or of the Earth, i.e. fertility, childbirth, abundance, crops, fate and death) realms, the astral regions and dreamscapes, the inner psyche. In effect, Hekate developed as the Guardian of these dark and lonely places and of their inherent occult Mysteries. Dark acts of sexual Mystery, Kundalini, prophecy, inspiration and divination all came within her gift. Creatures of the Night - owls, dogs and horses became her totems, as did all creatures of the aquatic Underworld - snakes, serpents, spiders, toads and frogs [*ibid.*]. As Mistress of Trance-formation, her Divine light of Gnosis is secreted by her chthonic powers of life and death; her all-devouring sexuality leads her victims in a mantic embrace of regeneration. Her legendary priestesses moved the dying through an ecstatic death by their orgasmic convulsions [George, 1992:111].

Ultimately linked to the Dark Moon, Hekate was ever a Goddess of the soul's illumination before this. Time and Destiny are within her dominion; many of her epithets reveal her numerous roles and forms - Wise One, Queen of Shades, Mistress of Initiation, Gatekeeper, Psychopomp and Shining One.[1] To mystics, the Dark Night is the depth of love (Eros) and light (Phanes). George [1992:118] asserts than within Eastern philosophy, black represents the formless state of pure matter and a unified whole, of no separation, a truism reflected within the Greek Nyx and the Egyptian Nuit, both of whom carry the eternal message of the universal matrix as an expression of true 'love' (wisdom and understanding/compassion), ignorance of which induces fear and emptiness.

Barbara Waterson [1999:190] has received much criticism from academics for promoting the idea that Hekate is derived from Hekt, the frog headed Egyptian Goddess of birth, death and resurrection, and midwife to the Gods. But her theory is worthy of closer inspection. This primal Creatrix is said to have helped raise Osiris from the dead, preceding the role later adopted by Isis. Furthermore, her symbol, the frog, was later adopted by Christians to represent the resurrection of Christ. It has been found on numerous terracotta lamps with the inscription… *"I am the resurrection."* The eminent Egyptologist, Wallis-Budge [1971:63] explains that within Egyptian funerary rites, the frog amulet was (along with the scarab) placed upon the mummified remains of the dead in order to exert her powers of resurrection over it.

Later Greek mythology has revealed that Hekate, like Lucifer/Lux (light) is born of Nyx/Nox (dark). Long before this however, she was originally a Thracian deity adopted into the Greek pantheon as a Titan, a pre-Olympian deity. Described as a beautiful maiden whose hair is adorned by stars, she illuminates the darkness; her flaming torch reveals her role as Illuminatrix and Psychopomp throughout her three realms: The Heavens, the Earth and the Seas/Underworld. As shown already, it was only later, when consigned to the Underworld, that she assumed the more sinister role of soul-taker. Curiously, her feast day of August 13th as Goddess of Fertility is one in which she is propitiated to avert disaster befalling crops, and is remarkably close to August the 15th, the Feast of the Blessed Virgin, who later appropriated this activity!

In each of her four hands (sometimes six) she wields an object: a key that unlocks occult secrets of the Mysteries and knowledge of the afterlife; a rope/scourge that represents both umbilical cord (birth) and noose (death); the dagger, symbol of true will, cuts delusion and serves to sever both cord (allowing birth) and noose (facilitating release of the soul). In her fourth and final hand (or remaining three) she raises the torch (es) of illumination and initiation. Therefore, in conclusion, she clearly fulfils all primary roles as Creatrix, Illuminatrix and Initiatrix - the (true) Triple (faced) Goddess [George, 1992:142-5].

Both Hekate and Hermes share the role of psychopomp and protector of the crossroads and by-ways of the mental and physical planes. 'Herm' posts often stood beside those of 'Hectarea,' the Triple-Formed Hekate, complete with three heads and six arms. Popular myth presents them as lovers or companions, as healers, patrons of Lunar energy and harbingers of death. Bridging the worlds, they reveal past, present and future simultaneously, bestowing prophetic visions and ancestral communication. From their shadowy twilight world of illusion their gifts of enchantment secure the rapture and bliss of their devotees. Another, less well-known epithet of *'Hekatos,'* meaning - 'Distant-One' (the airborne magic that strikes its target), is one that Hekate (as a form of Artemis), shares with Apollo. Legends also tell of her as a phosphorescent angel, shining in the darkness of the Underworld, where her hypnotic light of trance-formation is revealed within the decaying mounds of the dead. Here her role merges with that of Persephone and of Demeter, with whom she became associated within alternative Greek mythologies.

It must be remembered that the Greeks always saw Hekate as the youthful maiden; she became Crone only to the Romans when Artemis and Selene supplanted her in this form [*ibid.*]. Martha Ann & Dorothy

Myers-Imel [1993:157] also remind us that within the Eleusinian Mysteries, the role of Brimo (the destroyer of life - the terrible one), who births Brimos (the Saviour) is associated with Kybele, Demeter, Persephone and Hekate! She also guides Persephone back to the Upper world from Hades. Yet she is Phosphorous - Dawn and Twilight, Mother and Guardian, Bringer of the Dawn, of Life, Birth and Death, she is the Morning Star, the Bringer of Gnosis, the *'propylia,'* the one before the gate and *'propolos,'* the guardian of the threshold, and 'psychopomp' - the leader of the 'way'. [2]

The shadowy world of dreams is where Demetra George [1992:148] suggests we are cocooned; within the nurturing breast of Hekate, suspended in liminal Time, we reach a still-point (a magical praxis of non-being). This, our moment of becoming, is where she is true Mistress of Fate. Our total submission to her brings the rewards of true Gnosis. Hekate guides the true seeker, Hekate blesses the newly born child, and Hekate shields and guides the soul upon its final journey. Remember, this young and beautiful faerie godmother wears a crown of stars. It is noted that devotees of the Chaldean Oracles contrived to promote Hekate as Sorteira (Saviour), an epiphanic celestial deity and cosmological principle of the cosmic soul, not unlike the 'World Soul' of the Neo-Platonists.[2] In Asia Minor (c800BCE), Hekate was a member of the Mother, Daughter & Son trinity of Kybele, Hekate and Hermes. Yet by 400CE, her role had devolved into the dark and sinister stalker of graveyards, snatcher of souls, Queen of Witchcraft and Sorcery, Patroness of Circe and Medea [*ibid.*]. The Romans, who deemed her roles connected to female blood matters surrounding birth and menstruation as impure, had shifted her, allying her to Diana Triformus, once again shared with Proserpina (Persephone).

Picknett and Prince [1997:85] relate how the Magdalene is the form behind the Black Virgin/Madonna and how the Dominican Archbishop refers to her as both the *'Illuminati'* and *'Illuminatrix,'* traditional roles attributed to her within Gnosticism. Legends claim that she lived in a cave previously the focus of worship for Diana Lucifera (the Illuminatrix). The contentious 'Priory of Sion' revere the Black Madonna as *'Notre Dame de Lumière,'* [Picknett & Prince, 1997:101] yet hint at her role as priestess of Isis, a sacred Hierodule and Initiatrix of the Mysteries. But wait, isn't Isis misplaced here, shouldn't this association be with Hekate? Picknett & Prince [1997:111] go on to relate how in the Pyrenean Cathedral of St. Bertrand-de-Commings, a winged, bird-footed woman is depicted in stone birthing a Dionysian figure reminiscent of a Medieval Green Man. The mother of this Luciferian figure is tentatively suggested as being Lilith, and it may be. Remember though, how Hekate as *'Brimo'* birthed *'Brimos'* the Saviour. It is also noteworthy that legends abound within this region of Dame Herodias, the leader of Night Hags and Witches. Herodias is often a pseudonym for Hekate, who shares the same totem animals of the night. Moreover, French researchers link *'Pedaque,'* the Goose-foot Queen to the 'Queen of Heaven,' and thus by its modern associations to Isis. Yet this title is an older epithet for Hekate, and the bird's feet bring to mind another Queen associated with wisdom and Gnosis - Sheba, Shulamite Priestess to Solomon.

In the Nag Hammadi texts (Pistis Sophia/Virgin of Light), the Magdalene is associated closely with Sophia, the partner of God - she is both the word and wisdom. Scholars now believe strong elements of eroticism prevalent among the texts reveal the true Nature of this relationship. Serpents have always denoted wisdom and these too are totems of Hekate [Picknett & Prince, 1997:142-3]. Sophia is the judge of the dead, and this is another role attributable to Hekate, rather than Isis. Remember, it was (Roman) Christian Gnostics who first identified Sophia with Isis. From their Roman cultural viewpoint, Isis became the predominant 'Queen of Heaven' usurping several former claimants to this title. Isis shown suckling the young Horus pre-empted the Madonna and child effigies adopted by later Christian iconographers.

To the Romans, Isis represented more of how they perceived the Universal Mother to be, divorced from death and all matters unclean. The Roman world spread the popularity of Isis, who prior to this had been one of several female Egyptian deities less important than Nut, Neith, Maat and Hathor. As her popularity rose, Hekate's waned. Thus denigrated to Mistress of Witchcraft and Sorcery did she become immortalised, deprived of her true place within popular and public media. In every sense of the word, Hekate went underground, where her Mysteries continued to be appreciated by all those who knew her true origins. Disguised as Sophia, her role as saviour within the obscure realms of philosophy deeply affected scholars, alert to her true forms of Illuminatrix and Initiatrix. One Medieval scholar in particular, obsessed by Sophia as Initiatrix reports his tumultuous experience of her in Gerhard Wehr's [1990:77] seminal work, *'The Mystical Marriage'*:

> "...immediately after several emotional storms, my spirit broke
> through the gates of Hell to the Godhead born within me, and I was
> encompassed by love as a beloved bride as embraced by her

bridegroom. Just what spiritual triumph this was I cannot write or tell. It cannot be compared with anything except being given life in the midst of death; indeed, it was as life for one who is risen from the dead."

Anyone who has ever experienced this all encompassing elevation will readily empathise with these extraordinarily prophetic words. Yet beyond the beauty and philosophy of the noble Sophia, is *'Sophia Prounicos'* - the wanton whore, from her alone is complete wisdom achieved, a total fusion of spirit magically transposed via the sex act, the ultimate sacrament, a complete trance-formation of mind, body and spirit, enlightenment and full Gnosis - the gift of Hekate, Mistress of 'the Way'.

Picknett and Prince [1997:338-9] explain how Mary of Bethany anointed the feet and hair of Jesus with Spikenard, a ritual performed only by a hierodule, a priestess who by this act is proclaiming his 'Kingship'; his sacred sovereignty is enforced by the rite of *'horasis'* (whole body orgasm facilitated only through sacred sex). Again, these sacred rites were performed within all the ancient Mystery Schools by Hierodules in the King-making of Osiris, Tammuz, and Dionysus. Thus the whore becomes holy and the king becomes Divine. This sacred act allows the complete and ultimate Goddess (Hekate) to manifest in this case within the Magdalene, a priestess not of Isis, but of Hekate. She is the Dearly Beloved, the Black Madonna - the dark and terrible Goddess. Throughout Time her magic has seduced, destroyed and revived all who succumb to her embrace. Picknett and Prince [1997:430] also emphasise that the (Gnostic) Mandean Goddess 'Ruha,' ruler of the realms of darkness is perceived as the Holy Spirit.

Other writers of esoterica have long recognised the occult world of Hekate as existing beyond the superficial levels awarded her by popular mythologies. She is mistress of psycho-sexual magics, leaping between realms and planes, shifting between subtleties of flesh and spirit. Grant [1996:173] describes her role as Mistress of all Realms - of true Witches that traverse alternative dimensions. Her Lunar ophidian current offering magical renewal is germane to the Draconian Cult. Furthermore Grant [*ibid.*] reveals Nyx/Nox as key to the Abyss, guardian of the first Gate within Daath, the bridge between mind and body, the place of trance-formation and the place where Gnosis is achieved. This bridge when activated by (Tantric) Yogic practices, stimulates and sensitises the skin, organs and olfactory units, emitting Kalas of black light, by which all other lights are illuminated. Hekate is the ultimate sexual Initiatrix, the shroud of Mystery and knowing, she is Lady Wisdom, Star Maiden and Gateway to other worlds. Redgrove [1989:120] names Her the *'Aimah Elohim Shekinah.'*

So it is that Hekate's priestesses have performed the initiatory roles of psychopomp from Mari-Ishtar and Magdalena to Jesus and beyond. When trans-figurement is complete, the return from the plateau of Hekate brings Charis, Karuna and Samadhi - beauty, compassion and peace [Redgrove, 1989:125/6]. To Gnostics, Charis the Redeemer was the name of their female Christ, whose Eucharist of menstrual blood preceded that of Christ's [Redgrove, 1989:128]. Again it is Hekate who is mistress of all matters relating to female menstruation, fertility, childbirth and death. Today, within the practices of Tantric Yoga and some forms of Witchcraft, women priestesses continue to adopt the role of hierodule, channelling *'Charis'* into touch-magic *"performed within the circle, that produces a waking dream upon the skin, it is an entry into the astral by the act of horasis"* [*ibid.*]. The gift of the Initiatrix is the synaesthesia wherein the black theatre of the mind becomes a receptacle of light filling the vacuum created by the purged and depressed ego.

Redgrove [1989:156] further proclaims that Hekate is Mary Lucifer, the *'lumen naturae,'* the radiant darkness, and the illuminator of the soul. Mistress of the Psyche, triple-faced Hekate stands at the crossroads of our unconscious looking forwards and backwards into our lives. Her functions fulfil a paradox of criteria, of healing, of destruction, of wisdom, of lunacy and of life and death [George, 1992:145-7]. Here in this mental labyrinth, we face our demons, our negative subversions, here she strips us of our illusions, eliminating all those facets that deny our wholeness, loving her is loving yourself; the revelation of true Gnosis is the realisation of the inherent divinity of oneself.

No definitive form of Hekate exists, spatial representations of her reflect only the needs of the moment, yet she remains the Ultimate Dark Goddess, the primal serpent of cosmic illumination, a role she shares with Lucifer the Light-Bringer, together the twin beings of Phosphorous, the torchbearers of true Gnosis.

Bibliography:
Ann. M. & Myers-Imel. D. 1993 *'Goddesses in World Mythology'* Oxford Uni. Press.

George. D. 1992 *'Mysteries of the Dark Moon'* 1992 Harper Collins. NY

Grant. K. 1996 *'Nightside of Eden'* Skoob Pub. London

Picknett. L & Prince. C. 1997 *'The Templar Revelation'* Corgi. GB

Redgrove. P. 1989 *'The Black Goddess and the Sixth Sense'* Palladin. London

Rudolf. R.von. 1999 www.islandnet.com/~hornowl/library/Hekate.html

Wallis-Budge. E.A. 1971 *'Egyptian Magic'* Dover publications. NY

Watterson. B. 1999 *'Gods of Ancient Egypt'* Bramley Books. Surrey

Wehr. G.1990 *'The Mystical Marriage'* Aquarian Press. UK

1.   www.hecate.org.uk/history.html
2.   www.inanna.virtualave.net/hekate.html

Published previously in:
   The Cauldron #110 - November 2003
   The Hedgewytch #35 - Lammas 2006

5. The Wisdom of Courtly Love

"Pure philosophy is spiritual striving through constant contemplation to attain Gnosis of God...."

Hermes Trismegistus.

Philosophy questions our deepest assumptions and perceptions. It is a process of the reasoning mind (though it is not logic), an aspect of our psyche, our self-image, which guides our thoughts towards consciousness (awareness of the true essence), preparing it for true Gnosis. Indeed, the term Philosophy means: lover of Sophia - Wisdom [Freke & Gandy, 2001:43], the feminine emanation of God; as such she has been the lover and inspiration of all seekers of Gnosis for millennia. This Goddess represents the psyche within, that which we strive to integrate to achieve completion – a true life's work. Sophia, as wisdom, manifests as the higher self, the true self, taking the traditional role of female psychopomp, the light and guide through the initiatory Mysteries of Life: those of sex, birth, death and rebirth.

Within esoteric Christianity, founded as it was upon an amalgam of Jewish and Oriental Mystery traditions, the early Christians recognised in Mary the Mother of Jesus, one manifestation of Sophia; in the Magdalene, beloved of Jesus, another. As Virgin and Whore, they represent pure psyche and manifest embodied psyche - higher and lower aspects of the Goddess, separated by analogy within Mystery Schools to reveal the original Nature of the 'pure' and the later redeemed aspects of the united soul, the complete - wholeness - the perfect [Freke & Gand, 2001:92]. Gnostic inheritors of this infant faith reflected these beliefs in the following poem:

"I was sent forth from the power,
I am the honoured and the scorned one,
I am the Holy One and the whore,
I am the Mother and the Daughter,

72

I am called Sophia by the Greeks,
And Gnosis by the foreigners.
I am the one whose image is great in Egypt,
And the one who has no image among the foreigners."

In 431CE, at Ephesus, the Pagan site of Artemis, the title of 'Queen of Heaven' was bestowed upon Mary in recognition of her metaphysical role within the Mystery Traditions where it was already taught that as 'Bride' of God, she was not mortal. Within the wonderful Old English 'Dream of the Rood,' its heavy Christian overtones fail to subdue Mary in her role as initiator of the annunciation, for it is the gift of herself to God that prompts his response - *" bride of the most excellent Lord of Heaven, Lady of the heavenly Host...you alone ..."* Why these roles are relevant, will soon be made clear as we trace these ideas from the ancient world into that of the Medieval, where fusion of this knowledge formulated the greatest threat to the Church - that of Heresy, particularly that of the Gnostics.

Ancient philosophy held the Body, as physical form, to be the outer self; the Soul, as Psyche, or Mind, was the inner self. Pneuma/Nous or consciousness, perceived as the animating Divine spark was experienced as the 'knowing' principle. Therefore the true Mystery of Gnosis becomes a conscious awareness of God [Freke & Gandy, 2001:63]. Hence, he who truly knows himself knows God. In Greek myth, Psyche (the soul-self) is rescued by Eros (Love) personified in the adoration of the ideal woman; as the object rather than the subject of his desire, she becomes the vehicle for his Gnosis – his completeness, his perfection.

Gnostics believe that from our fall into gross matter, there are three stages by which we can return to Grace [Freke & Gandy, 2001:80]:

* The psychic – where through our repentance, we realise the need to change, and our wish to be purified.

* The pneumatic – our redemption, which hones our devotion, focus and will through its desire, its love of the Goddess.

* Finally, The Mystical Union, or marriage - true bliss. Full conscious awareness of self and deity.

These understandings were developed and incorporated within

heretical teachings of 10th century Gnostics - the Balkan Bogamils who founded the sect eventually known as 'Cathars' in France, Spain and Italy. Claiming to be inheritors of the true faith, heirs to the Mysteries and wisdom of the ancients, they paid the ultimate price - that of death. The hand of a fearful Church instigated one of the most vicious pogroms of all Time.

It has been suggested by many scholars and poets, Dante Gabriel Rossetti (Pre-Raphaelite artist) to name but one of them, that this deeply mystical faith influenced the literary genres of the Medieval period, leading Victorian academics in 1883 to subsume all forms under the term of 'Courtly Love'. It is argued that hidden within the prose and verse are the secrets of salvation, of completeness through the adoration of Truth and Beauty, of Wisdom, manifest in Woman, as the soul seeks to be 'pure,' to be 'perfect'. Nevertheless, there are problems inherent within this supposition; mainly those of variety of form and subject matter, ranging from the vulgar to the devotional, and from farce to adventure. What all these lyrical forms share, is a common interest in the joys, despairs, longings and satisfactions of the many forms of love, either requited or unrequited; a recognition of the magnetism, magic and Mystery of love. What we now need to do, is explore in depth, this enigmatic genre to determine its connection to the Cathars, Gnosis and Sophia.

Within the closing years of the 2nd millennium, modern academia recognised that previous pre-requisites for the term 'Courtly Love' were vague, erroneous and restrictive, and so the boundaries were moved, separating a genre that still avoids tight classification [Boase, 1977:117]. From their summative research, it was concluded that, for a few short decades, a concept later to be eclipsed by the popular 'Romances' emerged within the Southern regions of France, around the Languedoc and Provençal. These regions embraced the Cathar heartland, the heretical sect devoted to Sophia, Goddess of Wisdom. Here, Neo-platonic ideals of a fine love, a pure love of the highest Mystery evolved, that of 'fin d'amors' - the souls' nostalgic and insatiable desire to dissolve itself in the unity from whence it sprang

Troubadours and Menestrals transposed their mystical teachings, formalised in song, prose and verse. Ironically, numerous works recognised the irony of a world that dishonoured women, yet almost deified them as the virtual personification of Love [Grant & Kay, 1999:35]. Art, as life, reflected this paradox. Outside Provençal, the punning and satirising of love sought expression within various literary forms. In general, the mediating theme was one of ennoblement and perfection, acquired through the love of a 'gentil' woman. Of course, love as a medium for ennoblement had been widely acknowledged by the Classical Greek poets - Virgil and Plato; but the concept of woman as a focus, in whose devotion and inspiration engendered mans' elevation, appears to be a new innovation. This ran parallel to Church theology, where man was obliged to emulate Christ's humanity - to seek a 'perfect love' through the rising 'Cult of the Virgin,' a clever synthesis of Pagan (latent) sexuality and Christian morality, exploiting the conflict between body and soul as the highest dynamic. This was a massive paradigm shift from earthly to Divine love, from the profane to the sacred. Worship of the Virgin responded to a vital necessity for the Church while under threat and pressure - adapting what it could not suppress [Warner, 2000:135-7].

Folquet de Marseille, a Troubadour, wrote: *"God in whose power it lays, had made me standard bearer for my Lady of the Pure in Loves High Kingdom."* Although clearly dedicated to the Virgin Mary, its context is in her role as Sophia. Cogent to this, the infiltration of a miasma of Oriental ideas permeated the West via Arab texts and treatises, which, in the Church's haste to achieve *'Prisca Sapientia'* (ancient wisdom), they avidly translated. Perceived as heresies, their contrary doctrines were cleverly re-worked to conceal their truths. Despite numerous forms of this newly developing and popular style, salvation through love remained a collective theme. Nowhere was this more deeply imbued than in the lyrics of the Languedoc Troubadours. Here, perfect love reached its apogee in the genre 'fin d'amors,' and one upon which we may now concentrate. It is noteworthy that the term 'fin' within 'fin d'amors,' stems from the term 'fyn' - an alchemical definition that denotes absolute purity (without flaw or blemish) within gold and silver smithing.

Southern France was geographically close to Northern (Muslim) Spain. Thus it can be observed how the seeds of 7th century Greco-Arab love poetry *(Udhri)*, extolling unseen heroines as foci for aspiring Gnosis, germinated in the fertile sociological and religious grounds of the Languedoc. Guillaume, IX Duke of Aquitaine (1071-1127), a warrior knight, crusader and amorous lover is generally credited by most academics as the first Troubadour within Provence, the heart of the Aquitaine [Burrow &Turville-Petre, 1995:81]. His family held many dynastic ties with Muslim Spain and he effectively combined 10th century Arab *'kharjas'* (songs and refrains) with the contemporary styles of the 'Jongleurs' (wandering entertainers).

Themes of erotic love and mysticism introduced spiritual elements not present in earlier works such as the Edda's and Saga's, which were primarily tales of bravery, adversity and courage interwoven with praeternatural events, unfolding to reveal the spatial history and beliefs of migrating peoples. Kieckhefer [2000:105] posits that even here, women are often central to these plots, acting as healers and guides, albeit in the roles of seductresses and hags. Within the rich and illustrious courts of Southern France, 'fin d'amors' developed from 'Gai Saber,' a form of suave Paganism, a happy wisdom or gay science, rising to challenge the Christian ideal of fidelity, marriage, manhood and virtue. Both Eleanor of Aquitaine (1122-1204), wife of Plantagenet King Henry II of England (also known as holder of the Devil's crown) and her own daughter Marie of Champagne (d1198) endorsed the many forms of 'Courtly Love' centred around traditional themes of vassalage, fealty and love longing experienced as *'joy d' amour'* - the agony and ecstasy of frustration.

For a Time, Bisson [1999:220] believes that women suspended the reality of a tedious existence, where their status as mere chattels, plunder and loot, frequently subjected them to rape, defilement and abduction. Within matters of state and politics, they were ever subservient to their husbands and fathers. Instead, they now focused on more pleasant interludes, fictionalising men as *their* captives, subject to their every caprice and whim. Indeed, many impecunious knights, deprived of land through primogeniture, did receive 'gentil' tutelage, fully endorsed by the Church, from such ladies as these. However, themes of manners and coquette, intrigue and elaboration have obfuscated the true Nature of the Cathar wisdom native to these people. The eloquent wit of the Troubadours added piquancy to their sauce with themes of Gnostic and Islamic heresies rich in cosmological speculation and Hermetic principles, providing a sharp contrast to Christian pedagogy; wisdom was the highest prize, sought through the Grail.

Father Denomy [1947:59] recognised, nearly sixty years ago the inherent anathema to the Church within the 'Cult of the Beloved,' whose basic principles were:

* Ennoblement of human love.
* Elevation of the beloved to a superior position than the lover's.
* The concept of love as ever insatiate, of ever increasing ardour.

He further postulates them as distinct from all other forms of love explored by the Toubadours (Trouvères). By the above definitions, the surge of the lover to rise in worth and virtue towards the beloved, through the force and energy of desire, to seek spiritual elevation through her, was a heresy of the highest order. This compels everyone to love, since only through it can one be ennobled and virtuous. Conversely, it condones fornication, adultery and sacrilege as sources of virtue, since no bar exists. Its expression is both sensual and spiritual - an heretical paradox. Ferrante [1975:66] asserts that evident within this paradox, woman, as a unified construct, deified as Love, becomes its earthly manifestation. Unity with her on a psychological level brings man into harmony with the Macrocosm. But, she adds, later, this harmony is rejected in favour of fragmentation of the psyche; the individual questor becomes aloof from society, where woman tests and tempts, rather than inspires him.

Aristotelian influences replaced platonic idealism and as a symbol, woman barely held her status; as intermediary between man and his God, union is now sought through her, but no longer with her. In a truly narcissistic way, his ideal self is projected onto, then reflected back from her. Duncan [1995: xviii], further argues this was nothing more than a device adopted for mans' own idealisation of self, realised through projection of his 'anima' onto woman as an external focus for his elevation. Wholeness and integration of his feminine aspects and attributes, balanced and in harmony with natural male instincts, are thus tempered and conquered. Heer [1993:130] concludes woman as custodian of mans' soul - God's surrogate. This Jungian analysis reveals clues to deeper Mysteries behind such rationale.

Marcabru (fl.1135-50), himself a Troubadour, proposed that it was indeed the love of the lover, and not his beloved that ennobled a man [Denomy, 1947:60]. Nowhere is this more clearly evidenced than in the 'Tale of Gawain and the Green Knight'. Here the unknown author implies that women are untrustworthy creatures, whose devices contrive his failure. Gawain's love, more for himself than for his Lady, facilitates his denial and rejection of her gifts, offered for his salvation. Although the deceit he pays for is clearly his own, he denies responsibility for it [Newman, 1968: vii]. His failure to recognise her value and worth as an earthly manifestation of Sophia starkly contradicts the blazing pentangle of the five knightly virtues upon his shield, which when yielded, induce completion - perfection. For him, Eros (Love) and Psyche (Soul) fail to unite. His eternal reminder of this regret is symbolised in the acceptance of the green girdle, worn in the fullest sense of penitence, as a talisman into which it is hoped that all the grace and wisdom of 'woman' will be imparted. Seen by some as an ambiguous emblem of success (in that he lives and defeated the Green Knight), the following line taken from the poem clearly states otherwise: *"the token of untrawthe that I am tan inne,"* (the sign of that untruth which I am found in).

Later legends known as 'Romances' developed this theme, reflecting the highest ideals (spiritual) as subject to love, war, fate and fortune, heavily influenced by the *'Roman de la Rose'* and Dante's *'Divine Comedy.'* Germane to the 'Romance,' were the myths and legends of Arthur, once and future King, conceptualised as ('Celtic') King and supreme emblem of Honour. Now, the 'courtly' knight, magically empowered, began his epic spiritual quest depicted within numerous Grail legends, where women once more play strong, though no longer central roles within this emerging allegorical genre. It is important to remember that the Grail within Celtic myth confers the power of fecundity and wealth to he alone who prevails the true and correct understanding of the Goddess, expressed in their relationship with her earthly manifestations - women. Thus 'Sovereignty' represents autonomy for her and land and title for him, a Pagan concept ironically Christianised prior to the Churches purge against the Dualist Heretics c1209 [Jones, 1985:16]. Sovereignty as a principle is preserved within Irish legend of the 'Tale of Sir Gawain and the Loathly Lady' (Lady Ragnall). His rights to success and fulfilment, conferred through her, are dependent upon his recognition and honour of her own autonomy; love requires freedom of will and awareness of something not possessed. Chretien's 'Perceval' exemplorises these concepts; in it, he depicts the rape and abuse of Faerie maidens who provide hospitality to wayfarers, as the reason for their disappearance.

Of relevance also to many ancient Mystery Cults (particularly of Ishtar and Tammuz) is the principle of 'ritual' love of a woman, especially one of a higher status than the lover; his spiritual and physical fulfilment is possible only through her Love. Jones [1985:16] also confers the possibility of the Mystery Cult of the Grail as a survival of these descent myths where he is reborn through her Love and his subservience to her. Immortalised within their lyrics, each subsequent author reworked principal themes; Medieval troubadours, aware of such traditions maintained these powerful praxes. Original subtleties relating to sublimation of the male ego, however, became subsumed within Christian legerdemain, obscured from all but the alert reader. Many Troubadours were also clerics, whose depiction of women as hags, temptresses, nymphs and seductresses in distracting the hero from his quest, ironically fail to conceal their true role as initiators and guides. Kieckhefer [2000:17] suggests that allegory and mysticism were employed by the Church in their concealment of the role of women relative to man's fate, repressing the truth within their patristic works.

Total communion on all three planes of mind, body and spirit bound in truth to each other only, as a concept, is almost entirely absent from all love lyrics outside the Languedoc. Again, Denomy [1947:30] advises that in the mystical Neo-platonic philosophy of Avicenna (987-1030CE), sensual love is freely celebrated as a way to spiritual fulfilment. In his 'Treatise on Love,' human love of the sexes is perceived as a positive and contributory role in the ascent of the Soul on its journey towards Union. This ennobling power becomes the driving force to perfection - The Supreme Good. He believed that only through such pure love could man seek the source of Virtue. Common within Arab philosophy were the double truths, of esoteric and exoteric doctrines; yet the former were often at variance with the latter's orthodox teachings. Avicenna wrote:

> "This book contains indications on the basic notions of metaphysics and annotations on its propositions - He only who is endowed with the necessary aptitude may study it, while he who is deprived of that aptitude, may draw no profit from it."

Avicenna and his contemporaries expounded love as a vital source of Divine inspiration, yet this great good could also be considered a great evil by the Church. Certainly, Chretien, court lyricist to Marie of Champagne, expressed such concerns regarding the incompatibility of '*fin d'amors*' with the teachings of the Church. Mary becomes a Muse to mans' achievements, a foil for all his needs, pains and devotions. Boase [1977:126] maintains that Marianism was, to a great extent, both cause and consequence of the perceived decadence of Troubadour poetry. During the 12th century, the Church moved to consecrate marriage (something it did not actually achieve until 1563), a practice held in anathema by Cathars. This tension affected all literary motifs within the cultural phenomenon of 'Courtly Love'.

The Dichotomy of man as both a child of Nature and of God is clearly expressed within Chrétien's '*Lancelot*'; but, his later work - '*Perceval*,' provides further endorsement of 'fin d'amors' - pure, perfect love, the central tenet of Cathar Gnosticism. Within this tale lies the Grail at its deepest level - in the feminine mother symbol. His grief over her death is expressed through his failure during the encounter with the 'Mothers and the Lady' [Heer, 1993:146]; both Grail and Lance mature as sexual symbols. In their union, lies completeness, wholeness; this is why he seeks the Grail, the thinly disguised mystical symbol of the Goddess. Understanding facilitates his receipt. Jones [1985:5] stresses the irony of a Church that began its purge with the Albigensian crusade against Gnostic heretics in 1209CE who well understood the Grail's significance, yet adopted the 'Eucharist' into its own Dogma in 1215.

Wolfram's *'Parzifal'* and Gottfried's *'Tristan,'* both written in full allegorical style, also promoted the higher principles of love. Gottfried artfully reveals the essence of Catharism, through his descriptions of a shared sacrament by the (pure) lovers. True only unto themselves and a higher wisdom and placed above all earthly ties, this was a total binding - spiritually, physically and emotionally. In another work, *'Bel Inconnu,'* written in the late 12th century by Renaut de Beajeu, women are extolled as the source of everything that is good, a theme germane to *'fin d'amors'*; moreover, man must honour and serve her. Later, in 'Nekyia' (a work similar to 'The Inferno'), our hero descends to the Underworld Castle within the City of the Dead, to face rigorous trials that will engender his full growth. Triumphantly, his salvation from the severities of painful transformation is given through 'the serpent's kiss,' whereupon his work of perfection is complete [Heer, 1993:157]. Among Gnostic sects, serpents were of course, the ultimate and sacred symbol of salvation. Revealed within allegorical myths of a primordial mother and father are profound philosophical clues concerning our essential Nature that encode our transformational relationship with the Divine feminine - Wisdom/Sophia, especially its promise of *"...those who understand, will not taste death"* [Freke & Gandy, 2001:3].

C.S. Lewis [1979:48] considered allegorisation of pantheism within poetry a device pre-requisite to monotheism, illuminating the way forward. Instructional and heretical, it facilitated absorption of Pagan texts and themes. Allegory was thus utilised as a popular visual and poetic teaching aid. As a highly transportative media, it found expression in the Cosmos of ineffable archetypes, the pleroma of Mystery, and in that cosmos of appearances - the Kenoma of Manifestation. Love is revealed as the Pleroma of the Law - ourselves as products of God. One such 'Mystery' play allegorises an attack by the Devil upon the soul, as the siege of a Lady (Sophia-the soul) in a Castle of Earth (the body). Christ (to whom our hero is supposed to relate), in the form of a suitor knight offers to save her from her foe. First of all, he must face many dangers on her behalf, which finally inculcate his death (mirroring his own crucifixion/ initiatory journey). Christ is in effect, both lover and saviour of the soul (Wisdom/Sophia), redeeming her from all earthly bonds. Thus, true love of a man for a woman elevates them both! [Burnley, 1998:186]. These scripted explorations of the psyche on its journey towards fulfilment later synthesised with the 'Cult of the Virgin,' where Mary as Sophia, replaced woman as man's initiator.

Women as her earthly manifestations devolved slowly into marginalized stereotypes, reflecting once again the roles of hags and temptresses; for men, the message was clear - duty and honour before love. After the horrors of the Albigensian crusade, themes of love turned to those of either pious, vacuous love or idyllic earthly love. No longer was *'fin d'amors'* the focus of ennoblement, which had, since its inception been a synthesis of Gnostic, platonic, Pagan and Arabic ideals exemplified in women as representatives of the Goddess Sophia/Wisdom. Throughout the Medieval periods in England, France and Europe, beauty and grace had been the inspiration of the poet. Women evolved into fantasy constructs of idealised femininity, a noble virtue that masked her higher purpose. Complex rules of conduct, ritual and worship of womankind's many glories were given full expression. Only in the Provençal *'fin d'amors'* did this achieve its true literary purpose; of maintaining the Mysteries for all those with eyes to see and ears to hear. Transcendental expression induced metaphors for the Divine; mediating mechanisms for those esoteric yet 'courtly' circles of the lavish Languedoc.

Bibliography:

Bisson, L. M. 1999 *'Chaucer and The Late Medieval World.'* N.Y., Macmillan Press.

Boase, R. 1977 *'The Origin and Meaning of Courtly Love.'* Manchester, Manchester Uni. Press.

Burnley, D. 1998 *'Courtliness in Medieval Literature.'* England, Longman Press.

Burrow, J.A. & Turville-Petre, T. [ed] 1996 *'A Book of Middle English.'* England, Blackwell Pub.

Denomy, A.J. 1947 *'The Heresy of Courtly Love.'* U.S.A. The Declan &

McMullen Com. Inc.

Duncan, T.G. [ed] 1995 *'Medieval English Lyrics 1200-1400.'* London, Penguin Books Ltd.

Ferrante, J. 1975 *'Woman as Image in Medieval Literature.'* U.S.A. Columbia Press.

Freke, T & Gandy, P, 2001 *'Jesus and the Goddess.'* Great Britain, Thorsons.

Grant, S. & Kay, S. [ed] 1999 *'The Troubadours.'* Cambridge, Cambridge Uni Press.

Heer, F. 1993 *'The Medieval World: Europe 1100-1350.'* G.B. Butler & Tanner Ltd. Federation Press.

Kieckhefer, R. 2000 *'Magic in the Middle Ages.'* U.K. Cambridge Uni. Press.

Lewis, C.S. 1979 *'The Allegory of Love: A Study in Medieval Tradition.'* Oxford, Oxford Uni. Press.

Newman, F. [ed] 1968 *'The Meaning of Courtly Love.'* Albany, N.Y. Press

Warner, M, 2000 *'Alone of Her Sex; The Myth & Cult of The Virgin Mary.'* G.B., Vintage Press.

The Tale of Sir Gawain and the Green Knight.
Previously published in:
> *The Cauldron* #111 – February 2004
> *Pendragon* # XXXII no. 4 Summer 2005

6. The Dance of the Seven Veils

In seeking origins for the infamous 'Dance of the Seven Veils' supposedly once performed by Salome for the head of John the Baptist, we may have to concede an enigma. Many scholars consider that it most probably derived from cumulative Middle Eastern myths and folklore, particularly around the 'Holy Lands'. The Bible itself reveals little; its few clues are confined to a handful of verses in Mathew [14:3] and Mark [6:17-29]. These mention only the dancing by the daughter of Herodias that so pleased Herod he offered her anything she desired, even half his kingdom; Luke mentions only his arrest, and John makes no mention of the Baptist's fate at all.

Salome is known to us only through the writings of the 1st century Jewish chronicler, Josephus, who in his 'Antiquities of the Jews' tells us that after the death of John, both Salome and her scheming mother Herodias are exiled (along with Herod) to Lugdunum (near Spain). Salome is said to have drowned crossing a frozen river and Herodias survived in legend to become identified during the Middle Ages with *'Diana nocticula'* - Queen of the night hags. Here clear examples of Christian morality justify the fate of two women, so despised by the early Church.

However, despite the Biblical omission of this dance as being composed of 'seven veils' or its erotic associations, there is within academia an understanding that when 'dancing' is mentioned in the Old Testament, it does indeed refer to a long tradition of ecstatic dancing, upon which no prohibitions were placed. The sacred Nature of dance, perceived as a union of spirit with deity, was unabashedly erotic. Female dancers were often hierodules - sacred priestesses, assigned to specific deities within the temples. Co-incidentally, Inanna/Ishtar was the ultimate hierodule and her influential Eastern cult was eventually suppressed by pious Christians wishing to subjugate both the Divine feminine and all women who served her variant forms.

As an expression of female power and erotic beauty that once celebrated the ineffable Creatrix, dancing became increasingly virtuous under the direction of patristic oligarchies. In the New Testament, where mentioned at all, dancing was clearly devotional, yet even as the chroniclers endeavoured to conceal the former free licence and eroticism, by the 4th century, the Church Fathers admit to railing against it. In one of the earliest and most influential scholarly histories of dancing published in 1754 (written by Louis de Cahusac), is cited historical sanctions given by the eminent Church Father, Gregory of Nazianzus (330-390CE), who in his letter to Emperor Julian states: *"...if you give yourself up to the dance, I consent to it...but why revive the licentious dances of the barbarous Herodias, who spilt the blood of a saint..."* Damning evidence indeed for this early understanding of Salome's dance to have been an erotic one.

Historically of course, erotic and/or ecstatic dancing has been widely practised throughout the world by all ancient cultures as far back as the Palaeolithic (Old Stone Age) and was widely celebrated throughout the Mediterranean and Asia predominantly. Nude and erotic dancing is a common artistic motif utilised provocatively on ancient and classical Greek, Roman and Egyptian pottery. The pre-Islamic Middle East, cherished a close affinity with the Divine feminine, enjoyed through sexual fertility rites performed in all expressive media including poetry, dance, song and ceremony. Within Biblical historiography the eternal feminine is revered in a collection of erotic verses known as the *'Song of Solomon,'* and which are related to the *'Shekinah,'* the female aspect of 'Wisdom' and spirit-bride of God.

In Sumer, where tales of the seven wind spirits/winds originate, we discover the lil-itu (powerful spirit/wind) known from around 4000BCE. Not until circa 700BCE within Jewish folklore does this become properly gendered and a night-hag, personified in the now eponymous Lilith! Better, more recent academic translations place her as the indwelling spirit of the tree within the Epic of Gilgamesh. As patriarchy tightened its grip, Yahwist priests demonised numerous former female deities and otherworld entities, including (lilitu) into *succubae*. Instantly we can see where all this is going and how it begins to tie things up.

Lilith becomes a demonised Queen, a 'harlot,' consigned to the ranks of forbidden nocturnal activities. A thing unclean. Yet she, like Pazuzu had originally been a wind spirit who brought pestilence, disease and drought (hence the association with the killing of young mothers and babies particularly vulnerable during such occurrences), but who could also be called upon to *protect* life from their gruelling manifestations, to be overlooked, 'passed over' in fact. The pattern becomes even more familiar as that re-told through the lens of an antagonistic tribal patriarchal priesthood, the bane of the Western world for two thousand years (Not

Judaism nor Christianity per se, just certain aspects of theology/dogma) Suffice to say that Lilith is not at all the figure misrepresented by history, nor is she the personage suggested by the many icons erroneously associated with her.

She is clearly the indwelling spirit of the tree, the 'Shakti' of God, His source of empowerment and beloved. There is only one Queen who is described as the Queen of Heaven and the Great Below, the Queen of Love, whose Beauty is renowned yet whose war-like prowess demands her due as Tutelary Goddess. Holder of the sacred Me, she holds the Tablets of Destiny, the Fate of Mankind.

Gilgamesh rejects her guidance and has then to traverse a circuitous path to enlightenment and self-realisation. She is therefore the instrument of Chaos as Gilgamesh discovered - the aid to egress and evolution. She follows through to the needful clearing of debris. What we 'desire' is often a fantasy projection, or a whim; 'needs' on the other hand are often immutable.

Inanna/Ishtar once transformed into the debased and despised harlot - the 'Whore of Babylon,' the now separated Shekinah became virginalised and quietly disappeared, surviving only tentatively within the mystical Jewish Kabbalah. Consequently, these former Goddesses entered the realm of folklore and legend to exemplify all desired and detested states of womanhood. Cautionary, instructive tales abound within the Jewish Midrash (studies of Hebrew legends) of woman as seductresses and many are coterminous with those of the bible, including Salome.

The 'alphabet of Ben Sira,' written and collected during the 7-10th centuries, is a series of commentaries that pronounces stern judgements on the seductive elements of the Hebrew Bible (The Torah). Naturally, artists drawing inspiration from these and other ancient texts have created visual works that represent a record of how history has perceived Biblical and mythological events.

Renaissance Europe was no exception. With the fall of Constantinople, a cultural tidal wave enveloped the West, sloughing off its fascination with all things Oriental or exotic until the 19th century turned. Prolific images displayed the female form in various stages of undress, often subject more to the imagination of the artist than to historical accuracy.

Several of these images linked the concept of the 'descent of Inanna/ Ishtar with the wearing of and dancing with veils. Curiously, within Turkey, it is known that harem dancers used silken scarves to flirt and tease while dancing for the Sultans. This genre of dance is named the '*kaytan oyuna amoros.*'

Modern Turkish dance, despite changing cultural uses of the veil, still retains the half veil, which in Islamic countries is now perceived as a modesty garment. It is nevertheless imperative to assert that this was not requisite within the Biblical period known to Salome. Of relative fascination is a Persian dance of the nomadic '*qashqai*' in the 'fars' province (much persecuted by modern Islamists); enigmatically named the '*raqs-e haft dastmal*' - this is literally the dance of the seven scarves!

Such exotica enjoyed many theatrical influences. Consequently, it is not clear whether Oscar Wilde really did invent the term: '*dance of the seven veils,*' when writing his stage production of 'Salome,' though I personally feel this is extremely unlikely given that Wilde was a highly educated man, well versed in mythologies and traditions of the ancient world. In addition, he was on good terms with many Jews, of orthodox and heterodox persuasion, and therefore privy to a more liberal cultural viewpoint counter to that of the Western Christian world. He could therefore, have unconsciously inserted into his then controversial play 'Salome,' a simple stage direction, whereby she is asked to perform what to him was common knowledge.

Unfortunately for both Wilde (and the composer Strauss), moral outrage from a paradoxically sexually ambiguous society crushed the cumulative perceptions of artists and visionaries accrued over several hundreds of years. Pornographers and feminists still hotly debate the historical accuracy of this dance. Each generation of scholars will assuredly exploit those elements that support their own teleological viewpoint.

The 'descent' of Inanna/Ishtar through the seven gates is one of our greatest myths revealed from the ancient world. Historically, there are two main versions, written in cuneiform (simple texts made by pressing a reed stylus into wet clay) and found in the regions known to the Greeks as 'Mesopotamia'. The first of these dates speculatively from circa 4000BCE, the second version followed around two and a half thousand years later. Both relate how the Sumerian Goddess Inanna (who later become known as Ishtar after the Akkadian invasions) made an epic journey into the 'Underworld.'

In the first and oldest version, this Tutelary Goddess wishes to gain the secrets of death and the afterlife; the second tale however, is thematically distinct and relates how she seeks instead to rescue her lover Tammuz/Dumuzzi in a perennial fertility rite. Either way, her journey necessitated descent via a series of seven gates and is expressed by some modern scholars as representative of the seven mythical stages of our humanity. At each gate, veils are removed, one by one, to allow complete sublimation of the ego, or evolution of the self. These veils may serve as metaphors for either the substantive aspects of our material world that surround and encompass our material 'bodies,' or they may be viewed as levels of our subconscious that lay bare our true selves when removed. Poetically, both interpretations offer proper and valuable analyses of this ancient tale. Upon consideration, it is quite probable the original context reveals a more ritualistic, magical tool evincing a trance journey through seven stages of altered consciousness for a higher purpose. It is herein suggested:

The Descent of Inanna
'from the great above she opened her ears to the great below
from the great above the Goddess opened her ears to the great below
from the great above Inanna opened her ears to the great below
my Lady abandoned Heaven and Earth to descend to the Underworld
she abandoned her office of holy priestess
to descend to the Underworld
she gathered together the measures of
heavenly and earthly powers
she took them into her hands
with the measures of heavenly and earthly
powers she prepared herself
Inanna set out to the Underworld...'

And of Ishtar...

'To the Land of No Return, the realm of Ereshkigal,
Ishtar, the daughter of the Moon, set her mind.
To the dark house, the abode of Irkalla,
To the house which none leave who have entered it,
To the road from which there is no way back,
To the house wherein the entrants are bereft of light,
Where dust is their fare and clay their food,
Where they see no light, residing in the darkness,
Where they are clothed like birds, with wings for garments,
And where over door and bolt is spread dust.

When Ishtar reached the gate of the Land of No Return,
She said to the gatekeeper:
"O gatekeeper, open thy gate, open thy gate so that I may enter!"[1]

Inanna possessed not the dark secrets of death and rebirth; only the virtues of life and fertility…and so she sought entry to these Mysteries. At the gates of the Underworld she pauses to prepare and seek permission to enter. She is challenged at each stage to discard yet more of her material form, her jewellery, girdles, and royal regalia that bind her spirit to the manifest world, for it is only thus, 'naked' (without consciousness), that we may enter the void of eternity. Then as now, we approach the Underworld to encounter the 'other' and learn through the feigned dance of death to face our true self, and discover equilibrium - the balance of light and dark. To learn the true cycle of life is to discover our own worthiness to receive, understand and hold deity.

It is also noteworthy to remember how at Sais, Neith, a warrior deity similar to Ishtar, as the oldest and wisest of Egyptian Goddesses, also maintained significant links with the dead. Her symbol of crossed arrows represents the strife between opposites, the paradox of life and death, of destiny and fate, and of light and dark. She was the personification of the eternal feminine and holder of 'Her' sacred Mysteries. These roles were later usurped by the rising cult of Isis, whose followers spoke of their new and popular Goddess through many of phrases formerly reserved for Neith, including the most profound of all, that of - *"the lifting of the veil."*

Even so, 'Her' eponymous dance generates, like Shiva the eternal, cosmic rhythm of the Universe.

References

1. <u>E.A. Speiser. [trans] 'Ancient Near Eastern Texts'.</u>
   www.gatewaystobabylon.com

Previously published in:
The Hedgewytch #36 – November 06

7. The Hand of Fatima

Pre-Islamic mythology drawn largely from Arabic sources offers an enchanting cocktail of magic, sorcery, fable and illusion generously laced with glorious tales of genies (the 'fiery Jinn'), bewitched jewels, fabulous beasts and flying carpets, all extravagantly maintained in folklore through countless generations. Among these, the 'Evil Eye,' is a concept especially common across the Near and Middle East, India, Turkey, North Africa and Central America. Interestingly, the origin of the English word 'to fascinate' (to charm by enchantment), is derived from the Latin *'fascinum'* - the evil eye. Belief in the 'Evil Eye', more generally given as an attribute of Witches and sorcerers during the Middle Ages is known to have spread to the Celtic speaking peoples of Northern Europe via trade, migration and conquest.

Often maliciously, this covetous, all too human glance is deflected most effectively by a talisman or charm that incorporates somewhat sympathetically, an eye. Frequently ascribed to a deity, as typified in the Eye of Horus and/or Ma-at in Egypt, this glyph is popularly included upon the apotropaic 'Hand of Fatima' in all its stylised variants. Through obscure origins, this symbol reflects a complex synthesis of both tribal and universal acknowledgements to the eternal efficacy of female divinity manifest within simulacra of 'hand' and 'eye'.

Histories of faith, belief and superstition preserve the iconic hand as a manifest projection of Divine power, bestowing blessings, benedictions, providence generosity, grace and favour. When combined with an eye glyph, it signifies clairvoyance and aversion of the 'evil eye.' It transmits spirit, protection and justice. The right hand (dexter) signifies a blessing; the left hand (sinister) however, is held to inflict a curse or banishing. Since the dawn of civilization, hands articulate by gesture and are thus said 'to speak'. Countless religious icons consist simply of 'hands'. By extension, as a symbol they represent the power and might of 'God' to inflict or protect as willed or invoked.

Another combined representation of hand and eye, is encapsulated in the Hindu 'Humsa,' cogently named the 'All Seeing Eye of Mercy.' Its Tibetan counterpart is also used to ward off evil influences bringing protection to its wearer. Associations with the Goddess 'Tanith' forge further links to the Punic (Phoenician) religion in ancient Northern Africa,

'Khamsa - Fatae Dexter'

where apotropaic eyes were the design of choice, gracing prows upon sailing fleets built by these infamous Mediterranean seafarers.

More remote still in history and geography, are the prehistoric First Nation sites of Moundville, Alabama, and Mesoamerica, where comparable designs have been discovered, all portraying the unmistakable image of an eye embossed, painted or inlaid upon a 'spirit' hand. Most particularly, the eye itself is either painted blue, or is inlaid with semi-precious blue stones of either lapis lazuli or turquoise in alternate concentric circles of dark and light shades. Due to a common folkloric belief that (often fair or red-haired) people with blue eyes possess the power (witting or otherwise) to cast the evil eye, another of similar hue is required to deflect it!

Similarly known in Jewish lore as the 'Hand of Miriam' (Mary, bride of God) or 'Hamesh/Chamsa,' it appears in various stylized forms, most often as a hand decorated with fish and hexagrams with three fingers raised, having two opposing thumbs arranged symmetrically, depicting its dualistic ambiguity as both right and left hands, which banishes/averts evil influences and invokes a blessing simultaneously. Widely used in amuletic jewellery, as charms over windows and doorways, and in wall decorations, its sustained popularity attests to the continued belief in its efficacy. Part of the enduring myth now coterminous with these 'five' telesmic fingers concerns the holy teachings relative to each branch of the Semitic faiths of the Middle East. These are: The Pentateuch, The Torah and The Five Pillars of Islam, a testament to the synergistic evolution of parallel symbology. The evil eye (*ayin harah*) is equally significant in Jewish folklore. Ashkenazi Jews traditionally exclaimed against the evil eye in Yiddish, '*Keyn aynhoreh!*' to ward off impending misfortune in cases where providence was boasted of too rashly.

The Islamic 'Khamsa' (Arabic for five), is generally indistinct in design from the Jewish motif, but may occasionally incorporate additional calligraphy over the fingers (in preference to the fish and the hexagram of sacred Yiddish iconography) and more rarely in a natural form in which there is only one thumb. Archaeological evidence supports the principle of a downward-pointing protective 'Hamsa' pre-dating both Judaism and Islam, being indicative of an ancient Middle Eastern Goddess whose 'hand' (or 'vulva') averts the evil eye. Tradition associates this symbol with the fabled daughter of the Prophet Mohammed: Fatima Zahra. Who then was Fatima and why is she credited with so much power, especially over fate?

Traditionally known as the first wife of the first Shi'a Imam and the 'daughter' of the Prophet Mohammed, Fatima was the matriarch from whom all Shi'a Muslims claim their decendancy. In fact the Fatimid dynasty is named in her honour and remembrance. She is described as a faithful, pious woman and worker of miracles, the ultimate symbol of womanly virtue and motherhood, of holy reverence, somewhat akin to Mary, mother of Jesus. The intriguing epithet, 'Zahra,' is an Arabic word signifying illuminated, bright or shining; hence she is often revered as Al-Zahra, the 'Lady of Light'. However, the origins of Fatima herself are far more interesting, revealing a hidden treasure of considerable esoteric magnitude.[1]

Within Islam, women often feature as second-class citizens and yet in the figure of the fabled 'Fatima,' we find an unprecedented spiritualization of the feminine. In the *'Omm-al-Kitab'* she is described as seated upon a throne in paradise ablaze with a glorious myriad of lights, be-decked with two earrings, wearing a crown and carrying a sword.[2]

This regalia is said to represent:
Crown - Mohammed;

Earrings -her two sons (heirs to the dynasty);

Sword - Ali, her husband and chosen one;

Throne - Seat of Dominion, the resting place of God,
the most high (Allah)

She is revealingly termed as '*The **Mother** of her Father,*' the 'source of the Sun' and '*Fatir*' (which simply means, **Creator**). In pre-Islamic Arabia, before the austerity of the present patriarchal system, the Goddess was worshipped as the 'Old Woman' or *Q're* (Kore), the Virgin. She was, according to Barbara Walker, perceived as the threefold Moon, comprised of three main Pagan tribal Goddesses, '*Al-llat,*' '*Al-Uzza*' and '*Manat*'.[3] Her symbols of the crescent moon and the star of Venus adorn the united tribal Islamic flag. Many Sufis, including Idries Shah, uphold the supreme divinity as female. Although later subordinated as Fatima the alleged 'daughter' of Mohammed, her original 'character' was known as the embodiment 'Fate,' the night, the illumination that separates light and darkness, the pure essence of being and the red cow who suckles all her children of the Earth. Of the 'Hand of Fatima,' Barbara Walker writes that this amulet was pre-existent to Islam, but re-named after the Prophet's (possibly) mythical daughter.

The Arabic people worshipped this trinity of desert Goddesses who simply personified the three primary characteristics of the Ultimate Goddess.

* Al-Uzza ('the mighty') represented the 'Virgin' warrior aspect, who gave them strength, protection, power and purpose in battle. She was also a fearsome desert Goddess of the Morning Star Venus and the waxing, crescent Moon ablaze in the East assert the iconic symbols of Islam.

* Al-Lat, whose name means simply 'Goddess,' was the fertile Mother Earth and dispenser of all life's riches. Representing the Sun, she was the female version of the Aramaic Allah, known as the 'Lady of the Temple,' often associated with the Syrian '*Astarte*' the female Queen of Heaven and sole Goddess of the (Western) Semitic Arabs. She is mentioned by Herodotus; in old Arabian inscriptions; and in pre-Islamic poetry where she features as the 'Mother of the Gods,' likened to the '*Urania*' of Hellenism. Here, confusingly, these Arabs worshipped her as the Sun, not the Moon which was masculine in northern Arabia.

* Manat was the darkest element of the Goddess, ruling *fate* and death. Oldest of all three Goddesses, '*Manat*' is very possibly, the original Goddess of the Semitic Arabs. Even so, she was venerated beside several other deities in a temple called 'the house of the Gods,' as the regulator of fortune (in the shape of wells/oasis/land, plunder and slaves) in addition to the Mysteries of Time, life and death. She was revered and worshipped with the same ardour as the Greek 'Moirai,' the Goddess of Fate and the daughter of the Nox (the dark night). Her 'sisters,' named 'Moros' (doom) and '*Erinyes*' (*ancestral* furies) in the sense of the forces of life and power are comparable to '*Al-Lat*' and '*Al-Uzza*'.

Thus are her many diverse names, forms, and facets expressed throughout several cultures, spanning considerable geography and units of Time; but she is most closely associated with: *Astarte, Ashtaroth, Artemis, Asherah, Anath, Elat, Isis, Ishtar, Fortuna, Shamiram, Tanith*, and *Venus*.

The word '*Al'lah*,' which contains the prefix 'Al' of obscure origin, is either a Sanskrit derivative or more probably of Chaldean origin. Within Sanskrit, '*Allah*,' '*Akka*' and '*Amba*' are cognate terms for a Goddess or *Mother*. There is even a Sanskrit chant to invoke the Mother and warrior Goddess Durga (just one of her many titles or appellations) within which the word Allah is incorporated, suggesting its continued use and reinterpretation after Islamic conversion. It is of course, essential here to remember that both Arabia and India were settled by invading Aryan tribes, engendering significant fundamentalisms between them, most especially with regard to terms for deity and its attendant powers or qualities. The Koran makes reference to *'Eloah,'* which is a Hebrew name for God in the Old Testament; its Chaldean form is *'Elahh.'* Clearly, there are many similarities at play here. Most outstanding, is how the all exclusive term for deity includes the faculty of fate within its variable triplicities, which is borne out in the three phases of Time relevant to the three manifest realms of human existence and expression: past, present and future; Underworld, Earth and heaven!

Logically, this passage of Time has more recently, come to be associated with the three distinct phases of the maturation of womankind, the earthly representative of the ultimate female deity, poetically depicted by many as the maid, mother and crone. These three have throughout the myths and histories of the ancient world, been cited as the 'three mothers,' the 'three brides' or the 'three daughters,' reflecting this archaic triplicity of Time, Motion and Force. Ancient Middle Eastern mythology traditionally presented a trinity of Gods in which a nuclear family placed an emphasis on the 'Mother'-'Son' relationship, for example, that of Ishtar/Tammuz. Ultimately, this evolved into the 'Father'-'Daughter' praxis of early Islam as the former dynamic gave way to the latter. This shift in emphasis was in part due to a nomadic lifestyle of many of its tribes, who were more dependant upon trade and piracy than they were agriculture and its attendant fertility deities. Allah was, of course the 'Father'; his three 'daughters' were *'Al-Lat,' 'Manat'* and *'Al-Uzza'* being latterly combined in the figure of just one daughter - Fatima. Both the celestial Goddess and her earthly counterpart became transposed as 'daughters' to God and the Prophet respectively. And so, despite this demotion and sub-summation of the three (tri-form Goddess) into one, we can clearly see even through this patristic disguise, exactly how the beneficent 'Hand of God' or more properly, the 'Hand of Fate' extends throughout Time and across culture, manifesting supremely as the popular and enigmatic talisman: the 'Hand of Fatima'.[4]

References:
1. J. Campbell. 1991. *'Masks of God: Occidental Mythology'* pp 445-6. Arkana. USA.
2. J.C. Cooper [ed] 1998. *'Illustrated Encyl. of Symbols'* Thames &

Hudson. London.

3. B.G. Walker. 1983. *'The Woman's Encyl. of Myths and Secrets.'* pp 51-53 Harper & Row pub. San Francisco.

4. http://www.hinduism.co.za/kaabaa.html

Previously published in:
The Hedgewytch #42 - May 08

'Sila - Litha Grima'

8. Sila na Gigh

Mysterious crone. Cailleach. Hag! Christian depiction of corrupt vices of the flesh or simply a vulgar grotesque? Does her blatant sexual gesturing articulate fertility or something more inane? Is her crude form ancient or relatively modern? She has of course been indiscriminately presented as all of these by latter-day Pagans along with perplexed historians who share an uncertainty regarding her origins. Should we then view her according to our needs? Can we truly understand her, out of context? Possibly, but only if we are willing to suspend pseudo Pagan legerdemain for something less indulgent regarding this intriguing and overtly obscene figure - the 'Shelah na Gig'. Sometimes, according to the appropriately Medieval principle of Occam's razor (principle of parsimony), the truth is not only often bizarre, but blindingly obvious.

Notable examples of the 'Shelah na Gig' figures adorn archways and keystones, usually over the thresholds of churches. Later her apotropaic imagery became secularised within castles and mills etc, guarding doors and gateways from baneful influences. In religious and magical traditions, doorways are extreme liminal spaces, a vulnerable point betwixt and between, where natural and supernatural forces are either in harmony or flux. In matters of magic and religion, such a dangerous crossing point requires a strong guardian whose form is simple, clear and unambiguous. Yet it is frequently asserted how this particularly wizened figure resembles most the 'Cailleach,' the fearful and unglamorous Winter hag of 'Celtic' lore, leading to many erroneous associations with this genre of Goddess. But equally problematic are the claims of her prowess as a fertility 'charm.'

This scrawny, ugly figure could not resemble less the voluptuous images carved in stone, wood and bone for countless centuries in variant cultures across the globe. The only vital statistic of note is her grossly exaggerated vulva stretched into a lozenge shape indicative of older (Neolithic) Goddess symbols. Rarely do these austere carvings possess breasts, and where they do they are empty and sagging, shrivelled beyond usefulness or beauty. Her facial features leer and grin inanely, or grimace menacingly above a shrunken, deformed and often skeletal form. Bereft too of hair, she casts a startling representation of raw, condensed power, a fearsome symbol of focussed purpose. Truly, this is not a nurturing figure.

Unknown before the 11th century, these now iconic images first made their appearance upon Medieval churches on the continent, eventually arriving later to the British Isles between the 12th and 16th centuries. However, a number of these European (both North and Eastern) images are often placed in an altogether different context; but not always. Cogently, the meaning of a word is in its use; and so it is with symbols, that evolve to meet the needs of its subscribers. However, as we shall see, some are more enduring than others, remaining true to their original purpose. Pertinently, many folklorists, following the lead of common folk belief have accepted this little figure as a protective image, whose potency lies within her blatant sexual symbology. Such an association strongly links the purpose of this figure to that of popular folklore in which the deflection of 'evil' intent is achieved through exposure of female genitalia, particularly by women of ill repute (that is, one who is prepared to consider such and undertaking without fear of retribution!). Such forceful intimidation acknowledges a primal fear of womanhood within popular superstition, revealing the frightening force and power attributed to her sexuality.

Origins concerning her name remain speculative, offering little indication of her true purpose. The best retains etymological definition in the Icelandic derived Scottish word, 'Sil'[1] for shield, affirming perhaps the mode of protection extended by this image. Another plausible option is found in the word 'Silad' which describes the act of spreading. [2] Herons, storks and Cranes are birds known for their association with crones and hags (in 'Celtic' lore). Inhabiting the liminal marshes between land and water, these birds are named 'Síle na bPortach.' Gig is suggested as an Irish colloquialism for the female genitalia probably a slang word: 'gigh' or 'giog' for crouching,[3] all of which could speculatively render the term 'Shelah na Gig' as either the shield of the vulva or crouching hag. For those who wish to pursue this line of enquiry some researchers discuss many other possibilities.[4] & [5]

Already it appears unlikely these figures ever represented religious or deific carvings in any way, rather they begin to suggest a primarily protective purpose, unconnected (directly) with fertility, the land or Goddess worship. That these often crude 'dwarfish' figures prevailed in popular use is testament to the horary understanding of 'dwarves' as unique in their singular ability to avert malign influences and so were always envisaged as a protective presence, either real or as stone icons. Indeed, throughout the Medieval period, dwarves were considered a pre-requisite presence, gracing the courts of many esteemed courts throughout the British Isles and Europe.[6]

Progressive ideologies of the 18th century vilified these superstitious practises and demeaning motifs, causing their eventual neglect and abandonment. And in spite of the fact that many of these rudely carved stone images remained in their original locations, others were removed for re-use elsewhere, appreciably obfuscating their original function and significance.[7] Certainly, later records have even revealed their (not unconnected) use as 'birthing' stones.[8] Memories are fickle and it is said that it takes but two generations for a 'thing' to be lost; and so devoid of context and direct application we flounder in the mire of subsequent speculation. Nevertheless, we do have some means of investigating other clues, intrinsic to their structure and design.

Gothic or Romanesque architecture of the 11th and 12th centuries freely expresses the burgeoning influences of both Near and Middle East, especially the artistic flourish of high Byzantine style - a gift of the crusades, trade and intellectual expansion, appearing first in the Aquitaine and Northern Spain (areas prominent in Arabic influence).[9] Many abbeys and ecclesiastical buildings erected over previous Saxon buildings bear witness to this upsurge. It must though be stressed, how these were equally conditioned by provincial taste and cultural style, inculcating a wider range of ornamentation across the British Isles considerably distinct from those of a fashionable Europe that tended to exhibit more cosmopolitan (Greek/ Roman) influences. Gargoyles and other grotesques are superb examples of the evolution of the Romanesque into the High Gothic art, acquiring considerable status as a prophylactic sculpted in varying degrees of sophistication reflecting the style and scale of this genre. Continental carvings often included ithyphallic male figures whose 'contortionist' posturings are generally absent from buildings across the British Isles.[10]

It is unsurprising then how in Ireland especially, where the tradition of 'protectress' was extant, we find the greatest number of 'Shelah na Gig' carvings. Sin, lust and carnality were undeniably portrayed quite pornographically amongst other vices inveighed upon by the Church anxious for the moral turpitude of its largely illiterate congregation. Yet these examples remain quite distinct from the iconography of the 'Shelah'. Furthermore, the Middle Ages were abound in weird bestiaries, of griffins and chimeras and otherworldly creatures drawn from the depths of imagination fused with Nature to synthesise a metaphoric representation of supreme guardianship. Such mechanisms had been employed since ancient times, and were effective stimuli for such assurances.

Within popular folklore recorded in the 19th century, these stone sentinels were greatly revered as compelling charms perpetuated by an enduring belief in the ability of a wise woman (healer and/or Witch) to avert the influence of the evil eye by exposure of her genitals![11] Moreover, it was discovered that where their stone facsimiles could be reached, visible signs of 'rubbing' (for luck) can be detected, indicating the superstitious awe in which these figures, even today are held.[12] This ancient practice, popularised in the Middle Ages, not unconnected to the cults of relics and pilgrimages, extorted the efficacy of amulets, talismans and charming among the general populace.

Again it must be emphasised how the 'Shelah na Gig' images typically display the prominent eyes redolent of charms of 'fascination'; a hypnotic quality utilised to great effect by occultists, charmers, sorcerers, Witches and cunning-folk for innumerable centuries. And of course, where used in conjunction with an image of the vulva, its potency is unequivocal. Held in awe by many ancient cultures across the globe, the vulva, the scary 'dentata' of taboo, as the entrance to the womb, viz., life and death, generated the ultimate power symbol. Confirmation of this is furthered in the use of these stones named in folkloric use in Ireland as 'evil eye' stones.[13] In this context a direct parallel can be found in the Palauan Islands, where female images boldly revealing their exaggerated genitalia are placed above doorways and entrances to the chieftain's hut for protection from evil spirits.[14] Akkadian and Babylonian cultural art, later ascribed under the blanket term 'Mesopotamian' had gloriously valorised the lozenge as the magical and iconic image of the vulva and/or eye of their main protectress - the Goddess Ishtar, typifying the estimation of this symbol throughout the antique world.[15]

It must also be remembered in what extreme abhorrence the Middle Ages held the female genitalia, a superstitious fear so entrenched, vestigial remains permeate even modern popular culture regarding menstruation and childbirth. Yet paradoxically, no other 'thing' could be said to offer greater protection against perceived threats of 'evil,' than this singular organ of disdain. Even in religions (such as those of the Hindu) that worship the '*yoni,*' its power as a symbol is paralleled only by that of the '*linga.*' The yoni is variously represented by a crescent, an ark, a boat, a fish, an oval, a triangle, a cave, a lozenge, and various fruits dependent upon use and function, viz., a shrine or amulet.[16] The '*sakti*' power emanating from such a hallowed symbol offers protection par excellence and where depicted in buildings is often placed above doorways and entrances – a somewhat double pun! Before the advent of modern Witchcraft and Neo-Paganism, late 19th century studies of stone carvings now termed as *'Shelah na Gigs'* (then understood as a term for an immodest woman) similarly explained their significance in scholarly discourses and were expounded as 'protective charms' against the fascination of the 'evil eye' (*mal occhio*). Healing and protection attributed to holed stones of great antiquity (often free-standing) were termed not unsurprisingly as *'cunni diaboli'* (devil's yonies).[17] All are further proofs of this enduring belief.

Stone is a stable material and was the medium of choice for early depiction of archaic God forms from Shiva to Kybele, and Baal to Aphrodite. Invariably, all were in fact first represented by meteorites or aeroliths, holy stones that had 'fallen' from heaven. Many of these were ritually anointed and 'rubbed' for luck. Later, these rough, natural surfaces were hewn and worked to assimilate conceptualisation of a desired quality or function from the stone's correspondent. Where rock or stone was not itself overtly phallic or yonic, such imagery was carved into the rocky surfaces to form the apotropaic function of warding off evil spirits. Eventually smaller, more portable phallic charms were sculpted as proof against the evil eye and sundry influences, especially popular in ancient Rome. [18]

Sexual gestures were believed to distract such evil spirits, and less exhibitionist folk resorted to the use of their hands to form the symbols exemplorising male and female genitalia - *'mano cornuto'* (male 'horns'), or the *'mano fico'* (female 'horn'). The eye, the hand and the genitalia, male or female have been potent symbols of protection unprecedented within the history of religion and anthropology. Their continued use in magics high and low is equally well attested. Amongst other portable charms popular in the ancient world, against the evil eye, especially in Egypt, were cowrie shells. Though claimed to naturally represent the female genitalia, they had additional expression as 'eyes,' again affirming this overlap in use.[19]

Since the Neolithic age then, many of the oldest and enduring images have traditionally been depicted carved in or upon stone and rock as votaries, especially the genitalia of the Divine feminine, determining the assignation of presence. No exception to this, pre-Islamic Arabia revered a triad of female deities, worshipped in aniconic form in the black (meteoric) stone of the Kaaba at Mecca. Veiled, it was the universal symbol for 'yoni,' the point and source of tribal protection.[20] Clearly then, the yoni is undisputedly indicative of a potent force, effective against the maleficent, in form, thought or deed, and its attested use as a charm of protection demonstrates the most likely assignation of purpose for this much debated figure, the *'Shelah na Gig'*.

References and Bibliography:

1. http://www.bandia.net/sheela/SheelaFront.html
2. http://www.bandia.net/sheela/SheelaFront.html
3. http://www.bandia.net/sheela/SheelaFront.html
4. http://www.bandia.net/sheela/SheelaFront.html
5. http://en.wikipedia.org/wiki/Sheela_na_Gig
6. J. Black & A. Green. 2003 *'Gods, Demons and Symbols of Ancient Mesopotamia'* British Museum Press. London. pp.73 NB. Term 'Dwarf' used in folkloric sense only.
7. http://www.whitedragon.org.uk/articles/sheela.htm
8. http://en.wikipedia.org/wiki/Sheela_na_Gig
9. Ronald Hutton. 1997 *'Pagan Religions of the Ancient British Isles'* Blackwell. Oxford. pp.310
10. http://www.whitedragon.org.uk/articles/sheela.htm
11. http://www.whitedragon.org.uk/articles/sheela.htm
12. http://www.whitedragon.org.uk/articles/sheela.htm
13. http://en.wikipedia.org/wiki/Sheela_na_Gig
14. http://en.wikipedia.org/wiki/Sheela_na_Gig
15. J. Black & A. Green. 2003 *'Gods, Demons and Symbols of Ancient Mesopotamia.* British Museum Press. London. pp.153
16. G. R. Scott. 1996 *'Phallic Worship: A History of Sex and Sexual Rites'* Senate London. pp.155
17. G. R. Scott. 1996 *'Phallic Worship: A History of Sex and Sexual Rites'* Senate London. pp.190-3.
18. Ronald Hutton. 1997 *'Pagan Religions of the Ancient British Isles'* Blackwell Oxford. pp.314
19. Geraldine Pinch. 1994 *'Magic in Ancient Egypt'* British Museum Press. London. pp.107
20. B G. Walker. 1983 *'The Woman's Encyl. of Myths and Secrets'* Harper & Row pub. San Francisco. pp51-53

Previously published in: *Hedgewytch* #41 February 08

9. Dia de los Muertos

"The Devil, who is the enemy of everything good, enjoins that these unfortunates should eat him, or allow themselves to take possession of him by eating him in those small idols."

Ruiz de Alarcon - 1926

Celebrations honouring the dead are prevalent among many ancient cultures, sharing similar religious commonalities, sadly lacking in modern European religiosity. For many here in the West we are offered 'Halloween,' a glib and vacuous consumer driven farce, a travesty, devoid of any spiritual significance; it is as empty as it is expensive. Of course, history is replete with the variant ways in which Pagan and Christian peoples have ritualised death, most of which include some form of ancestral worship. In this regard, books, leaflets and articles extolling the virtues of our supposed cultural 'Celtic' heritage, wherein Samhain is disconcertingly accepted as the 'true' Halloween, are practically falling off the shelves. Nevertheless, I have to agree with Prof. Hutton [360-5:1996] who states that Samhain has now acquired a significance totally removed from its original function - the celebration of 'Summers End,' a Time for culling cattle and careful storing of the recent harvests for the Winter ahead.

Contained within this festival were contentious elements of sacred sex and sacrifice that accompanied great feasting, bonfires, games and fayres. For those magically inclined, propitiation of mischievous spirits believed to taunt and haunt those foolish enough to ignore them is requisite at this liminal Time when the gateways of the 'Sidh' are once again acknowledged. Of course, folklore holds fast to the concept of magical gateways, mischief and mayhem, the duality of which clearly underpins modern 'Trick or Treat' activities popular at this Time. During the Middle Ages, prayers for the dead (including family members) offered around November's hoar frosts, allowed people opportune contemplation of the many terrors of Purgatory and Hell. Traditional Catholic Masses held for 'All Soul's Day' truly maintain the 'feasting' essence for our ancestral dead as three masses are recited to beseech these souls to act as antecedents between the living and their God. Pious prayers are sung out for those residing in Purgatory to speed them upon their way. Soul-cakes too, are bought and eaten by those more fortunate as dour and depressing charitable acts for the poor [*ibid.*].

Scandinavian people celebrated 'Winter Nights' around 11th-17th November, a Time when the *'Disr'* (female spirits and Goddesses) were honoured. Some believe these spirits are past female family members dedicated to watching over their progeny after death. Certainly the Goddess Freya has a strong connection to this festival. In Egypt, Isis and Osiris are central players in a Mystery Play of death and resurrection held around the end of October/beginning of November. February was the month in which the festival of 'Lemuria' meant acts of propitiation for Romans in fear of harm from angry neglected spirits. Curiously, these gentle magics and other popular acts of divination are of course still celebrated in many 'Samhain Rites' conducted by both Witches and Pagans. But what of Death? Where does this feature in our modern concept of a sanitised Craft? How few of us really confront our mortality or seek to coerce and appease ancestral spirits? How many of us even honour our creators or mythical progenitors?

These issues very much occupied my thoughts during a pilgrimage to Mexico where I was privileged to witness and participate in the *'Dia de los Muertos'* held November 1st –2nd each year throughout Hispanic America. Originally it would have been celebrated in the Aztec month of *'Miccailhuitontli,'* roughly equivalent to the Gregorian months of July/ August. Naturally, the colonising Spanish prohibited this festival and moved the greatly sanitised theme to November, supplanting it by their own Feasts for All Saints and All Souls. Despite the obvious Catholic overlays, this festival remains primarily Mesoamerican, revealing many indigenous celebrations of death and ancestry.

Preparations begin in early October with the cleaning and repairing of family tombs. Many roadside shrines are built for those killed in traffic accidents and from natural disasters (Salinas-Norman, 2003). Over the last few years, these have been extended to honour the memories of the many victims of vicious attacks, including those who were killed in the 1999 Columbine massacre by two (allegedly) Neo-Nazi, Fascist, racist boys, whose killing frenzy also ended the life of one boy who had spent some Time in Mexico helping with rebuilding programs for the poor [Cullen, 1999].

When festivities finally get underway, the 1st of November is dedicated to *'los angelitos,'* the little angels: the souls of departed children. Flowers and candles adorn the gravesides as the family hold their evening vigil, storytelling and singing until dawn. Native Creation accounts maintain a frequency of stories relating to the first human couple as the ancestors of mankind. These are honoured today in the tales told to their descendants during the '*Dia de los Muertos*' celebrations. As dusk falls, the 2nd of November is dedicated to '*Los Muertos*' the dead adults to whom food, tequila and cigarettes are offered alongside ritualistic flowers of the dead - '*cempazuchitl*' (marigolds) whose perfume blends perfectly with copal, burnt upon graves and altars throughout Mexico. Mariachi bands accompany masked dancers, whose grinning skeletal faces gleefully mock death in this ceremony that celebrates our mortality as a beginning rather than an end of life. My diary records the evocative beauty of this pageant to death, and of the devotion and veneration of death itself who comes almost as a saviour from the toils of life. Fireworks and folklore drama full of sexual innuendo complete the carnival atmosphere. Children pull playfully on skeletal marionettes of death, the stark reality of which parallels every day. There is no Catholic duality here, no fear of death, just a dynamic unity in opposition.

Colour pre-dominates the scene as fire and candles illuminate the night glowing orange, the colour of the flower of death. Fruits, costumes and masks appear in abundance decorating the doorways of shops and houses everywhere. It is still believed that flowers given as sacrificial offerings are at the behest of Quetzalcoatl who instructed his people to give only these and butterflies in lieu of human flesh [Miller & Taube, 88:1993]. Upon entering the San Miguel cemetery in Oaxaca, we were offered steaming bowls of rich, dark hot chocolate and '*pan de muertos*' (bread of the dead), which is a shared consumption between the living and the dead. After blessings, these 'dumb' suppers are removed from '*offrendas*' (private altars) for the public in what anthropologists recognise as the ancient tribal activity of 're-distributive' feasting.

Spectacular, imposing shrines line the quadrangle of tombs, dedicated to past dignitaries and revered members of the community. My gardenias were laid at the shrine of Maria Sabina, a much loved and missed '*curandera*' to her people. Constructed of arched reeds and sheaves of corn, the shrines are adorned with garlands of tangerines and flowers. Water too is set out to slake the insatiable thirst of the dead. Immense national pride and civic prowess among competing teams guarantees a magnificent display, mindful of disqualification for the introduction of foreign elements i.e. pumpkins and cauldrons.

Candles illuminate photographs of all persons honoured and are often accompanied by *'Calaveras,'* poignant yet satirical eulogies extolling pertinent virtues and vices of the deceased. Delicate lacy paper patterns of figures and symbols relating to death also decorate these shrines in honour and remembrance of intricate paper hats worn by *'Mictlantecuhtli'* the Aztec Lord of Death (synonymous with the Mayan *'Ah Puch'*). Marzipan and candied fruits sit among sugar and amaranth skulls, symbols of the Gods of death, highlighted with red and black spots, redolent of putrefaction, convincingly depicted in decorative coloured icings. Hundreds of years ago, during the months of *'Panquetzaliztli'* (approx November) and *'Toxcatl'* (approx April), amaranth seeds of the *'huala'* plant were finely ground and mixed with blood and honey to form a stiff dough. Shaped into deific skeletal figurines, primarily of *'Tezcatlipoca,'* but also *'Huitzilopochtli,'* they were hung high upon the Xocolli tree and worshipped. Finally, they were taken down and consumed by *'tecuelo'* (meaning quite literally - God eaten) participants, a ceremony with such a startling similarity to the Eucharist, it was suppressed by Spanish missionaries [Miller & Taube, 40:1993 & Hutchinson, 14:2003].

Pulque, a milky alcohol, likened to the mothers' milk, fermented from the sap of the maguey (Agave) cactus, is still consumed as a ceremonial drink in place of ritually revered traditional hallucinogenics such as datura and morning glory. Nevertheless, during a private conversation with a local guide in which we refreshingly discussed several compatible issues of deep significance within our individual cultural magical practises relating to the 'Cult of the Dead,' he confirmed that hallucinogenic flowers and fungi are indeed accepted as a continued and vital link to the ancestral spirits in all aspects of religious life, especially in the more rural areas of Mexico. This fact was later verified during a visit to a remote Indian village high up in the Chiapas Mountains, where a wizened old *'curandero'* (popular folk healer/ charmer) performed a healing for a young girl that involved much chanting, gesticulation and animal sacrifice.

Magnificent sand 'rugs' decorate the stone slabs of the courtyard satirically portraying skeletal brides, bandits, dancers and musicians: death here, is a welcome inevitability. Included in these intricate designs are the images of butterflies and humming-birds, reflecting the Aztec belief in the immortal soul returning from the Underworld, now visually celebrated in the Autumnal return of the monarch butterfly in from Canada and the USA. For the Aztecs, the Underworld, though fraught with trials and tribulations was no Catholic Hell. After a harrowing journey and judgement, Mictlan was the final destination of nine levels in the Land of the Dead with many Classic funerary pyramids constructed of nine levels reflecting this.

However, the terms of a person's death was accepted as being pre-determined at birth and the soul was thus dependent upon this death, rather than the life lived; this conditioned which of the nine regions of the Underworld, known as *'Xibalba'* to the Maya, they would inhabit. Soldiers killed in war, women who died in childbirth and all children go to *'Tonatihuilhuac'* - the 'House of the Sun,' then to the *'Land of the Clouds,'* two of the thirteen Aztec Heavens. Perceived as eternal paradise (*Tlalocan*), arriving souls become transformed into butterflies and hummingbirds, to co-exist with the Gods [Nicholson, 41:1967]. *'Xibalba'* (the place of fright), inhabited by male and female paired deities related to death, was not a reserve for sinners, but one for those who had not died violently, irrespective of social standing, or moral fortitude. Laying to the West, Xibalba could also be entered through caves and bodies of water known as 'cenotes,' sacred water cisterns, places of ritual sacrifice to the Lord and Lady of Death - *'Mictlantecuhtli'* and *'Mictecacihuatl.'* Bodies were buried with grave goods of Jade beads, food and chocolate to be offered as payment upon reaching *'Mictlan,'* the final level of the wandering soul [Miller & Taube, 177-178: 1993].

People reflect and embody regenerative process and so death is perceived as a cyclical symbiosis, from which life evolves. In this ancient agricultural society, propitiary acts of sacrifice and cannibalism convinced the Spanish they maintained unholy pacts with Satan. Yet baptism, penance and the use of incense inferred religious piety. Moreover, the regenerative life cycle is connected to that of the maize, which is seen to Spring from the ground nine days after the seed is planted. Mirrored in the emergence of life from the nine fleshless realms of *'Xibalba,'* death was thus viewed as a descent into the world of spirit. Skeletons as powerful symbols for new life are depicted in many art forms, more commonly as masks where skeletal faces are drawn back to reveal the fully fleshed life latent within. Bones, like seeds are cyclical; hence life comes from death and is not to be feared. Complex cosmologies emerged woven around the life giving maize, life from the Earth and the fertilization of blood spilled upon it by the first couple and the creator Gods. Ancestor worship in Meso-America is celebrated in Classic Mayan art, filled with scenes of priests and rulers offering back their blood and other sacrifices to the honoured dead [Miller & Taube, 26-33:1993]. Death Mysteries formulate a subtle but powerful eschatology. Represented by primal symbology, it facilitates magical expression manifest within the subconscious, freeing the conscious mind to act upon matters more mundane.

Pre-Hispanic cultures dominated by cults of death, considered life a slow putrefaction; a corruption ended only by death, 'soldiers of the sun' contributed their energy to maintain the 'right order of things'. Life offered in mutual symbiosis established the 'Order of the Universe,' a state they firmly believed would end if sacrifice ceased - the Gods are nourished by prayer and sacrifice. Death was deemed to serve the collective good, for it justified creation. The body dies as a pre-contracted debt to those who gave us life; death comes almost as a lover to liberate mankind from the pain and anguish of life [Laura de-la Vega, 2003]. A belief that 'only in death are we truly awake,' confirms extreme Gnostic principles of life as a dream [Salinas-Norman, 2003]. Therefore, it is not feared but welcomed, flirtatiously as one does an affectionate relative. Even now, many hundreds of years later, in their enduring fatalism, they tenaciously make a joke of death.

Paralleling these ancient concepts clearly evidenced within *'Dia de los Muertos'* celebrations is the recent rise in popularity of the *'Cult of Santisima Muerte'* (Saint Death) who has subsumed the role of *'Mictecacihuatl,'* the Aztec Lady of Death. As a robed female skeleton she is unashamedly called upon for all kinds of material comfort - in life. Reflecting the rise in Neo-Pagan/Hispanic syntheses over recent years, various commonalities prevail. Candle magic and colour correspondences dictate votive offerings for use in 'requests' to her; cloaks worn may for example, be black for power and vengeance, or red for affairs of the heart. Household shrines to her are lit daily with relevant flowers, food, water, tobacco and even where necessary, liquor. An evening kiss secures her good favour and fortune throughout the night. Her popularity is fast exceeding even that of the Virgin of Guadalupe in Mexico City, with thousands buying water and holy incense dedicated to her, though she is not, of course, recognised by the Catholic Church. There is even an annual ceremony for worshippers to celebrate her birthday [Martinez, 5:2003].

Sadly and perhaps cynically, this re-emergence of the ancient concept of a 'Lady of Death' may be no more than a need by modern society to exploit and supplicate materialistic desires, as everywhere people increasingly covet the riches and comforts of a greedy consumerist world wherein our spiritual and eschatological needs are ignored. Traditionalists within Mexico are increasingly fearful for the survival of indigenous culture in the advent of Halloween as forecast by N.A.F.T.A.'s saturation campaign.

One journalist labels it as it 'Gringo imperialism,' corrupting the sanctity of the 'Day of the Dead' [Blackman, 9:2003].

From my own perspective, despite very real and appalling poverty in Mexico, the transcendent beauty of this festival is indeed a treat for the soul (pun intended). As a participant in this highly evocative festival, its ability to express tangible magics is attested. Its depth and poignancy provides an insight into our real heritage as human beings, from Mysteries of our creation to the power of death, reflecting Gnostic perspectives of but a few remaining Sabbatic 'Cults of the Dead.' In a spiritually blanched society such as ours, I think that sometimes in order to understand what we are doing here and where it is taking us, we have to take a shift backwards to move forward. Perhaps it is fruitful too to remember the immortal words of Robert Cochrane that: *'all ritual is prayer.'*

Bibliography:

Blackman, James 2003 *'Halloween Raises its Ugly Head'* Oaxaca Times. Oaxaca. October Issue no. 157.

Cullen, Dave 1999 *'Inside the Columbine Investigation'* www.salon.com/ news/feature/1999/09/03/columbine/index.html

Hutchinson, Alice 2003 *'Dead Heads'* Oaxaca Times. Oaxaca. October Issue no. 157.

Hutton, Ronald Prof. 1996 *'Stations of the Sun'* Ox. Uni. Press, Oxford.

La Vega, Laura 2003 *'Origins of the Day of the Dead'* www.azcentral.com

Martinez, Carlos 2003 *'Cloaked Lady Death'* Oaxaca Times. Oaxaca. October Issue no. 157.

Miller, Carlos *'The Arizona Republic'* www.azcentral.com

Miller, Mary & Taube, Karl 1993 *'The Gods and Symbols of Ancient Mexico and The Maya'* Thames & Hudson, London.

Nicholson, Irene 1967 *'Mexican and Central American Mythology'* Newness Book, Yugoslavia.

Salinas-Norman, Bobby *'Day of the Dead'* www.peoplesguideto mexico.com

Previously published in: *The Cauldron* #114 November 2004

Male Mysteries

10. Abbots Bromley, the Wild Hunt and Saint Nick

Every year, a strange procession winds a circuitous route for approximately twenty miles around the Staffordshire countryside, through the satellite village hamlets of the Abbots Bromley parish. Twelve dancers, dressed in exquisite Elizabethan styled costumes of muted red and green wool decorated with Oak leaves move solemnly and ritualistically. Prior to Queen Victoria's Jubilee in 1887, the much simpler costumes were tailored from strips of coloured ribbon and rag roughly sewn upon old clothes. A single file then proceeds silently into each allocated area before circumambulating first one way, then another weaving a serpentine figure of eight before lining up to face each other in two opposing rows. Advancing three steps towards the 'opponent,' they bow down to the left, allowing the light horns to cover the dark ones. The bowman shoots at the snapping horse, the Maid faces the Fool, and the boy with the triangle faces the musician. Moving onwards, each dance is punctuated with refreshments offered to all performers and onlookers with considered honour and acknowledgement culminating in a grand finale at the Buttercross in the Market Square.

Named by Violet Alford[1] as the most primitive dance in Europe, it is performed during 'wakes weeks' and is indeed the oldest surviving known ceremony in Britain. A royal charter of 1227 granted rights to hold fayres annually (except during plagues which amazingly avoided Bromley) most commonly in August and November, and occasionally in December through to January. These annual 'wakes weeks' holidays now occur at the end of August and the first week in September, with the dance taking place pedantically upon the first Monday after the first Sunday after 4th September. The intriguing reason for this is because the *'Bartlemy Fayre'* at which this dance is said to have been historically performed occurred during late August. After the imposition of the 1752 calendar reforms by Pope Gregory, the popular August date shifted to early September.[2] Yet, in 1686, one Robert Plot recalls the dance in his 'Natural History of Staffordshire,' as performed 'within memory' at Christmas, New Year and Twelfth Day; this most definitely establishes it as a Midwinter Custom. Later in 1790, Lady Bagot of Bromley also records it as a Christmastide performance.

Unfortunately, due to a lack of substantive records, it is not known when this custom became shifted from December/January to September, though it is most likely to have occurred in the mid 18th century.[3] Moreover, to further complicate matters, the 'wakes weeks' were in fact originally held, not in August, but in early November.

A Medieval Staffordshire custom of keeping prayer vigils over the graves of the dead reflects the Catholic custom of annual Vigils for patron, parish saints. After the Reformation, many customs were abandoned; others became transposed to more secular dates. This particular custom moved to Midsummer (end of August) and from the graveyard to the Market Square, becoming established within the commercial fair and market celebrations, effectively removing from it any religious overtones. [4] Naturally, these revels devolved into riotous festivities with a whole host of games ranging from horse racing to tugs of war, complete with ale and hog roasts. Harvest games and activities were also often incorporated into these 'fairs.'[5]

Robert Plot also strangely describes the performance not as the Horn Dance, as you might expect, but as the 'Hobby Horse Dance,' the horns he affirms are 'reindeer heads (the horns were painted red and white with the arms of the three prominent local families - Bagot, Paget and Wells and were mounted on 16th century carved wooden deer heads) that merely accompanied the 'hobby oss' on its rounds. This suggests the prominence of the horse over the horns during this period. No mention is made of the Maid, the boy, or the Fool. The bowman was incorporated into the horse, suggesting either a mounted hunter or a mythical centaur. A cooking pot/cauldron was carried by the Reeves or towns' chiefs into which food and alms were gifted for later distribution among the poor and needy of the parish and the upkeep of its church.[6] In 1976, these horns were carbon dated to approx 1065 and are of a species long extinct in this country.

It is believed that either the Danes or later Vikings brought these magnificent horns with them into their settled territories, which by the 11th century incorporated Saxon territory across the whole of the Midlands (Northwards). The village hamlet of Bromley finds its root in the Saxon terms 'brom' and 'leah,' meaning broom and (forest) clearing respectively [7] and is recorded in the Doomsday book, along with its original Saxon parish church of 'Bromleigh.' At the back of the church a list records all the priests and vicars dating back to 1086[8] all of whom promised in perpetuity to provide annual charity (of bread and meats) and doles for the poor. In all that Time, the horns have, significantly, been stored in the parish church.

Six horn bearers, traditionally all male, each carry a set weighing between 16 1/2 lbs and 25 lbs. Three sets are painted white/cream, and three are painted black/brown. The remaining revived troupe now consists of a cross-dressed Maid (Marion) who carries a ladle, a boy with a triangle, a bowman/hunter, a Fool with a bladder, a musician and a wooden 'hobby horse.' Most prominent is the 'Hooden Horse' described by Christina Hole as a seasonal character appearing nationally and traditionally accompanied by several men to auger good luck, fortune and fertility to all folk encountered upon their way.[9] Originally a real skull, the horses head was replaced with one of wood, mounted upon a pole with snapping jaws; a cloaked body concealed the man animating it. Hallowtide and Mid-winter were the favoured times for its appearance, particularly during the twelve days of Christmas.

In Wales, the 'Mari Lwyd' (the Grey Mare/Holy Mary or Grey death) traverses the neighbourhood, jaws snapping from door to door demanding cakes, ale, and alms during the period around Twelfth Night. In Yorkshire the 'Haxey Hood' game or (head) trophy hunt became a feature of the Winter festivities.[10] Curiously though, in rural areas only those men who worked with horses were allowed to 'play' the roles associated with them. Interestingly, in Cheshire, the 'Horse' known as the 'Wild Horse' appeared at 'Hallowtide' accompanying the 'soulers' on 'All Souls Day' as alms known as 'soul cakes' were sought to secure masses for the dead.[11] This activity, popular throughout Staffordshire, Shropshire and Yorkshire is reminiscent of the original 'wakes' vigils.

Tradition asserts how Henry 1st granted certain hunting rights to the villeins (peasants) of 'Bromleigh' in his forests of 'Needwood'. But the 1125 records of the Cartulary of Burton Abbey confirm only grazing rights granted to five men for an annual rent of 10 shillings (this was, in all probability 'doled' back to the villeins at the appropriate Time). No mention is made of hunting rights. Speculation abounds then, how this dance can be said to celebrate the communal joy of an unprecedented privilege that ensured Winter fodder for their animals, fuel for the home and possible salvage of wounded game (not poached) as additional food.[12] Christina Hole further speculated how the origins of this dance may relate to a pre-Christian fertility rite,[13] inspired no doubt by the impressive antlered headgear found at Star Carr in North Yorkshire, also linked tentatively to the prowess and success of the hunters. Nevertheless, though this theory has since been de-bunked, I hope to show how she may have been right, but possibly for the wrong reasons.

Because of the great antiquity of the horns and the dance, we cannot be certain of its origins or purpose, yet it is clear that it remains a unique expression of traditional and communal spirit. Other speculators have compared the dance to the Deer Dance of the Navajo people of the Americas and even to the Horned Dances of rural Frenchmen, whose maiden chasing antics in no way resemble this serious and solemn ritualistic performance. Some draw comparisons from act iv of Shakespeare's 'As You Like It,' wherein the actors celebrate a victorious hunt by sporting great antlers upon their heads.[14]

Of course we must remember that Shakespeare was more than familiar with legends of the Wild Hunt, led locally by the antlered 'Herne,' immortalised within his own work. Though more anciently the Hunt is led by Odin, the Norse God (or Saxon - Woden) who rides the Midwinter skies, conspicuously between All Hallows and Candlemas, upon his great horse, *'Sleipnir.'* Paradoxically, he gathers the souls of the dead, and distributes small gifts to those he considers deserving. In fact, Midwinter celebrations and customs disintegrated by the Reformation had commonly focussed upon these ancient vestiges of Pagan belief. Just the passing over of the Wild Hunt was believed to fertilize the fields ready for the Winter ploughing to come. Odin has many other Midwinter folk affiliations including links to the Sword Dances of Yorkshire.

So the truth is probably simple and very close to home. For instance, we must consider how two families, the Bentleys and the Fowells retain sole rights to its enactment through an inherited family tradition (the Fowells reverted to this maiden name of a daughter married into the Bentley family after some acrimony a 'long Time ago'). They remain staunchly opposed to its commercialisation and sponsorship, refuting any secular associations despite ceding the Parish Council legal ownership of the Horns in 1981.[15] It is an oral tradition, passed between family members with no surviving written records. The horns are never allowed to leave the village. If the dancers perform elsewhere, then a spare set of horns are used in their stead.

If we analyse the clues we can determine then a plausible and sensible solution.

*   The date of the horns of over a thousand years corresponds to

Danish/Norse settlers and the establishment of grazing rites and the origins of a crude church.

*   The dance itself appears to 'beat the bounds' around the forest circuit in honour of the original early village grazing ground, a Pagan territorial activity continued by the church.

*   Village owed allegiance to the Abbey to which it was willed by Wulfric, Earl of Mercia in 1002, and not, as was the common practice, to a liege Lord.

*   The dance retains characters that reveal a more ancient affiliation or association, i.e. the horse, who was originally noted as the main character, particularly important amongst Saxon people.

*   The dancers gather alms and charities for later distribution amongst the poor. A custom upheld by the parish church in honour of its patron Saint.

*   The horns have always been stored within the confines of the Parish church to which they are dedicated and annually blessed by.

*   The Patron Saint of the parish church is unsurprisingly Saint Nicholas, the Patron Saint of Midwinter bounty, of gifts and charity!

*   These several noted references to 'Hooden Horse' traditions are linked to parish churches dedicated to St Nick. (see ref:18)

*   The dance is still performed 'religiously' during 'wakes weeks' that initially celebrated the annual feast day and vigil by the parish in dedication of its Patron Saint. Notably, the Feast of Saint Nicholas was abolished during the Reformation.

* The horns are in fact Reindeer antlers, a beast of great significance to Scandinavian settlers to these Isles, and which are now irrevocably associated with Father Christmas.

Expressed simply, it is not unreasonable to assume an original dedication by migrant Saxons and later Scandinavians of the horns to a Pagan tutelary deific form of Woden/Odin and his power animal, the great horse - Sleipnir. For a short period this dance could have expressed a simple ritual, marking out territory granted them in the privilege of Henry 1st. In its simplicity it marks the lemniscate movement of the Sun,[16] suggesting the eternal shift from light to dark, life to death, fertility over sterility etc.

This could later have been subsumed within the church politic as a victory over Paganism without any significant change in the format of the dance. The 'light horns cover the dark,' remains a dual Pagan and Christian theme of mutual compatibility. There is no contradiction and no conflict. The dance shifts from honouring a tutelary deity (the gift-giving Yule Father) to a tutelary Saint (the gift-giving Saint Nicholas and later Father Christmas), both of whom share similar characteristics and is performed seasonally as appropriate to either/both during different periods of emphasis and appropriation over several hundred years of calendar changes and religious transformations.

After concluding these simple facts, corroborative details were discovered in a booklet about 'Obby Oss' customs of Cornwall and Somerset and Dorset that offers astonishing comparisons. [17] Not insignificant is the translation of 'oss' as 'God.' These ancient dances are held annually in May, also in honour of Patron Saints, namely St. George and St. Mark. It is also celebrated in Ireland at Midsummer in honour of St. John; celebrants are also 'tapped' for alms. The Sacred Female is honoured as May Queen, correlating with the 'Mollie,' the Maid Marion of Abbots Bromley. Mention is given of the ladle, once suspended from the horse's jaws for the purpose of alms collection, now removed into the hand of the 'Mollie.'

Significantly, the horse is a sacred totem of the Celtic language confederates, being emblematic of Epona, the mare, or mother; a form no doubt embodied in the darker celebrations of the Welsh 'Mari Lwyd.' Embedded within Saxon culture, the horse as a cultic object remains prolific within Teutonic folklore; against these examples of cultic totemism, a worried Church had placed a proscription on animal guising since the 4th century. It is well attested throughout Britain and Europe how men have reverently adorned themselves with great antlers, horns and horses heads with unknown purpose. Reaching back into the Neolithic and Bronze Age cultures, they are often discovered as esteemed grave goods. Horses' heads on poles were also used by the Vikings for magical purposes and were sported as good luck talismans, often stored in the Earth between seasons for increased influence.[18]

Fertility aspects of these celebrations are echoed within heathen beliefs of Saxon and Scandinavian people that the return of ancestral spirits during Hallowtide and over the term of the 'Wild Hunt' could bring blessings for their kith and kin. These 'evolved' dead were powerful ancestral spirits and guardians of the land, and would be honoured by dances and offerings to the boundary markers or cairns/mounds of family territory. Fertility then and abundance were imparted by these spirits to all those who remembered them at this Time. Again this echoes the Hallowtide (November/December) soul vigils of 'wakes weeks' activities. Obviously, the complete celebration as expressed here determines it as primarily Christian, in spite of possible Pagan origins which must remain entirely speculative. This is true of most folklore extant in modern society. There are exceptions, but these are far and few between.

Yet the facts are too obvious to ignore. Even so, it has been suggested these highly cultic and ritualistic objects, the horse and the elaborate horns, were devised for purely theatrical engagements, for raucous caperings and mundane entertainment devoid of any religious significance, Pagan or otherwise.[19] Whilst we must concur the need for caution, it is extremely improbable that those people prior to the industrial revolution, whose very world was steeped in and revolved around religious custom, who lived and breathed superstition and folklore, would have placed no spiritual value on the objects, the dance or the celebrations. Of course, my tentative summation may be seen as anathema by some, it may also be wrong. Nevertheless, it offers food for thought and invites all you readers to review this ancient and intriguing dance for yourselves.

Notes and References:

1. Christina Hole. 1976 *'British Folk Customs'* 1976. Hutchinson & Co. Pub. Ltd. UK
2. M. Alexander. 2002 *'A Companion to the Folklore, Myths and Customs of Britain'* Sutton Pub. UK

3. Christina Hole. 1976 *'British Folk Customs'* 1976. Hutchinson & Co. Pub. Ltd. UK

4. M. Alexander. 2002 *'A Companion to the Folklore, Myths and Customs of Britain'* Sutton Pub. UK

5. Roy Palmer. 1995 *'Britain's Living Folklore'* Llanerch Pub. UK

6. M. Alexander. 2002 *'A Companion to the Folklore, Myths and Customs of Britain'* Sutton Pub. UK

7. E.R. Shipman. 1996 *'A History of Abbots Bromley'* Benhill Press Ltd.

8. E.R. Shipman. 1996 *'A History of Abbots Bromley'* Benhill Press Ltd.

9. Christina Hole. 1976 *'British Folk Customs'* 1976. Hutchinson & Co. Pub. Ltd. UK

10. Roy Palmer. 1995 *'Britain's Living Folklore'* Llanerch Pub. UK

11. Christina Hole. 1976 *'British Folk Customs'* 1976. Hutchinson & Co. Pub. Ltd. UK

12. E.R. Shipman. 1996 *'A History of Abbots Bromley'* Benhill Press Ltd.

13. Christina Hole. 1976 *'British Folk Customs'* 1976. Hutchinson & Co. Pub. Ltd. UK

14. E.R. Shipman. 1996 *'A History of Abbots Bromley'* Benhill Press Ltd. GB.

15. Private conversations with Tony and Carl Fowells. *My gratitude for this information.*

16. Eddie Cass & Steve Roud. 2002 *'An Intro to the English Mummers Play'* English Folklore Society. UK

17. Thurstan Peter. 1997 *'The Cornish Obby Oss'* Oakmagic Pub. UK

18. Geof & Fran Doel 1992 *'Mumming, Howling and Hoodening: Midwinter Rituals in Sussex, Kent and Surrey'* Headly Bros Ltd. Kent. UK

19. Ronald Hutton 1996 *'Stations of the Sun'* Oxford Uni. Press. New York.

Previously published in: *The Hedgewytch* #39 August 2007

11. Summer and Winter Solstice Customs

Investigation into the qualities of 'Holly' and 'Oak,' trees sacred to and represented by the Young and Old Horn King respectively, inspired through folk observance of Nature's seasonal cycles of renewal and decay.

The 'Holy' Tree - Holly:
Solar fire
Mid-Winter
Pro-creative force of Nature.
Youth, vigour and vitality.

Used for over 2000 years in Mid-Winter celebrations and religious observances that lauds the seasonal Solar return. Gifts of holly were presented during 'Saturnalia,' a Winter Solstice festival whence vegetal 'spirits' immortalise the 'Wild Holly King,' covered in Holly and evergreen foliage, dispersing His blessings of light, life and fertility for the seasons ahead.

This 'erotic' Holly God evolved into the 'Green Man,' the May King and the popular folkloric 'Jack-in-the-Green.' His dark, yet highly reflective leaves reflect the immortal 'light' of spirit within Nature. Twinned with the Oak King, they together represent the waxing and waning aspects of the Solar year, guarding portals at transitional Solstices.

Twelfth Night, known traditionally as 'Holly/Holy Night, is where blazing Holly branches carried as torches, retrieve 'light' from the darkness. Gaelic tradition maintains how the 'Wildman' or 'Wodewose' spirit, carrying a holly club and a lump of coal (carbon – unit of matter, ergo life) becomes imbued within the dark-haired first footer, as he leaps over the threshold imparting his special gifts of (fiery) light and life.

The ethereal Holly is used in dream magics, divinations and enchantments. Holly wood is also used to make concentrated charcoal for smith-craft, where hotter temperatures are required to smelt metal, especially for arms and armour, hence association with Tubal-Cain, Tutelary deity of smith-craft. The smith as magician possessed all the wisdom and cunning of the Gods.

Holly is equally associated with Saturnalia, fertility, sex, magic, thunder, light, power, Thor and thus by default goats (who pull Thor's chariot). Nature herself accents Holly's power in the midst of Winter, when all else lies dormant, stark and dry; its dazzling waxy leaves, vibrant fertile berries and myriad points sparking light, full of Solar power, last right through into late Spring. The red berries suggest the colour of blood and of life a poignant Noel.

Its true totem bird is surely the Robin, whose own red breast clearly reflects the sacristy of blood, both in birth and sacrifice. A Royal emblem indeed!

'Father' of all the Trees - Oak:
Lunar, Solar and stellar
Mid-Summer/Autumn
Doorway to alternate dimensions.
Old age, wisdom, longevity, stability and strength
Preserver and keeper of the Mysteries.

In late May, as the Holly leaves begin to lose their lustre and diminish, (its many berries much depleted), those of the Oak begin to unfurl, gaining size and colour by June (circa Summer Solstice), fruiting in early Autumn, retaining its leaves into late Autumn, losing them only around the Winter Solstice. Oak is sacred to Dagda, Taranis, Odin, Dionysus, Cybele, Diana and Rhea and is popularised in groves venerating all archaic father and mother deities. In popular myth, the stag-antlered Lord of the All Hallows Hunt is the Saturnian 'father.'

Most widely revered and most ancient of trees on Earth it is one of the first trees to colonize Earth. Believed in myth to be the first tree created by God, from which all human life sprang. It is the wood of oracles and prophecy, carrying and manifesting the word of God. The mighty Oak was seen as a channel through which the sky God was able to communicate to mankind, hence the reverence for 'gospel' Oaks and sacred groves of Pan and Hermes.

Many ancient Oaks were carved with the ancient symbol of sovereignty (the equal-armed cross within a circle) to symbolise their protective power and magical associations. More over, where an Oak displayed the abundant fertility of the sacred mistletoe (sacred sperm seed of God), it was revered as sole reproductive force within the Universe. Oak represents the ultimate ruling power of Nature, and inherent Spirit of God in all life. A myth relates how if mistletoe is laid upon an altar during a Mid-Winter rite, it will bring the spirit of God to Earth, a manifestation that renews its synergistic power! Herne, another mythic leader of the Wild Hunt is said to inhabit the Oak. He is often compared to the more archaic Hermes and Pan (the Universal Father).

Oak is the liminal guardian of the threshold.
Oak is a focus for Time and memory.
Oak symbolises the mightiness of Time.
Like the Holly, it too is associated with Thunder.

Great fires of Oak burn at Mid-Summer, its bonfires honouring the gentle power and glory of this slow but sustaining wood, its life giving abundance (acorns provide food, fodder and balms) in the season ahead. Oak also represents unseen virtue, a mystical quality of the Sun (God), who at the cross-quarter day of All Hallow's, stands silent sentinel to the 'lars' or ancestral fey, during their remembrance.

Within Druidic tradition, the Robin and the Wren, rival birds symbolic of the Oak and Holly year kings, are immortalised in two rhymes - *'Who killed cock robin,'* and *'We'll hunt the cutty wren'.* Dual themes of sacrifice and submission. The Wren is sacred to Bran, Celtic deity, synonymous with Saturn, Father Time and Mid-Winter monarch extraordinaire.

Collated information from myth and history support this observation of Nature, confirming symbiotic intricacies between archaic and folkloric custom and those traditions that hold in regard the perennial wisdoms of the Young and Old Horn King; concealed within symbologies pertinent to Holly and Oak, inseparable, counterparts that combine within all potencies of Nature, the Universe and being. These attributions offer an alternative more representative of Nature than the more popular but ill-conceived expression of the Oak King as God of the waxing year falling at Mid-Summer and the Holly King as God of the waning year, falling at Yule. This may be a misunderstanding that probably arose from the complex and confusing misalignment of the seasonal changeover between Divine 'Kings' as celebrated in the more ancient Middle East and their folkloric revival in the modern West over a lacuna in Time.

Earth births the Solar/holy child at Yule!
He grows in strength, waxing through our Winter and Spring:

Holly King 'dies' at Midsummer. (Life/regeneration)

Oak King 'rises' at Midsummer, reigning during the waning Solar year, throughout our Summer and Autumn to 'die' at Yule. (Hibernation/renewal)

These mythical and highly symbolic roles are fully cognate with those of the Young and Old Horn King, ancient deities affiliated to virtue throughout the Middle East. Despite climatic differences (i.e., their fertile growing season was during the cooler auspices of the Lunar deity), the archaic Father/Moon (Old Horn King), ruled from the Autumn Equinox to Spring Equinox. The arid scorching heat of Summer was the province of the archaic Son/Sun (Young Horn King) whose reign lasted from the Spring Equinox to the Autumn Equinox, it is clear that in *both* instances, the Oak/Old Horn King remains God of the *waning Solar* year, while the Holly/Young Horn King reigns supreme throughout the *waxing Solar* year.

Of course this means that Holly is still the predominant cumulative deity during May's Eve celebration of fire, light, growth, all gifts within his remit as the fecund 'Green Man,' the 'Jack in the Green,' the shamanic Wodewose of the woods. His dark counterpart is the Man in Black, the Harlequin, the Trickster, the Holy Fool, Saturn - wise old Father of Time, typified in the 'death' and introspection of all Yule and Twelfth Night celebrations. Naturally this shifts considerably the emphasis central to both Yule and Twelfth Night, now seen as the beginning and end of a dual celebration in addition to the more obvious ones of Summer and Winter Solstices. Of course this has even deeper significance for anyone working with the complexity of the father/son relationship to the void that enigmatically is not a void, and to light and dark matter, keys to the Universe that continue to unlock the wisdom of ages.

Previously published in: *The Wytches' Standard* #2 Litha 2005

11. The Wild Hunt

Beginning with an explanation of the Wild Hunt as it is known today, the historical processes by which we acquired that view shall then be closely examined, exposing original and formative myths that remain pertinent to the Craft today. From these we may conclude with a brief summary of the significance of 'Twelfth Night,' the height of the Hunt activity.

Belief in the 'Wild Hunt' or 'Furious Host' being generally Teutonic in character was at one Time widespread all over northern Europe, specifically Germany, Northern France and Great Britain. Traditionally, it occurs between All Hallows and Candlemas, the fallow season of hibernation and introspection. Significantly, folk tales of all Scandinavian countries have Trolls or Elves making their appearance at Yule during this Time of shadows, death and natural deprivations. Of course, to Norsemen, the ancestral dead were known as Elves, and are divided into two types according to Jacob Grimm, Teutonic compiler of Faerie lore: '*Svart Alfar*' (dark Elves) - Gnomes and subterranean dwellers, metallurgists and guardians of treasure, (representing a more archaic form of being) and '*Lios Alfar*' (light Elves) - or shining ancestral souls (fey), reminiscent of Vanir deities who were subsumed and vanquished by the more patristic 'Aesir.'

A 17th century writer records how *"neither good nor evil spirits that are in the air, particularly around the holy birth-*Time *of Christ are called (Juhlafolker) 'Yule-folk' by Laplanders."* This name is suspiciously similar to the Old Norse '*Jolnir*' for 'Gods' from which '*Jol,*' or 'Yule' is derived.[1] Stormy nights were said to herald the Hunt with claps of thunder, fiery flashes and the pounding rain, all evocative of the baying hounds and pounding hooves of dark spectral riders in their primal cavalcade. Such tales of the furious host abound in folklore, myth and legend of airborne spirits flying through ion charged clouds. But it is hard for us to view this world in the manner of our Medieval counterparts, so we must remember the child-like way in which their worlds both natural and supernatural were not as clearly delineated as are our own. For them, the existence of otherworld spirits and daemons was indisputable; more than mere archetypes of mind, or denizens of magical realms, these wraiths personified archaic beliefs in a world where every moment held the possibility of death from disease, deprivation or dispute, where every moment was ripe with potential for manifestations from a parallel world that coexisted indistinctly from their own.

The Wild Hunt is popularly held to be a troupe of spectres and demons, usually depicted as mounted hunters; sometimes accompanied by hounds that trawl the sky at night gathering departed souls, sometimes even to a cacophony of 'rousing and rough musick.' Seeing the Wild Hunt was and often is considered a very bad omen, usually foretelling a Time of strife, misfortune, madness or death. In some story variants, the Hunt directly achieves its end by fright or exhaustion. And according to much folklore even the living unfortunate enough to cross its path, are to be seen swept up within its infernal train. This strange and awesome folk belief was particularly endemic during the early Middle Ages. In each region, the spectral rider is often described as dressed in black, occasionally headless and is generally a local figure in folklore, a past hero or mythical figure from legend. Accounts report how 'fire spurts' from the hooves, mouths and noses of phantom horses and hounds, which are often only two or even three legged.

An appearance of Herne the Hunter in Windsor Forest is often followed by tragedy or disaster, often of national importance. Herne is probably the most famous stag-horned leader of the Hunt and is often linked to the Gaelic deity 'Cernunnos' (who in turn has been tenuously linked to the striking Palaeolithic wall painting of a 'sorcerer' figure at Les Trois Frères cave complex). Although the mythological origins of this cult may be reasonably placed within Iron-Age Europe, there is no tangible association between Herne and the Gaelic deity 'Cernunnos' that should push those origins of the Wild Hunt back into pre-history. Herne is a hunter, 'Cernunnos' is not. Their roles are in fact entirely different. But what is particularly relevant is how the Hunts seem to frequent the same territory: these are generally corpse ways, spirit paths, ancient forests and other liminal places. These processional ways are interstitial points of commune with discarnate forms. Lights, magnetic phenomena and eerie sounds denote places of especial power, profound and subtle points of interaction between the human psyche and its environment, induced by radon gas, ions and sonic vibrations indicative of these geomantic centres. Funeral processions and the 'Wild Hunt' are also linked in many traditions at sites all over the country. In fact, Saxon spirit paths and ritual causeways named 'daeda-waeg,' formed the later 'corpse-ways' [Jackson, 1996:51].

In later Medieval funeral processions, the bier/byre or wagon was hailed as 'Gabriel's Wain' and it is likely this psychopompic angel subsumed the horn blowing 'Hunt' leader, gathering in all errant or lost souls [Jackson, 1994,24]. Traditionally, other leaders of the Hunt are variently listed as Auld Hornie, Herne, Hran, Odin, Woden, Dame Holda, and Herodias, to name but a few. In the Scandinavian traditions the Hunt is often accompanied by Valkyries, female warriors who ride with Odin astride his eight-legged steed, Sleipnir, the true and original leader of the 'Wild Hunt' in his guise as giant storm God of death and wisdom [Branston, 1974:94]. Indeed, as it was thought that souls of the dead were wafted away on the fierce winds of Winter, Odin became regarded as leader of all disembodied spirits - the gatherer of the dead. Suggestive already of spirit flight, surely?

Eventually, all storms became associated with his passing. In this role he became known as the 'Wild Huntsman' and is mentioned as such within the Peterborough/Anglo-Saxon Chronicle of 1127 [*ibid.*]. The passage of his Hunt, known as Odin's Hunt, the Wild Ride, or the Raging Host (*Asgardreia*), eventually acquired increasingly sinister associations. Other common names for this raging or furious host were Cain's Hunt, Herod's Hunt (Medieval appellations indicating the theme of a penitent Wandering Jew unable to find respite from their alleged murderous crimes), '*Oskorei,*' and in England the '*Herlathing*'; the latter named for the mythical King Herla, whose bizarre encounter with the Faery Rade recorded by Walter Map circa 1190, is certainly worthy of further investigation [Oldfield-Harvey, 2002:57].

Not all accounts are so doom-laden and anomalies do exist of Wild Hunt traditions existing in areas away from Norse influence that hint of earlier more benign beliefs. In Wales for example, the leader of the Hunt was '*Gwynn ap Nudd,*' 'Lord of the Dead', whose pack of white hounds with blood-red ears bayed loudly as they rode out [Jackson, 1996:28]. Known as the '*Faery Rade*' in 'Celtic' mythology, the 'Hunt' relates more to their ancestral train riding out from Annwyn's depths via liminal portals within fabled hollow hills to gather recently departed souls to join their throng, particularly when seen in the waning half of the year (Autumn and Winter) and to augment the renewed spirit of re-generation in the waxing half of the year (Spring and Summer). Hence the 'bi-annual' polarity of kings relative to their 'magical' year expressed within the tale of '*Pwyll*' (Lord of Dyfed) and '*Arawn.*' This theme is also reflected in the wild-man or green spirit of Faerie, the true potency and cyclic patterning of Nature. Though feared it was not seen as demonic or in any way penitential. In fact, it should be understood as a heritage of otherworld states within ancestral streams of Craft historiography.

In supernatural and nocturnal worlds, Time and space warp the temporal order of perception; ethereal forms normally banished to these liminal fringes manifest within the conscious mind, heightened by trance states induced by fear, exhaustion, or more sensibly auto-suggestion. In the zoomorphic form of the White Stag, '*Gwynn ap Nudd*' as psychopompic leader, guide and freer of all souls during their spiritual evolution, he releases the 'mind' from the steely grip of life's realities. Modern esoteric terms articulate a perception of such ecstatic visioning as one induced by the poetic metaphors of the tales themselves. Each leader is a primal liberator of mundane consciousness, bringing a death-like trance state to the seer. Reversals of world order are often geomantically associated with specific inter-dimensional portals, astral gateways to otherworldly realms whether of mind, land, dimension or reality. The choice is ours. However, these interstitial places are potent catalysts for empaths, psychics and seers.

Mortals are lured into Faerie realms where Time is commonly quantum (King Herla presents but one example). A moment there, is as the passing of hundreds of years in mortal Time. In this twilight world, supernatural deities and totemic animals exist in a strange other world outside normative bounds of Time and space. Many Medieval legends within the Mabinogion, the Arthurian Cycles and Irish legends from the Book of Leinster relate many such events. Typically, only restoration from khaos ensures victory or survival. This is an ancient motif indeed and it forms the basis for many later Hunt legends.

The Northern Wild Hunt also had a strange connection to canine myth in that sometimes after it had passed, it left behind a small black dog that had to be kept and carefully tended for a full year unless it could be frightened away. This forms a curious but very interesting connection to Hekate, the Greek Goddess of Death, Mystery and Sorcery (and later Witch Goddess) which can be explored in connection with the Norse Wild Hunt viz - the Black Dog. Her followers are claimed to have sacrificed black dogs (and lambs) to her. A Greek myth also has Hekate roaming the Earth on Moonless nights with a pack of ghostly, howling dogs. Enigmatically, she too is encountered at special corpse ways, usually crossroads - popular places for gallows.

As Pagan religions died away, Odin's place in Wild Hunt folklore was taken by others. In later themes the Hunt is commonly led by a nobleman or king doomed for either his sins or blasphemies. Similar to

Britain, this theme is common to both Scandinavia and Germany, being post-Medieval in origin straining under social narratives grafted onto original legends. Such men are doomed to suffer the eternal wrath of a higher judiciary. These anarchic allegories assert the peasant's impotence to act within mortal realms, of their suppression and incumbent resentments and their entreaties for supernatural aid.[2]

Cogently, the expression used by Medieval historian Walter Map to describe the Wild Hunt is - the household of *'Herthelingus'* which contains a curious Old English word: 'thing' in its sense of 'troop', hence *'the troop of herle.'* Herle may be linked etymologically to *'Herian'*, a variant epithet for *'Woden'/ 'Odin'* as Lord of all warrior troops.[3] However, others assert that Herle's distinct root is traceable to other related forms. For example, the household of *'Herlechinus'*, rooted in *'Hel/a'*, Norse Queen of the Dead, evolved many centuries later into the male form of Harlequin, a rombustuous character who led wild jousters or *'Charivari'* through the streets and villages of Europe in their wild celebrations [Olfield-Howey, 2002:57].

Folklore retains legends of those who have died violent or early deaths whose traumatized souls then become the furious hosts within the Wild Huntsman supernatural train. The first full description of a procession of such ghosts was written by a Parisian priest in January of 1092 (recorded in the *'Ordericus Vitalis'*) who saw a swarming crowd led by an extraordinary and menacing figure armed with a club, followed by spectres that wailed and moaned over their sins. Following this was a seething mass of corpse-bearers laden with some fifty coffins upon their backs. Women on horseback, seated on saddles with glowing nails stuck into them hastened them ever onwards. Finally, a host of ecclesiasticals also on horseback brought up the rear! The priest exclaimed his recognition of many recently departed souls, concluding that he had finally witnessed the infamous *'familia Herlechini.'* His scepticism firmly banished, he believed he had finally seen this ghostly train.[2]

European accounts of the 'Hunt' primarily involved spectral forms of such discarnate souls, moaning and bewailing their fate. Again this view typifies an overlay of Christian morality and penitential social-conditioning. Many elaborate themes developed from these early reports into fantastic and often gruesome tales of masked and zoomorphic figures terrorizing the countryside. Clearly both Time and history has polluted the Hunt, transformed by pious zeal into a spectral train of the doomed - a cruel warning to all who flaunt the Church's doctrines. Sometimes it was claimed the Devil lead them, hunting for lost souls; though in Devon, the hounds themselves were thought to be souls of un-baptized children. Many lurid tales were expounded by monks and clerics intent on feeding the natural fears and superstitions of the peasantry, exhorting real scare tactics with tales of horror and diabolism suggestive of the Witches Sabbat. Naturally, all were banished by their own superior powers and dispositions.

By the 19th century in England, the demonic huntsman might be any one of a number of local heroes or villains, usually of the landowning class - often a hunting squire and his dogs, condemned to hunt for evermore for hunting on a Sunday, or someone who had otherwise achieved fame or notoriety. One typical local folk hero known as Wild Eadric is said to lead the Hunt in rural Shropshire. For ever more he is destined to gallop furiously across the Stipperstones in search of his wife, Godda, a Faerie Queen who mysteriously disappeared one day. This ghostly pair are said to appear on the eve of war. Eadric was seen as the Crimean War broke out, making further appearances in 1914 and 1939 [Westwood, 1986:248-9].

Another important folklore inclusion is that of the Seven Whistlers, (usually geese or Swans) whose flight augers ill fortune and death. Folktales declare that when all seven are heard together, they herald the end of the world. In North Yorkshire the grisly Hunt procession consists of long deceased spirit shades accompanied by either human headed or red-eared dogs known as the '*Gabble Rachets*' or 'Gabriel Hounds'. Cognate with the hounds of '*Anmvyn*' that bound forth from the hollow hills (ancestral sidhe) they bark like geese in full fury overhead. In fact, the old northern name 'gabble rachet' is believed to have little to do with the psychopompic Angel Gabriel despite his tenuous links to Anubis. Close examination of the phrase reveals an old word for 'corpse,' yielding a literal meaning of 'corpse hounds,' which readily explains all associated traditions, in particular, the actual sound of the 'geese,' whose eerie cries we may recall echo the impending doom heralded by the seven whistlers [Westwood & Simpson, 2005:670-1 & 434-435].

So where can we begin to search for the real truth behind the Wild Hunt legends and thereto discover its true origins? One theory suggests an ecstatic cult of Scandinavian warriors dedicated to the (Norse deity) Odin known as berserkers, whose wild, shamanic behaviour does indeed engender the fury of 'ecstatic' entrancement [Jackson, 1996:41]. Odin's name is derived from the Old Norse '*Odhr*' which means *'Fury, ecstasy, inspiration';* Woden is similarly derived from the related Indo-European word - the Saxon '*Wod,*' both immediately suggest ecstatic trance and spirit flight. Berserkers are most commonly associated with the cult of Odin from 9th century Norway onward. Entranced from ingestion of specific hallucinogens (generally Fly Agaric) and donned with animal skins, they believed themselves 'transformed' into animals (usually wolves or bears). Thus enraged they could easily be perceived as the hounds of Odin's in his ecstatic Wild Hunt.[2]

A comparison of 'Berserkers' with wolves would make them symbolically dead. Wolves are synonymous in Old English with outlaws and criminals, and those outcasts of society who exist on its peripheral fringes. It is easy to see how a Wild Hunt of the dead could be derived from their exploits. The dogs of the Hunt can be traced via wolves back to Odin (and curiously also to both Hermes and Hekate, both known psychopomps). The death-dealing chaos of the Berserkers in action relates to the dark, unruly side of Nature, particularly the liminal privations of Winter. Clearly then, the Wild Hunt myth suggests its part in a cyclical drama of both annual and terminal existence, enacted by Berserkers as part of an Odinic cult. Furthermore, usage of the term *'das wutendes heer'* (wild army of Wotan: the Germanic form of Odin) implies a phrase essentially hostile to Christianity, of an opposing host embodying active forces of darkness. This supports interpretations by early folklorists such as Grimm, that *'das wutendes heer'* might originally have been *'Wotan's Heer.*' [2] So much for folklore, but what of Norse legends themselves, what do they reveal?

Most intriguingly and not unsurprisingly, the Old Norse sagas mention neither Odin's Host, a *'Furious Host'* nor even a *'Wild Hunt'*; though some references infer a shared commonality. The *'gandreidh'* described in *'Njals'* saga reports tales of black riders, carrying flaming sconces. However, it must be emphasised that these appearances were seen not as portents of doom, but as portents of great or auspicious events! In this Saga, Odin boasts of how he is able to confuse the 'hedge-riders' of the skies [*ibid.*]. A clear distinction is here made between Odin as leader of the 'Host' and a train of 'hedge-riders' or evil spirits, he wishes to avoid. It is important to remember that although Witches are also called *'hedge-riders'*, *'mirk-riders'* and *'evening-riders'* these appellations could refer to oneiric nightmare-riding, rather than to the activities of Valkyries in *'Njals Saga'* [*ibid.*]. It must be stressed that even allowing for some Christian glossing within these tales, Witches were very much perceived as malignant forces by Norse and Saxon peoples.

Primary sources are silent regarding ghostly trains of either the unfortunate or premature dead due very probably to Norse conviction of a contrary fate within the mythical realms of Valhalla and the Everlasting Battle story in which the fallen are resurrected each day anew. A possible association of Odin is tentatively made in a Medieval Norwegian ballad *('Draumkvaede')* with *'Grutte Gray-Beard'*, who rides upon a jet-black horse wearing a black hat and mantle. *'Grutte'* is posited as meaning to look angrily or fiercely [*ibid.*]. His name, countenance, garb and steed have all clearly suffered adversely from bias (Christian) annotations.

Early Swedish and Danish myths, wherein a supernatural Hunt was active, focus upon a quarry that could be anything from beautiful white breasted maidens, mermaids and wood nymphs to wild boar or horse. More characteristic of separate myths confused over Time involving *'Thorr'*, they are indicative of a cultural paradise rather than a penitential haunting! [Oldfield-Howey, 2002:52]. A lacuna of several hundred years bridges these early reports with those of avid 19th century folklorist collectors, which more properly record the fusion of evolving concepts rather than individual examples that inculcated their conclusions. In fact, many legends actually support the belief held by 'heathens' that Odin and his hosts (perceived as ancestral dead/spirits) distributed blessings and boons to the deserving.[1]

Yet another variation of the Hunt legend concerns the female leader *'Holda'* (*Perchte*/*Holle* in Germany) or *'Freja'* (*Frien*/*Freki*/*Frik* in Sweden and Northern Germany) and *'Frau Gaude*/*Gode,'* which stems from the same root as *'Wode'* (fury/ecstasy). However, *'Holda'* (*Perchte*) leads a very different train of souls, for her followers are young children; usually those she has allegedly 'stolen.' More probably, these are souls of poor children who having died prematurely, are gathered up within her immortal train. As a strict Matriarch, she meters punishment for lazy women who have not completed their allotted tasks, yet is benign and generous with her conscientious brood [*ibid.*]. As Earth-Mother and Mistress of Death - *Hela*/*Holda*, is leader of the 'Hunt,' formed from migrating yelping Winter Geese; hence her appellation as 'Mother' Goose. Importantly, the goose is a shamanic totem of arctic shamans and magical steed par excellence of visionary travelling. Again as a poetic metaphor it is crucially not a strictly specific occurrence. Unequivocally, the Wild Hunt or Furious Host appears most commonly and consistently over the Yule season reflecting deep-rooted Germanic cultural traditions often involving supernatural hauntings.

In Norway, fascinating tales relate how those who lay as if dead, entranced and enchanted, have their 'souls' snatched from their stiffened carcases by the furious host. These folk later awake unharmed to tell of how they had ridden with the '*Asgardreid*' [*ibid.*]. Depending upon attitudes of those encountering the Wild Hunt and whether or not they laugh, mock or leer at the apparent misfortunes or dispositions of those caught up in it and whether they engage with or help the Hunter or members of his train, such persons are punished or rewarded with obscure gifts, the truest treasure of the Gods. Cogently, both '*Gaude*' and '*Woden*' hold the powers of fate and thus the presentiment of good or bad luck!

While these tales show the Hunt as folklore, legend, myth or fantasy, modern scholarship seeks to explain these events as subject to natural phenomena. In centuries past, the Wild Hunt/Furious Host was habitually compared to the storm-winds of Winter and seasonal migrations of geese maintaining elemental associations yet neither mythical nor psychological rationale behind them. These legends only really make sense if we can accept them as a multi-layered truth composed of facts, history, myth and poetic visioning. Often these spectral Hunts actually flew over land and the last example intimates we should look again at birds and flight in myth and magic. Geese are common symbols of magical flight in Europe. Indeed, Medieval Witches often used the fabled goose fat as part of their flying ointments. Feathered skins of Cranes were used in shamanic flight in both Siberia and in parts of northern Europe. So could we in fact posit magical flight, and can specific routes be discovered?

Although the Hunt is usually peopled by the dead, Witches' testimonies in Europe during the 16th and 17th centuries presumes their belief as co-riders of the Divine huntress Diana, the direct equivalent of Holda, Hekate and Hela. Revellers in the 13th century were described by Etienne de Bourbon as the '*bona res*' - bringers of the 'good things.' Mortal and supernatural followers of Diana, Herodias/Abundia were popular in Medieval myth and were associated initially with the Faerie folk, who though fickle, would distribute and share gifts of abundance and wealth among those they had taken a shine too (or who had propitiated such acts). A humorous poem written by Alexander Mongomery in the 17th century lampoons the '*Faery Rade*' at All Hallows, and although the descriptions are clearly of Faerie folk, Witchery is explicit. Three sisters of '*Wyrd*' (Fate) morph into the Triple Godmother of Faerie. Nine nymphs accompany '*Nicneven*', bringer of the cold, deprivations of Winter, riding within her Faerie Train. This Great Queen or malignant hag of Scottish myth is often likened to Hekate. Political expediency, fear and superstition eventually transposed these folk beliefs into flights of the 'Witches Sabbat.'

The assimilation was complete, the 'Land of Fey' had become integrated into Satan's Kingdom [Macculloch: 1921].

Another common belief among scholars is the idea that a high percentage of Medieval records regarding the Wild Hunt/Furious Host were actual descriptions of ritual folk-processions, related perhaps to the *'Charivari'* or khaos jousters, rough revellers of wild music and song, disrupting and upturning all in their path. Again folklore and history merge to support an underlying myth of mystical origin. In fact the late Gerald Gardner [2004:145] suggested how he believed where Witches following in the wake of Witch-craze hysteria could easily have capitalized upon earlier folkloric legends by riding and guising to Sabbats. If true, this would have instilled fear and keep prying eyes from activities centred upon the many places of power surrounding ancient burial mounds, stone circles and crossroads etc. Legend proclaims how the baleful host could appear by both day and night, converging upon city streets in addition to harrying lonely travellers in dark woods. A recorded description of a masked procession held in honour of 'Holda' (Perchten) sheds some light onto the possible origins of his theory:

> "The wild host, very strange figures, horned, beaked, tailed ... roaring and shouting ... behind, on a black, wild steed, Frau Holda, the Wild Huntress, blowing into the hunting horn, swinging the cracking whip, her head-hair shaking about wildly like a true wonder-outrage."

Horrific folktales also relate how their benefactress would come among them in the guise of either a beautiful, masked figure or in the form of terrifying spirit that seized and possessed them, a wild spirit, a fury who could tear them apart in her frenzy.[2] Is this another reference to shamanic *'seething'* or garbled folklore? Remember of course, glosses aside, that as 'death-mother,' she would gather up all recently departed souls, which is not at all the same thing as stealing a soul from the living! It must also be stressed that *'Holda/Hulda/Perctchen's'* procession was considered to be a visitation, a procession heralding the (Faerie) Queen arrival; it was a gathering, not a 'Wild Hunt' *per se* [Macculloch: 1921]. A critical investigation into Norwegian sources concludes the possibility of assimilation between wild tales of drunken revelry and those of the carousing dead.

Belief in Faerie Folk and eldritch creatures originates in ancestral and racial/cultural memory, perceptions of divinity, imagination, hallucinogenic and/or oneiric experiences. Witchcraft is after all, rooted in primitive magics and sorcerous rapport with the dead, with shades and wandering souls. These two quite separate beliefs finally merged during the 16th and 17th centuries, especially in Scotland [*ibid.*] lending their own weight to a burgeoning morass of myth surrounding supernatural and nocturnal activities. Myths of the 'Wild Hunt' have fascinated generations of people encompassing history and geography with considerable variations reflecting cultural, political and religious affiliations.

However, and this is absolutely crucial, it may be heard, even felt by many, but only seen by those it 'takes,' either literally, as with dying souls, or metaphysically in respect of visionary seers, psychics or otherworld travellers. Already we can see a true esoteric significance of the 'Wild Hunt.' Or perhaps, since the Hunt rides out on stormy nights, a mundane explanation for the Gabriel Hounds might just indeed derive from flights of wild geese. But then Mother Goose might just be the chthonic gift bearing Earth Mother to those deemed worthy and who punishes the lazy that are not. Ancient shamans might just fly in the train of ancestral souls; we must each decide.

Mythology has always served a social and political purpose, and meanings alter in order to suit contemporary mores. Myths exampled in the Wild Hunt have simple meanings of natural death and regeneration yet can easily be harnessed to sinister and subversive ends. Use of myth in the service of history has and will always be open to abuse. And so if we remove the bias and gloss of ages, what do we see? That it evolved from possible vision questing of Palaeolithic hunters, progressing through myths of the 'Faerie Rade' and its commemorative ancestral trains, merging culturally with Nordic gatherings of slain warriors led by the powerful Odin and Frau Gaude. Northern traditions of shamanic practices of spirit flight further enriched the blend before the scaremongering of the superstitious Middle Ages demonized these processes. Ghosts and shades of evil-doers became the next form of the Wild Hunt, rampaging and terrorizing the countryside. This theme especially may have been compounded by alleged activities of Witches themselves. In later, more enlightened times, beguiling principles of the Wild Hunt are once again expressed through poetic metaphor, intimating the modalities of astral travelling, spirit flight, mystical visioning and initiatory experiences etc.

It is very important to remember that the Hunt always occurs during times of great flux in which the powers of air (flight) are most prevalent; indicative of Wintery thunderstorms, it holds immense significance for

Hallowtide, Yule and Candlemas. The Wild Hunt is traditionally led by a psychopomp, leader of souls to the Underworld during Yule and early January occurring at all the places we have been taught to fear - all those places of geomantic instability: crossroads, high places, running water, corpse ways, graveyards, lonely track-ways and ancient cairns and burial mounds.

What does this mean magically for Witches and Pagans of the 21st century?

The Wild Hunt originally signified a Time of commemoration, of remembrance for the ancestral dead, especially our historical and mythical progenitors. The Wild Hunt of Winter heralds a period of inactivity, hibernation and introspection. These magical tides are the most potent magically, not for spell-casting, or creative pursuits, but for rites of necromancy, for divination - for communion with the dead. This can be achieved directly for those well versed in such arts, or via oracular and divinatory means for those more cautious in their enterprises. At these times when the ancestral train rides out to be amongst us, their energies, insights and inspiration can be utilised for our magical evolution. This is the Time of Saturn, the primal study-master, a Time for cerebral activity, for learning, for reaching out to those mighty dead who have gone before us for aid and guidance. At these liminal times when their closeness is never again equalled, we should take full advantage of their communion. This is why when we gaze into the fire, the cauldron, a mirror, or cast runes and yarrow sticks, or read tarot cards, tea-leaves, the flight of birds or whatever we feel appropriate and have a gift for, we connect with spirits of Air - the element of Mind. The once shining cavalcade of airy spirits in both 'Celtic' and Teutonic lore bear the torch of illumination - the light in the dark and wisdom of ages. This 'dark' magic is what the Church feared most - that of our connection to a heathen ancestry, that of continued communication with it, and that of accrued wisdom and Gnosis through it.

This is why the ancestral train became demonized, the once white horse and hounds turned black as ebony. This is why shining spirits became the bestial and tortured forms of sinners, and why liminal places of power where spirits could be engaged were branded as cursed - places where the 'Divil' himself would steal your soul. All nothing more than horror stories to frighten away the curious or remotely cynical enquirer. Ironically, the name often used in common parlance for the Devil - Old 'Nick,' is a synonym for *'Hnikkr'* a title of Wotan/Odin [Jackson, 1994:24-5] and not as is generally supposed, a derivative of St Nicholas.

Most particularly, the highest concentration of energy is to be obtained over the twelve nights of liminal suspension during the period of Misrule from around Solstice/Yule eve to that of 'Twelfth Night' culminating in a 'true' Epiphany (manifestation of the Divine). Then, with normality restored, the gates of Khaos will slowly diminish before closing again for one more year. Khaos here, must be understood as an archaic utopian state, of the Golden age of Saturn, a Time of knowledge, of man's true state in which he lived in harmony with all life around him, in all states of being; a Time before corruption and his 'fall' (correctly perceived as a 'state of grace' and not a disembodied state).

Our ability to regain this state is thus offered through mystical visioning by seers during this Time of true inversion, a return to this primordial condition. Once over, it is the mundane order that is restored; in other words, our common state, the one of life on this plane of being with its attendant ignorance and finite views. Twelfth Night is specifically the eve signifying the zenith of the previous twelve nights of foray into mystical realms of the nocturnal hunter of souls, psychopomp of magico-ecstatic trance and death wisdom. On this night, the primal hunter summons the fetch (our body double) to ride with him through the cosmic realms with other souls on their journey home. Through this wild ride we may enter 'initiatory' death, the ambiguous ecstasy of the shaman.

Transported, we may journey through alternative realities and dimensions, seeking and obtaining the wisdom of ages. Fittingly, New Year's Eve, is ruled by the bi-faced God from whom the month receives its name - Janus, Oak deity and male consort of the huntress - Diana. Worshipped by the Basques (peoples including gypsies), as Janicot, he is the dual faced Lord of the Oaks in paradoxical rites where self-sacrifice and the sanctity of Life was and is central to their beliefs. As dual doorway between dimensions and Master of Time, he looks backward to the old and forward to the new [Jackson, 1996: 20-23]. As Master of Destiny and a product of *'kairos'* he can remove the veils, suspend Time gauged reality and transport us upon transcendental journeys to Sabbats past and Sabbats yet to come. Twelfth Night, a date sacred for millennia, augers the epiphanic moment, beginning with a celebration of the new son/Sun, and culminating with a renewal of blood awareness, covenanting our archaic ties to the Gods.

Throughout Old Europe, Greece, Rome and Egypt, Midwinter festivals celebrated this darker aspect of life in death - of sacrifice. Saturn, the dark Roman Lord of Misrule, has a Gaelic counterpart in Bran, Lord of Death, oracular wisdom, prophecy and necromancy, to whom the wren is sacred. Related to this is the myth of the twin waxing and waning year kings, the youthful, vibrant and wild Holly King of the waxing, Solar seasons and the wise, old 'Father' and Oak King of the waning, Lunar seasons, whose origins and truths were garbled in the mists of Time. They are here represented by their sacred totems: Robin (Holly) and Wren (Oak). Robin and Wren, totems of the waxing and waning year; but note they are both birds, signifying flight.

We advance these principles throughout our ritual year, which at its heart exemplifies the eternal flux between life and death, between light and dark; each part conducive to the whole, a true victory of the Sun, a celebration of the light from the dark, from ignorance to awareness. And so in spite of the origins of the Wild Hunt, and all its attendant superstitions, Time and custom have allowed us to develop magical traditions that may now be utterly removed from them. Yet, in reaching back through history, to study these curious myths we can determine how we have reached an understanding by which we can retain that primal link to our Pagan ancestors. Enlightenment dawns only in the light of Gnosis, never from the depths of ignorance. It is pertinent that Twelfth Night is also known as Holly/Holy Night.

Bibliography:

B. Branston. 1974 *The Lost Gods of England'* BCA London

G.B. Gardner. 2004 *The Meaning of Witchcraft'.* Wesier Books. New York

N. Jackson. 1994 *The Horned Piper'* Capall Bann Pub. Berks.

N. Jackson. 1996 *Masks of Misrule'* Capall Bann Pub. Berks

M. Olfield-Harvey. 2002 *The Horse in Myth and Legend'* Dover Pub. New York

Canon J.A. Macculloch 1921 *The Mingling of Fairy and Witch Beliefs in the 16th and 17th century Scotland'* Folklore, vol. xxxii [December - Folklore Society]

J. Westwood. 1986 *'Albion: A Guide to Legendary Britain'* BCA. London

J. Westwood & J Simpson. 2005 *The Lore of the Land'* Penguin Books. England

1. www.home.earthlink.net/~wodensharrow/yule.html
2. www.vinland.org/heathen/mt/wildhunt.html
3. www.members.tripod.com/GeoffBoxell/hunt.html

Previously published in: *The Cauldron* #126 November 2007

'Al Khidir - Viriditas'

13. Green Knight
- Dark God of Light

"The perennial agony of man, self-fortuning, deluded, tangled in the nest of his own tenuous delirium, frustrated yet having within himself, undiscovered absolutely un-utilized the secret of his release..."
Joseph Campbell - *'Hero with a Thousand Faces'*

Prose, poetry and other dramatic media of the Medieval period including the spectacular 'Mystery Plays,' inherited narrative traditions of 'Celtic' and Norse 'Paganism.' Preserved within these were collective mythologies and cultic practices of an ancient world, the apparent diversity of which reveal fundamental occult praxes of a common origin. Classical concepts, adapted from *Mithraism, Zurvanism, Shi'ism, Druzism* and *Gnosticism* were skilfully re-woven to suit Medieval Christian sensibilities.

During the 1400s an unknown author penned a beguiling synthesis in his enigmatic - *'Sir Gawain and the Green Knight.'* Common motifs evocative of archaic traditions prevail throughout, leading us into otherworldly realms where Time and space develop quantum qualities, affording us a window into another 'reality.' Set within the confines of liminal Time, spanning twelve days of ritual reversal gateway from the old year into the new, key players direct us to observe the dilemma of fate. Popular topics for celebration included mythical motifs of the slain and resurrected God, of challenges, the beheading game, typical New Year celebrations of renewal and regeneration, love and betrayal, the wasteland and the castle, all utilising varied themed magical symbols and emblems conflated within the popular Grail 'Quest.' These were explored via easily recognised archetypes, beyond whose superficiality may be discerned the deeper Mysteries; clues to a higher Gnosis.

A brief synopsis discloses an elegant yet deceptively complex plot wherein the Green Knight, personal champion of the Goddess as 'Fate', here represented by *'Morgana,'* challenges the King's mortal champion within his court, to a beheading game. The head of the Green Knight is taken by Gawain's valiant blow, but in return, his own must be offered up, one year and one day's hence. During that Time he is honoured and feted by the whole of Camelot, receiving a hero's send off several months later as he ventures forth to meet his nemesis in the Green Chapel. Travelling through a bleak wasteland, Gawain encounters a strange ethereal Castle where his hosts, Lord and Lady Bertilak are more than they seem. Promising to show Gawain the whereabouts of his assigned rendezvous with the Green Knight at the Green Chapel, Gawain is persuaded to tarry a while thereto partake of their hospitality. Gawain and Bertilak engage in a strange bargain, agreeing to exchange the prize and fortune won by each over three consecutive days. For Lord Bertilak, these are the spoils of the hunt, paralleled in the affections and kisses Gawain receives from Lady Bertilak.

Time passes and Gawain must ride out to the Green Chapel; but he is remorseful and guilty, for he had not exchanged his gifts truly. He'd withheld the gift of an enchanted girdle, given by the beautiful Lady Bertilak, in her role as the Goddess of Fate to protect him from the Green Knight's deathly blows, who was in truth, his host the Lord Bertilak. Three blows are delivered to Gawain, two thunderous, death-blows are swung to miss; the third alights upon his neck, inflicting only the lightest of flesh wounds, a reminder of his fragile mortality. This then is the tale of a deceit that cost him the ultimate prize.

Metaphoric landscapes of stark, ethereal beauty provide the devotee a place wherein they may encounter the Divine through archaic Mysteries long known as initiatory pathways towards self-knowledge. Enlightenment is attained only after oneiric mystical visionary experience generates profound transformations of consciousness, transcending all perceptions of faith. Various themes pay homage to the Dark Mother (Nox) and the Light Son (Lux). Furthermore, they reveal the true sacrifice of our Creator and our individual part in the anarchic process of redemption.

Simplistically, myth and ritual combine to inculcate an awareness where Earth is the Mother and the Hero who must 'enter' Her, both physically and symbolically as son/child and lover. Her compassion alerts him to a conscious breakthrough, pushing him into a wider Cosmos, to the stars themselves, back to the source. Indeed, we are truly all 'stars' and children of the Earth; our initiator is the son and child of the Earth. Masked and cloaked in Her resplendent greenery, primal colour of regeneration emblematic of fecundity. He is guardian of Her wisdom, the true treasures of our Earth. Beyond death there is hope, but only for those who see beyond the mask and who perceive its light concealed within. He is our

'Father,' and like all children, our love should be unconditional, total and pure.

Within the Mysteries, priests are consigned to awaken aspiring souls to Gnosis; however, each person of necessity bears their own karmic responsibility. Each of us must work to earn our redemption; salvation is not for sale. It is a gift beyond intellectual appreciation, achieved only through direct experiential transmission - interaction with the Divine. These rewards are not easily earned, nor are all pathways to them always comprehensible; the aspirant must be forever on their guard not to err. One slip and all is lost. That is why, without exception, it is often emphasised that only the 'pure of heart' may attain it.

Laced with high drama and pathos, the poem: *'Sir Gawain and the Green Knight'* invites us to participate in a central conflict wherein our Hero, Gawain, endures many trials upon his quest for Gnosis. Gawain is in effect, the anti-hero, champion of the common man, whose intentions, though good, are flawed with his own 'humanity' as he confronts the forces of Nature both within and without himself. He is a vehicle for many tales within the Grail Mysteries of errant souls seeking salvation. It is within this tale most particularly, that Gnostic, Luciferian principles shine through the brightest, forcing us to face our own eschatological needs. Human endeavour is presented to us as superficial constructs, juxtaposed against the primal purity of Nature.

Gnostic metaphors relate perils of fate, free will, true will and duty, a message revealed through the eyes of Gawain. He is hunted and challenged by the Green Knight, a figure coterminous with 'Arawn,' psychopomp and dark God of the Celtic Underworld. John and Caitlin Matthews, in their book on Irish Mythology [1995:80] emphasise the associative translation of Gawain's name in Welsh - *'Gwalchmai,'* the 'Hawk of May' as a plausible correlation to traditions of challenges between Summer and Winter Kings. They also discus how similar this tale is to the possible source tale of *'Bricrui's Feast'* [*ibid.*, 86-87]. 'CuChulainn' (hero and prototype of Gawain) is challenged by mischief maker *'Cu Roi ma Daire'* (also analogous to *'Hafgan'* in the similar tale of *'Pwyll'*) to a beheading game; though within this cycle of 'Celtic' tales, CuChulainn later defeats this club-wielding giant [*ibid.*, 28, 54]. Boars and deer as sacred totemic animals of challenge and transformation are artfully used to great effect, conveying high drama to an audience still familiar with analogous subtleties, especially apparent in the comparison between the 'stinking fox' caught by Lord Bertilak and Gawain's devious concealment of his prize from Lady Bertilak.

Brian Jones [1964:9] also cites the epic *Fled Bricend'* as probable source for the beheading game, emphasising three component actions shared by both tales. First, after 'CuChulainn' is challenged by *Uath mac Imomain'* (Terror, son of great fear) to strike off his head, three return blows are inflicted without detriment to 'CuChulainn,' declaring the hero as champion. Second is the inclusion of woman in her definitive role as temptress. The third and final element explores archaic traditions of gift-exchange, a formality among warrior classes and chieftain kings of old, affirming fealty and honour, the courtesy in fact, of developing knighthood under feudalism. Tribal customs in Africa, Madagascar and New Guinea still practise this custom, vital to their social stability. Beyond Time, religion or creed, these represent universal truths and are therefore common motifs within storytelling.

The author has successfully preserved the mystique of the three-day trials between Gawain and Lord Bertilak; a crucial factor common to traditions that maintain ancient links to purposefully broaden the scope of comprehension. Within the Tale of Lady Ragnall, [1] *'Gromer Somer Joure'* (Lord of the Summer Day), who like the Green Knight is under service to Morgana, Mistress of Fate, offers a challenge to Arthur [Matthews,1995:87]. Yet, intriguing though these similarities are, selective details separate their inherent message and purpose, requiring us to look deeper and further afield than this amorphous 'Celtic Twilight.'

To Nigel Jackson [1996:112-115], this Faerie-hued Woodwose initiatrix and inspirer of apotheosis is suggestive of fecund sexuality of Earth and water. His 'Summer King' guides initiates through verdant realms of an otherworldly landscape of fey. As Jack-in-the-Green, this ubiquitous woodland sprite evokes Silvan, Bacchus and Pan, embroiled in Oak, vine and evergreen leaves of the forest glades. Ancient images of this Divine shaman of the woods can be traced as far afield as Hatra in Mesopotamia and pre-Christian *Baalbek'*; carved in stone, they present a stoic testament to their timelessness [Basford, 1998:9]. Wildman and giant (Grigori?), his death inducing stasis engenders Gnosis of the Horned Master. Tendrils whisper prophecy and wisdom. Only if we listen with the 'true ear of the heart,' will such secrets quicken the soul to graceful union within the 'Ultimate Creatrix' - a *Unio Mystica.'*

Hildegard of Bingin, Medieval nun, Christian mystic and confidante to the Pope, faithfully recorded her numerous experiences wherein she offers the word - *'viriditas'* (greenness) to explain 'the word made flesh,' the evocative manifestation of spirit into matter.[2] This single word inculcates for her this state of Kenoma, where the ineffable becomes tangible. It is noteworthy that during her lifetime, carved, foliate heads adorned many churches and cathedrals throughout Europe [*ibid*.]. The verdant effulgence *viridios/viridius*[3] signifies a deified masculine spirit worshipped in ancient Britain. Of course, in the Middle East, this role was reflected in the Hindu God, Rama, consort of Sita, Goddess of Nature.[2] Cogently, both Lord Bertilak, and Rama are hunters, brandishing their great bows and arrows whose wives are also integral to their own roles. Curiously, Rama is the 7th incarnation/avatar of the great creator Vishnu, God of water and Earth and as such he acts as lineage bearer for the houses of the Sun and the Moon [Jansen, 2004:85]. Within the Indian epic, 'Ramayana' (circa 600CE), tales unfurl of heroism, brotherly love and of devotion, chastity and fidelity within marriage - all 'knightly' virtues [2004:78]. Parallel to the pan 'Celtic'/Irish myths, Rama, through mistrust and betrayal lost Sita, Goddess of sovereignty, accentuating the dilemmas of free will, itself a dichotomy of enlightenment or material pursuit [*ibid*.]. Philosophically, these tracts exceed their cultural and moral value.

In the '*Masks of God*,' Campbell [1991:31] places source material for the tale of 'Sir Gawain and the Green Knight' in these early Vedic mythologies circa 375-950 and heavily influenced by the 'Shakti' cults of India. Typified in the *'Festival of Sabarotsava,'* orgiastic revellers cover their bodies in mud, leaves and flowers to celebrate the extraordinary fecund sexuality of Shiva [Jackson, 1996:120]. Campbell [1991:31] maintains how later Sufi mystical poetry added even greater import to the significance and character of the Green Knight, especially in the figure of Al Khidir. This pre-Islamic prophet, as representative of Divine wisdom throughout the Arab world acted as guide to Moses and Alexander. [2] Reverence for the Green Crawler - *'Nabi Khizir'*, the living green man of waters and ponds is evidenced in shrines near natural springs throughout Kurdistan, confirming the esteemed role of the *'Nagas'* (wisdom serpents) once prevalent throughout India. Fortuitously, the feast day of *'Al Khidir'* falls in Spring, coinciding with Nature's own renewal.[4]

The main goal of a Sufi is to attain alchemical transformation, and the intercession of Al Khidir is integral to that process. To the *'Shi'ite'* sect in particular, this messianic redeemer is perceived as a 'Time' lord whose sphere of influence upon this plane determines one's fate: at-one-ed or annihilation at the end of Time.[4] Gnosis is achieved through faith, devotion and wisdom after trials of seemingly senseless riddles, each designed to test perception, breaking down rational processes of the conscious mind. Only the righteous will prevail, assured of their Gnostic passport into the kingdom of light [Jones, 1964:135]. Pertinently, the alchemical *'Tabula Smaragdina,'* the wisdom imparted by the emerald stone from Lucifer's crown, *'Lux Mundi'* is also green.

Indigenous Kurds practising *'Yazdanism,'* the 'Cult of Angels,' also perceive their Lord Creator God - *'Haq'* (not to be confused with the Arabic word for truth - *haqq*) as a 'Time' lord, whose atavistic presence within *'Baba'* (Father) as gateway and portal reveals his true Nature and purpose between noumenal and phenomenal realms.[6] He is eternal spirit made flesh; a teacher and guide offering redemption through wisdom. Shams, legendary poet, Sufi mystic and mentor of Rumi, was afforded gifts of prophecy, wisdom and poetry at the end of a long vigil by the shrine of *'Baba Kuhi.'* [7]

Heaven and Earth combine in the colours of yellow and blue to create green, sacred throughout Asia, India, Middle East and Europe, expressing life and renewal on a mundane level, whilst supernatural powers of spiritual transformation augment the occult realms. Thus all Gods exhibiting this hue: Osiris, Rama, Al Khidir and the Woodwose Jack-in-the-Green are all exponents of this duality, being at once a psychopomp, leading the souls through the darkness into the light and symbol of fertility and 'renewal'. In the *'Masks of God,'* Campbell [1991:502] even posits green as the colour of the Holy Spirit/Ghost.

Furthermore, the commonality of Spring as the ancient New Year is temptingly allusive to *'Shavuot,'* Hebraic forerunner of *'Pentecost'*, (the 5th feast of the year or 50th day after 'Pesach'/ Passover) when the 'word' (Law/Torah) of God was given to Moses in a *'Surah'* of Fire, and where the Holy Spirit descended as tongues of fire upon the disciples of Jesus respectively.[8] Note, that Moses, the disciples and Gawain all encounter these manifestations within Nature's own 'Holy' Temples viz, mountains or gorges. Spring as the commemoration of such revelations formulates the inspiration behind the Pentecostal Grail Legends and Quests within Christian Arthurian Cycles. Numerologically, both 5 and 50 are cogently associated with Mars/Teutates, a Romano-Celtic God of vegetation, agriculture and healing.

Bacchanalian sexual promiscuity and orgiastic revelry were charges levied at the Anatolian celebrations of *'Mum Sondü'* and the Iranian *'Chiragh*

Kushan,' practised within Yazdanism.[6] Resembling the Luciferian, Waldensian and 12th century Cathar cultic activities, these Tantric praxes fused spiritual fertility together with mystical union. Renowned 19th century academic Henry Rawlinson believed remnants of these fertility cults exhibiting aspects of Mithraism that celebrated the sacred union of *'Mitra'* (Time) and *'Anahita'* (Fate/Space/Void) were evident as late as 1818 [*ibid.*].

The Green Knight, initiator and key-holder to the Mysteries serves the supreme Mistress of Fate, testing and leading the Hero on through his many trials, purging him of all material desires in order to achieve his destiny – *"to win a good fate"* [Campbell,1973: 118-121]. This would declare him master of his own destiny wherein Lady Fate would announce his victory and freedom from her bonds. Gnosis of inherent divinity cedes the highest order of the Universe, acknowledging Truth and Beauty, the Holy Spirit that moves all. Divested of mundane mortality, the Hero becomes *'twice-born'*, subsumed within the *'Father'* - *'at-one-d.'* Thus enlightenment cedes true apotheosis where: *"Hunter and Hunted are but One;"* there is no separation and universal truth is realised. Victorious, the Hero becomes the guide, the *'sun-door'*, the initiator - but, Gawain fails and finds only despair, desolation and confusion. Loss of faith induces his long, dark night of the soul [Campbell, 1973:136-7]. For those who attain at-one-ment, the world ceases to be a Hell (place of profound transformation), a vale of tears, but a true paradise of *'bliss yielding, perpetual manifestation of the Divine presence'* [*ibid.*, 148].

As a brief aside, we may note that in the Spring Rites of ancient Babylon, the King, once stricken across his face by a sacred Hierodule had to weep, to shed tears of compassion and understanding, exhibiting an astute awareness of life and death, and the hereafter. If his tears were judged to be sincere and genuine by the Goddess as Supreme Mistress of Fate, she would indeed grant him and his people a *'sweet fate.'* Re-instated, he is fit to reign again as fecund ruler for another year. Campbell [1973:147] believes that only through sufferance and abnegation, will the light of Gnosis be imparted to those aware of the *"living waters as the tears of God."* Quoting extensively from *'Hero of a Thousand Faces,'* he eloquently adds:

> "In full, awareness of the life anguish of the creatures of his hand, in full consciousness of the roaring wilderness of pains, the brain-splitting fires of the deluded, self-ravaging, lustful, angry Universe of his creation, this divinity acquiesces in the deed of supplying life to life. To withhold the seminal waters would be to annihilate; yet to give

them forth is to create this world we know. For the essence of *Time* (my emphasis) is flux, dissolution of the momentarily existent; and the essence of life is Time. In his mercy, in his love for the forms of Time, this demiurgic man of men yields countenance to the sea of pangs; but in his full awareness of what he is doing, the seminal waters of the life that he gives are the tears of his eyes. The paradox of creation, the coming of the forms of 'Time out of Eternity' is the germinal secret of the Father. It can never be quite explained. Therefore, in every system of theology there is an umbilical point, an Achilles tendon which the finger of mother life has touched, and where all possibility of perfect knowledge has been impaired. The problem of the Hero is to pierce himself (and therefore his world) precisely through; to shatter and annihilate that key knot of his limited existence. The problem of the 'Hero' going to meet the 'Father' is to open his soul beyond terror to such a degree that he will be ripe to understand how the sickening and insane tragedies of this vast and ruthless Cosmos are completely validated in the majesty of Being. The hero transcends life with its peculiar blind spot and for a moment rises to a glimpse of the source. He beholds the face of the 'Father,' understands - and the two are at-one-d."

Solemnization of the holy ritual year, of life resurrected from sacrifice, underpins the Spring Rites of Attis, Adonis, Osiris, and Mithras in themes regarding a *'slain redeemer.'* No simple act of barbarism, this exemplifies death of the self, of gross matter, thus freeing and elevating the spirit towards Nirvana. Triple death blows are profligate within myths and legends from pre-history. Druidry, Freemasonry, Neo-Paganism and Wicca celebrate these concepts in various ways, honouring perhaps unwittingly esoteric practises of these ancient Mysteries. Initiatory blows are received upon the cheek and neck in some idiosyncratic practises. Knighthood confers similar points of contact where blows are struck representing first: the rite of confirmation, second: baptism, and third: the sacrament of the Eucharist - atonement by which:

> "man, since the beginning of his day on Earth, has dispelled the terror of his phenomenality and won through to the all transfiguring vision of immortal being." [Campbell, 1973:142-143].

Thus he dies and is 'resurrected' again in God the redeemer.

Clearly this is not as some would believe a veiled or simplistic tale of Pagan rites or of a battle between year kings - Holly and Oak. For Gawain fails, he does *not* defeat the Green Knight; neither is he himself killed. His life remains a token of his loss. However, allegorical tree lore and legends pertaining to these two majestic trees form integral clues, almost overlooked, so subtle is their inclusion. Oak is the tree of the waning Solar year; a Hero's tree, a tree of sacrifice (Herne and Robin), prophecy and wisdom, (i.e. it manifests the 'Word'). Revered as the tree of longevity, it represents the cycles of 'Time and Eternity'. Sage of all trees, it is a doorway/gate/portal that represents the ultimate ruling power of Nature conferring abundance upon man and beast.

Holly is the wild, erotic force of regeneration, of light and life during the Winter Solstice. Wildman of Saturnalian festivals, his power and thunder reflect the forces of Tubal Cain, God of smith-craft, magic and cunning. Known to Druids as Tinne, Gaelic, for fire, He truly represents the Solar Year deific force, bringing heat and light in the depths of Winter. Yet the folk name for Holly is 'Holm Oak', the evergreen Oak, revealing Oak and Holly to be one and the same, dual aspects of the one Sun/Son, who is his Father, another paradox of the Mysteries [Oates, 2005].

Furthermore, within the Druid tree calendar, the passage between Oak (Duir) and Holly (Tinne) is perceived as portal and gateway, emphasising again the suspension and liminality of Time, and the freedom to move through all realms via these powers of Nature. Despite much speculation and ambiguity surrounding correlations between pan 'Celtic' and Roman deities, Anne Ross [1974:474] makes it clear that unnamed Horned Gods of the broad spectrum of 'Celtic' language groups were generally associated with Jupiter, Mars and Mercury, and that these three share mutual qualities of fire and thunder, are related to smith deities and have *severed heads* dedicated to them.

Tangentially, we may observe how optical phenomena known as '*Fata Morgana*', resulting from a temperature inversion, cause objects on the horizon to appear as elevated and elongated, suggesting 'Fairy Castles' to those of a poetic persuasion.[9] Nevertheless, poets and mystics have for millennia accepted this domain of the Goddess of Fate and her Castle that spins between the worlds as a destination of aspiration. Fate, aspected as many Goddesses over this Time, has accorded her many names: '*Morgana,*' '*Morgan la fey,*' '*Morrighan,*' '*Macha,*' '*Three/Triple Mothers,*' the '*Norns,*' the '*daughters of Allah,*' '*Kybele,*' '*Kali*' and '*Hekate.*' She is the organizing principle behind the narrative text of the 'Green Knight' tale.

She is Lady of the Castle and her presence, though limited, is significant. As Goddess of Sovereignty and Fate she tests Gawain both here and in the tale of Lady Ragnall, though in the latter he does become her lover and champion. Matthews suggests this implies Morgana as the dark, Winter Queen, with *Launcelot* championing Guinevere as the Summer Queen [1993:41-42]. Whilst this has great symbolic significance within 'Celtic' folklore relating to forces of Nature and its changing seasons, it masks the praeternatural - the spirit realms beyond what we can 'see.' Morgana tests Gawain in both worlds, in Camelot and in the otherworldly Castle of 'Lord and Lady Bertilak de Hautdesert', the wasteland of dread.

The marshy wasteland encountered by Gawain symbolises decomposition of spirit [Cirlot, 1983:205]. Here the elementals actuate the 'Hand of Fate' in a pre-determined theatre of spectacles. Air and fire (active) are absent from the marshland, but Earth and water (passive) are prevalent, both aligned powers to Al Khidir/Nagas/Green Knight. Immediately, Gawain is out of his depth in an alien, hostile landscape. Seriously disadvantaged, peril looms and the balance is tipped against him. As a pawn of the Goddess, he must stave off his own reckless and impatient Nature; if he loses his wits, he is doomed to failure.

14th century literary allegories had returned to the devolution of women, incorporating them only as vehicles of lust and temptation; they had lost their higher purpose as spiritual guides and initiators. Thus marginalized, they represent sin and the call away from duty and honour. Yet the poet does in fact warn us of the 'fate' that Lady Bertilak holds within her concealed Nature. It is obviously far more than a play for love. Her purpose is abundantly clear. Parallel barren landscapes serve to reflect the barren psyche and thus highlight his inability to conclude his mission. Unable to recognize this scene as Hell (place of transformation), Gawain is truly doomed.

Spiritual elevation/enlightenment is perceived by Heer [1993:147] as attainable only via transformation through 'Hell' precipitated by encounters with the 'Devil' himself, the catalyst for evolutionary change and empowerment. Painful, rigorous trials facilitate a breach beyond the abyss towards salvation. Enchanted castles, fearful domains and the Underworld are all classic motifs with this ancient process. Heer [*ibid.*] further postulates Gnostic influences as germane to the Medieval literary genre, providing an associative crisis of conscience within the reader. Examples of this may be found in the poem, *'Nekyia,'* in which influential and sophisticated Oriental traditions are fused with elements of depth psychology, paralleling Gawain's trials. Rationalising conceptual devices as indicative of a return to archaic ambivalence and the mystical power of Paganism, Heer [*ibid.*] concludes them to be a clear rejection of Christian preaching on morality.

John and Caitlin Matthews [1995:162] adopt a more popular view of the wasteland as a punishment for loss of sovereignty, a consequence of power abuse, restoration of which they believe will occur only when the 'Goddess' spirituality is once again accepted as the prime mover. Through union with her (Gnostic) priest, the Fisher King, (Pelles - hence pellar for 'wise man') the land will be replenished and fecund once more. Again, though relevant on one level, this oversimplification, paradoxically, obfuscates the true motive and goal of the Grail legends. Although the Grail is not mentioned explicitly within the 'Tale of the Green Knight' text, the author would have expected his audience/readers to be familiar with the many earlier Grail legends through the works of 'Chretien de Troyes,' 'Wolfram von Eschenbach,' 'Robert de Borron,' the 'Mabinogion' and others.

In these, we encounter a significant recurring occult motif in the number five, the Grail has five forms and there are Five Grail Knights: 'Gawain,' 'Perceval,' 'Launcelot,' 'Galahad' and 'Bors.' Within this tale, Gawain's shield is emblazoned with a pentagram, a five sided symbol that uphold five knightly virtues: generosity, courtesy, chivalry, chastity and piety.[10] It also represents the five senses, but this endless knot also denotes another link to Mars/Teutates - of severity yet harmony through strife and conflict. Symbolic of many initiatic requisites, the initiate is instructed to face their demons, to integrate the shadow/darkness in order to become whole/holy and perceive the light.

This ancient symbol, discovered among the rubble and dust of Sumer is depicted as part of the insignia of imperial power, a principle that was later developed by Babylonians into a representational graphic of the five directions (four cardinal points of the plane compass together with the upwards central pole of the all enveloping and peripheral heavens, supreme abode of all Gods) and the five major planets. For Druids, this symbol represented the highest Godhead. Most intriguingly, the Greeks associated this graphic with the 'pentemychos' (five chambers of the heart), esoteric gateway between liminal realms of Time and space, from the earthly plane of being to those of Tartaros - boundless deep and darkness of the abyss.[10] Hades, both a place and (Greek) God of the Underworld, represents '*Lux Mundi*' in the fullest sense. All earthly treasures of place him cognate with the Naga King, whose serpentine form correlates as the 'Serpent of Wisdom,' avatar of Divine mind (nous), imparting enlightenment and immortality to the Hero within '*Nekyia*' after his successful descent into the Underworld Castle and survival of rigorous trials within the 'City of the Dead' [Heer, 1993:157]. His requisite salvation and re-birth confirms his accession as '*perfectii,*' a priest of the pure.

Hekate, Mistress of Fate rules the Underworld as Lady of Tartaros; key holder, gateway and guardian she is invoked by Medea in the play by Euripides with the words "*she who dwells in my inmost chamber*" - the '*mychos.*'[10] By association, this relates to the soul as vehicle as it travels the wheel of life that she spins. For Pythagoras, this innermost chamber was the seat of the soul and true core of being [*ibid.*]. Of course, symbolically the pentagram device upon Gawain's shield may simply represent the soul (*psyche*) as it journeys towards love (*eros*) as it yearns for enlightenment (*Unio Mystica*). Upon the reverse of Gawain's shield was an image of the 'Virgin', which if black would relate to her role as Mistress of his Fate on a much deeper level. Serving then as an emblem of fate and of truth, his destiny was assured.

Conceptually, the beheading game is significantly more than a defeat of one 'king' by another; or even more than the life and death aspects of the cycle of Nature. It maintains elements of archaic beliefs associated with the 'Cult of the Head.' Throughout the ancient world, the head was revered as superlative seat of power, will and intellect. To take someone's head was in effect an act of sub-summation. Warriors and priests who carried heads as trophies or oracles as in the legend of Bran the Blessed, were able to directly receive inspiration (literally in-spirit) from communion with and through them. A similar prophetic form of spirit possession is also associated with Sufi traditions through '*Al Khidir.*'

Sufis frequently use the term 'dancing headless' to denote a spirit entranced state, reached when passion overwhelms the intellect or mind, the rational seat of power. Such love under (true) will motivates apotheosis. In Mithraic rites, a crown is removed and/or rejected by the aspirant, indicating removal of the seat of intellect and submission of the heart (Fate), to the highest Love. Within Sufi initiatory traditions lies the ritual of 'removing' the head to provoke realisation before replacing it as an act of re-birth into the sacred Mysteries. Destroy in order to become. Beheading of initiates is also prevalent within the Cult of Kali, dark Goddess of Fate, Destiny and Time; she is depicted holding aloft the severed head, exclaiming "*he who loseth his life for me shall find it.*" Wildly she dances upon the body of Shiva, maintaining ecstatic union as she performs her dance of creation from destruction [Campbell, 1973:170].

In all these things, the soul yearns for release, seeking as lover, union with the beloved - *'Unio Mystica,'* the alchemical fusion of the heart/soul (*mychos/psyche*) with the mind/spirit (*Nous/Pneuma*) of God. Within the litanies of the Greek Magical (London) Papyrus, is an invocation to the 'Headless One,' frequently cast as the 'Born-less One' whose climactic rite of true apotheosis is one of the most arresting ever noted. Adapted from a rite of exorcism by Aleister Crowley, it exemplifies the principle of at-one-ment with the 'Father' [Goetia, 1997:12]; that so many ancient God-forms have animal masks or heads of beasts symbolic of certain pre-requisite qualities suggests a greater than totemic relevance. Association and identification with each head/mask facilitates elevation of consciousness into a spiritual scion, where the wearer's identity is suspended and replaced by that invoked.

Medieval alchemists regarded the first stage of the process as death of matter, the removal of flesh from the bone, revealing the true *'heart of the matter,'* a metaphor for the destruction of bodily passions that impede progress of the soul... *'if any man cuts off his head...'* refers to essential decay for transmutation of matter/ hyle [Seligman, 1997:136]. It is the mind of God, (the Divine self-nous) that replaces our own in the be-heading. As the seat of intellect, the heads' removal leads to death. Re-birth occurs when it is replaced by deific sentience, by thinking, seeing, feeling and becoming that deity: dancing headless, the body is ravaged by ecstatic union, as heart/soul (*mychos*) animates the body in the bliss of *'Premdeha'* (union). Persian Muslims retained much of their former mystical heritage from Mithraism. Regardie [1970:107] describes an initiate's three day death trance in the *'Osirion'* that culminates with the Crown of Glory emblazoning their head as a mandorla of Solar light - *'Xvarenah,'* Divinely bestowed light nimbus of magical sovereignty transfigures the mystic, separating the soul from the profane body; momentarily they are *'cit'*, pure consciousness. Love and death are not a duality, but a unity: *"The Lover, beloved and lover are one, for in the world of unity, all become one"* [Campbell, 1973:162].

Submission to the Goddess and at-one-ment through the Father binds and formulates two mythical concepts: Yin and Yang form an holistic holiness, the true meaning of androgyny as a spiritual not physical condition; Truth and Beauty as the Mother and Father 'Gods,' whose Mysteries inculcate our creation, destruction and evolution into perfection/

enlightenment -'Nirvana.' The female principle is 'yum'/Time; the male principle is 'yab'/eternity - the Tantric principle of Oneness, the union that creates the Universe. Here, Campbell [1973:136-7] believes the Green Knight to act as Mystagogue, and cogently, this final rite of the fully realised soul within the Mithraic litany entitles each aspirant with the grade of 'Father', priest and earthly representative of the Celestial (Solar) Father, spouse of (Lunar) Anahita; a union of Sun and Moon. They are spiritual fire and heart of the Universe, representing the Holy Grail within Arthurian legends. Glorious visions are activated by the 'questors' as they interact, engage and temper their passions in and beyond these material realms.

Analysing the interplay of archetypes within the Grail legends, it is clear that Gawain, like Launcelot submits to worldly gifts and temptations of the flesh rather than spirit, a theme the author of 'The Green Knight' uses to great effect. Being too worldly, Gawain only glimpses the Mystery and so fails to find the Grail. Only Galahad, son of the flawed Launcelot and the Grail Maiden is pure enough to attain his spiritual goal. Perceval is assigned the role of guardian within the 'Castle'. Launcelot the fallen and Bors remain on the periphery, having faith and vision but not the steadfast purity of the other three, most ostensibly manifest within Galahad. Yet Bors receives his mission to bring the wonder of the Grail Mystery to the outside world [Matthews, 1996:5]. Matthews [*ibid.,* 36] posits independent salvation as an idiom of the Mysteries, wherein all 'questors' are inherently mystics seeking apotheosis. Galahad was therefore pre-destined to succeed where others had failed. As the Angels carried him aloft, his parting words to the others were *"...remember me to my father, and as soon as you see him, bid him remember this unstable world...."* [*ibid.,* 106]. This statement invites comparison with the Buddhist principle of impermanence. By successfully combining heart and mind, Galahad achieves enlightenment. Perceval, ascetic Holy Fool, impetuous but ignorant of his destiny, innocent and impervious to the distractions of the world is the bridge by which we all have access to the path and thus he is in opposition to the earthly passions of Bors, the singular pathway of heart. The prize requires total harmony, equilibrium of spirit within the absolute face of divinity [*ibid.,* 107-112].

Unlike modern psychoanalysis, where the process of individuation releases patients from their private 'Hell,' removing obstacles of assimilation and friction within a mundane existence, the purpose of the Mysteries is not to place individuals back into a 'safer' environment, but to open their eyes to waken them from the sleep of ages, to procure for them a true vision detached from delusion, achieved by destruction of urbane impulses [Campbell, 1973:164-5].

> "Life therein, begotten by the Father is compounded of Her dark and His Light. We are conceived in Her and dwell, removed from the Father, but when we pass from the womb of Time at death (which is our birth into eternity) we are given into His hands. The wise realize, even within this womb, that they have come from and are returning to the Father, while the very wise know that he and she are in substance One." [Campbell, 1973:169]

Gawain, blinded by his desire to live, rejected this gift of harmony offered through his ennoblement in acceptance of women as initiators and psychopomps. As handmaidens of fate, his trust and surrender to them would have engineered his success. Perceiving them only as worldly creatures caused him to accept the gift of the enchanted girdle, failing to see the spiritual impedance in this act.

Within Hindu mythology, both male and female Gods wear belts/cords denoting sacrifice, puberty, manhood, initiation and protection, fertility respectively. Cords also represent reality, passion and inertia, all fundamental qualities of matter [Janson, 2004:31-32]. Exploring these concepts further, Campbell [1973:100,129] interprets the symbolism of these bindings as representative of the threshold or sun-door, indicating the wearer is at once in Time and Eternity. Lady Bertilak's gift of a girdle/cord becomes significant in this understanding; its relevance no mere enchantment. Moreover, it is green, the Faerie hue of both Green Knight and his Mistress (Fate) and therefore represents his initiatory powers of death/eternity and her protective powers of life/Time. Girdles are of course strong literary devices, indicative of magical dominion and the binding love/eroticism of the Goddess. In this later tale, Gawain clearly rejects 'Her' love in favour of saving his skin.

However, Lady Bertilak's role is ambivalent; she does not judge him, serving a higher purpose as initiatory Hag, rather than temptress. She simply acts out her role as instrument of his fate. Evil is not distinct from good, the boundary is blurred; only the goal renders the cause pure. She wished him no malice, nor harm; there was no hostility, the choice was his and free will must prevail. So, blind to his fate, he lost his salvation. Pure love above lust (in the broadest sense) exalts the initiate beyond the mundane into spiritual realms.

As Gawain lay down and bared his neck within the Green Chapel, he failed to grasp the irony of his own observation of this dark and terrible place where one: *"might meet the Devil himself"* [Jones, 1964:111]. He also failed to recognize and assimilate his passion for life, suppressing rather than embracing it, concealing rather than revealing it. He shunned death; flinching, he drew back from its Mysteries, shrinking from its embrace. He balked at the Sun-door, the gate of wonders. He de-faulted his vision of Eden, even as the Grail slipped away from him. A vacuum gnawed at his wretched soul. Out of step with his true will, the prize eluded him. Thus he retained his 'head', for his struggle was with life, not death.

Occult maxims constantly pronounce that we must give all to receive all, nothing short of total surrender and trust, and to burn always with passion. The Green Knight invites and challenges us to become, to embrace fully the Mysteries of life and death, the agony and ecstasy of union and separation, which is the knowledge and horror of Truth and the awesome Beauty of being. Androgyny is of spirit, not flesh, a common misunderstanding; it is perfection and that can never occur in the physical realms of matter for once achieved, spirit, beyond gender classification is freed from it. The sufferer within is that Divine being, the redeemer waiting to be redeemed, the protecting 'Father' and we are one - the *"hunter and hunted are but one"* (Robert Cochrane). The enemy, the challenger, the guardian at the gate is both God and Satan, bound within Fate, the Luciferian Gnostic principle of Light, Truth and Beauty.

Both paradise and hell co-exist upon this plane; we create and live with either, dependant upon our actions. This is Karma, the law of cause and effect, in the here and now, not some nebulous or speculative future. Only the righteous shall prevail to become one with the Universal Spirit - Haq, all others will be annihilated into eternal oblivion. Love is thus revealed as the 'Pleroma' of the Law, ourselves as products of God. Love is submission. Love under (true) Will. Love is the Way, the Tao, should any of us offer anything less?

Yet this arduous path was never more so than during the Medieval period, when Thomas Aquinas headed the intellectual camp of hard Aristotelian reason and logic; the mystical, intuitive, experiential camp was led by Francis of Assisi, fired by Rumi's passion. Yet intellect is distant and cold; passion is chaotic and destructive. For true Gnosis, one must harness passion to intellect, a marriage of heart and mind - *'evolove'*, in order to truly know and understand God, the *'Unio Mystica'*, allegorised as the sacred and alchemical marriage of the Sun and the Moon.

There are three alchemical stages in which we may approach the *Unio Mystica*:

1	2	3
matter	soul	spirit
body	heart	heart/head
action	devotion	contemplation
ritual	prayer	mediation
service	worship	reflection

The final stage is mystical perception: at-one-ment; *Nirvana; Samadhi; Premdeha; Unio Mystica* - the crown achievement of all mystics. These basic principles filtered into literary motifs that utilised allegory as a vehicle of illumination, of spiritual instruction, and the author leaves us in no doubt of Gawain's miserable plight. His lament of failed attainment is not however as Brian Jones [1964:11] asserts, an anti-climax, for the Mystery revealed is one of great subtlety. It absolutely matters not whether the message is Pagan, masked by Christian ideals or vice-versa, for it is delivered intact. Neither is it about the *'sin'* of imperfection. In fact sin does not mean that which is wrong or evil, it simply represents those 'things' that keep us from God, in other words the 'things' that distract us, bar our way, shift our focus from a higher purpose. Rather, the poem is about the failure to attain one's destiny, to be blind to the choices that Fate offers us - to miss the mark - *'hamartia'* (sin). Gawain's free will allowed him to reject and lose the ultimate prize; this tale is therefore cautionary. Mankind is given free will by the Creator and in order to receive the ultimate prize it must first be fully surrendered - the real meaning perhaps of 'perfect love and perfect trust.'

Bibliography
Basford, K. 1998 *'The Green Man'* G.B. Whitstable Litho Printers Ltd.
Campbell, J. 1973 *'Hero with a 1000 Faces.'* U.S.A. Princeton Uni. Press.
Campbell, J. 1991 *'Masks of God - Creative Mythology'* U.S.A. Arkana Books.
Cirlot, J.E. 1983 *'Dictionary of Symbols'* U.S.A. Routledge & Keegan Paul.
Jackson, N. 1996 *'Masks of Misrule'* Berks. Capall Bann Publishing.
Jansen, E.R. 2004 *'The Book of Hindu Imagery'* Netherlands. BinkeyKok Publications.
Jones, B. Trans. 1964 *'Sir Gawain and the Green Knight'* U.K. Hazell, Watson & Viney Ltd.

MacGregor Mathers, S.L. Trans. 1997 *'Goetia - Lesser Key of Solomon'* Maine. Samuel Weiser

Matthews, J. 1993 *'The Arthurian Tradition'* Australia. Element Books Ltd.

Matthews, J&C. 1995 *'British and Irish Mythology'* G.B. Aquarian Press.

Matthews, J. 1996 *'The Grail Tradition'* Australia. Element Books Ltd.

Regardie, I. 1970 *'The Garden of Pomegranates'* U.S.A. Llewellyn Pub.

Ross, A. 1974 *'Pagan Celtic Britain'* London. Sphere Books Ltd.

Seligman, K. 1997 *'The History of Magic'* New York. Pantheon Books.

Oates, Shani. 2005 'Summer and Winter Solstice Customs' The Wytches' Standard #2 Summer Solstice 2005

1. www.uidaho.edu/student_orgs/arthurian_legend/hunt/ragnall.html
2. www.spiritpassages.com
3. www.wikipedia.org/wiki/viridios
4. www.ancientworlds.net/aw/Post/171007
5. www.absoluteastronomy.com
6. www.ancientworlds.net
7. www.avatarmeherbaba.org/erics/glossh-j-html
8. www.biblicalholidays.com/shavuot.htm & www.biblicalholidays.com/pentecost.htm
9. www.absoluteastronomy.com/encyclopaedia/f/fa/ fata_morgana.htm
10. www.mysticalplanet.com/lib/pentagram.html & www.absoluteastronomy.com/encylopedia/p/pe/pentagram.htm

Author's note - Throughout the previous essay, several salient points have been highlighted as relevant not only to the poem but to my own Clan Mythos. During his life Robert Cochrane made several key statements that ring out again and again as esoteric truisms. He believed that *"all ritual should be prayer,"* a belief reflected in the beautiful 'Mask Prayer' he devised for use at May's Eve in which a foliate mask is built upon the face of each person receiving this special blessing, during an invocation to 'Fate', expressing the Virtues of Time, Space, Creation, Eternity and Unity in Love and Faith. This cosmic order of Truth (Maat) is the absolute made manifest. The relevance of this poem to our own Mythos is even more startling when one recognises the landscapes within it resembling those of Staffordshire, Cochrane's own county of origin. *'Lud's Church'* in the Dane Valley, a vetivert rich and eerie place is thought by many to have been the inspiration behind the poet's description of the Green Chapel. Having worked this poem as a Mystery play there with my own group, I can attest to its authenticity in terms of both topography and geomancy.

Previously published in: *The Cauldron* #120 May 2006 - # 121 August 2006

Pendragon #XIII no.4 Summer 06 - #XXXIV no.1 Autumn 2006

Priestly Mysteries

14. The Fisher King - Gnostic Priest of the High Mysteries of the Grail

Intrinsic to the Grail Mysteries, this enigmatic figure has long baffled and intrigued both mystics and scholars alike. Literary genres of 12th century Europe reflected lingering artistic mores of influential Medieval metaphysics. Contemporary mystics such as 'Hildegard of Bingin' and 'Bernard of Clairvaux' whose studies into the realms of individuation were in ever increasing danger of encroachment by rising Scholasticism symptomatic of the Middle Ages. Logic and reason were to replace the existentialism of faith and being. Jewish and Muslim philosophies merged with Greek and Latin studies, reconciling classical teachings with Christian theology, eventually minimising the free practice of Christian Mysticism. Within this conflict of the higher arts, the Grail Mysteries evolved and developed sequentially, typifying each stage, increasing our inability to capture the true essence of the Grail in a universal moment of Time. Perhaps this is precisely why this Mystery lures us still, captivating all seekers within its thrall.

Appropriately, because it is a Mystery, no general consensus of opinion purports to be the definitive answer, leading to considerable yet stimulating speculation. Naturally, certain studies are more academic than others, but this should not preclude those sourced more insightfully; all are valid in the holistic Nature of the Grail Mysteries. When we fail to seek it, the Mystery dies, and then the Grail truly serves no-one. Discussed within this brief discourse, are but a few, selected only by personal interest and for no other particular merit. My opinions and impressions of these will supplement their succinct rendition throughout the unfolding text. We must too be mindful that Medieval tales invariably prove to be a demonstrable amalgam of Christian theology, Oriental philosophy, 'Celtic' myth and alchemical treatises, laced with metaphors that adumbrate the questors' search for Universal Gnosis.

Renowned mythographer Joseph Campbell [1991:405] avers primarily a context of synthesised chthonic Near Eastern Mystery Cults, evolving from the Bronze Age into the Iron Age, wherein animated tales of conquest and heroes overlay earlier myths of fructifying Gods, spirits of the land and inherent fundamental harmonics. Tirelessly, he explores these themes from Mesopotamia, through India into Ireland, the fruits of which yield promising analogies between the Grail and early sacramental bowls (worthy of greater study than is permissible here). His study refutes the Grail as a Eucharistic vessel, dismissing it as readily as Jessie Weston's theory of the Grail being indicative of Pagan fertility rites. Initiation, a Grail Castle, a forfeit and promise of redemption formulate the nucleus of several Grail legends; so where within this exactly, does the 'Fisher' King's salvation lay?

Campbell [1991:407-8] suggests the Fisher King's origin may be found in sea Gods of antiquity, of '*Poseidon*', '*Manannan mac Lir,*' '*Nuada/Nodens,*' of '*Vishnu*' and '*Oannes,*' and especially in the Mesopotamian serpent God, '*Ningizzida*' who was known as 'Lord of the Tree of Life' and whose qualities included healing and magic. All these deities represent graphic models for this priestly figure, many of whom may be traced through diverse artistic representations. These include mystic 'fishermen' depicted on a 2nd millennium BCE Babylonian seal and more interestingly, a 3rd century sacramental bowl. The latter, displaying the figure of Orpheus (also 'fishing'), is believed to be a baptismal vessel indicative of the watery abyss, through which ones soul is reborn as pure thought, as Truth, garnered with knowledge of life and death. Gnostic Mysteries confirm a lineage of priest-kings whose esoteric form, from Oannes to Jesus, was commonly portrayed as a 'fish.' Mesopotamian reliefs depict this sacred vessel carried by the (fish) priest-king as an inverted truncated cone, a chthonic reflection of the sacred *omphalos*, the mound of creation [*ibid.*,12-17].

Deities of the formative world and life giving waters of the abyss were aspected within each initiate of the sacred Mysteries to be experienced and realised as the Divine within. Each aspirant becomes a 'Mystes', a full initiate, a 'fisher' priest, a bearer of the bowl, representative of his acquired capacity as a 'true' man. With this truth, he is able to generate fertility and abundance from the land that sustains life (the corporeal element) to complement his role as liberator of the soul (non-corporeal element). He is both creator and destroyer, maintaining inverse reflections of the paradox of existence. Effectually, as Orphic Mysteries merged with those of Christianity, this tragic figure becomes the sacrificial king, transforming a concept of the unity of all consciousness with the totality of being and thus the cycle of life, to the literal physical death of an avatar. This fusion lead to a mystical teaching within Christianity that flourished within the Grail Mysteries; Christ replaced Orpheus as supreme *'Mystagogue'* whose 'death' and 'ascent' was understood by Gnostics to refer to his re-attainment of at-one-ment and not in any orthodox sense of literal reparation for our perceived 'sins' [*ibid.*,25-26].

In myth, water is seldom referred to without recourse to the Moon, and Campbell [1991:409-10] highlights the magical and scientific connection between them. Water and all tides are governed by this celestial body; it waxes and wanes, having two vital modes. When waning, it is perceived as 'lame', its incapacity apparent. Yet, this dark mode conceals Mysteries attributed to it. Since ancient times the Moon has more generally been considered as 'male' (especially the lame smith, Cain - hence, the appellation of 'man in the Moon'); its dark and light qualities are aspected in Wagner's opera as the old (unseen) king and the younger (visible) king who must become 'whole' viz, healed and renewed, to full strength in order to yield the oceans into fruition, to inspire truth and vision, to think and know 'Truth.' This wise head, whose face we see in the Moon is none other than that (significant) head carried by Grail maidens upon the platter in the Grail Romance - 'Peredur.' In Wolfram's version of the Grail, he writes of the Fisher King - "*at the* Time *of the change of the Moon, his pain is great...*"

Chrétien's Grail Castle is the womb of rebirth, perceived by many esoteric scholars both ancient and modern in myth and history as resident within the Moon's sphere, guarded by two kings – one of great age and one though old, is younger than the former. Together they control the axis of this spinning castle, recycling souls in perpetuity both from and to the Earth, all except those souls freed by Gnosis. Mankind can thus achieve his destiny. Only self-induced apathy leads to impotence to act. This is the lesson of the Fisher King, of Orpheus, of (the Gnostic) Jesus and all other Lords of Higher Consciousness within the Greater Mysteries. Transcendence engenders *'claritas'*, a realisation free of anguish and ignorance, torment and uncertainty empowered by (free) Will, the aspirant shifts through grace from neophyte to crowned and resurrected (re-born) 'king.' He becomes his own true self. Though Chrétien's unfinished tale does not reveal the attainment of this by 'Perceval' (meaning - pierce through the middle, i.e. 'understanding'), his alter ego 'Parsifal' in Wagner's opera does [*ibid.,* 428]. It is indeed noteworthy at this point to emphasise the actuation of the Grail, not as a cup, platter, head or stone, but the

Gnosis borne by its bearer, the realised soul! Essence and completion of life is in death a harmonic of unity of spirit and soul within the living body - alchemy of Truth. Parsifal's integrity and desire to truly serve proves him worthy of attainment; acting upon the purest of emotions, of spirit awoken in love, rather than acquisition, his 'celestial caritas' is assured within this highly moralistic adaptation [*ibid.,*461].

The Grail Hero is named variously as 'Perceval' (in the earlier version by Chrétien de Troyes), or 'Parzival' (by Wolfram von Eschenbach, the basis for Wagner's opera) and 'Galahad' in the later Vulgate Quest. This young hero (neophyte) is given entrance to the Grail Castle thereto encounter the Mystery whereupon he is asked the meaning of the rites unfolding before him which again closely parallels Oriental tales in the *'Panchatantra,'* suggesting a common source or inspiration [Campbell, 1991:424]. In both cases the correct answer heals the 'maimed' king and the young questor/aspirant 'becomes' the next guardian or keeper of the 'Grail'; in other words, a fully realised initiate, having become at-one within the pleroma of the Mystery. He is then able to preserve and nurture this knowledge for the next aspiring seeker with whom he is obliged to teach. It is attained only by he who understands; that is, who has achieved Gnosis - the apprehension of Truth. *'Logos is deeper than Logic'* [*ibid.*] Succession is from one master/priest to his student/neophyte.

Essentially, these 'neophytes' are to come to terms with 'being', its acceptance and continuity rather than interpreting literally the bizarre puzzle of the events within life as ordered by higher powers. They have to see, feel and know by direct and active engagement, not passive meditation, but its resolution. Yet to inherit Gnosis without the disillusion of the paradoxes of life and its incumbent 'wound,' each questor must first understand the joys of existence; to lose these is to forfeit power of Will, manifest within his incapacity to act, to fulfil his sacred filial duties.

Returning our attention now to the Fisher King whose 'wound' has deprived his kingdom of abundance, we learn that his enigmatic 'wound' too is a debatable issue. Is he lame or impotent? Chrétien makes clear the devastation of the land is due to severance of the King's 'magical' attachment to it. Wolfram, however, later explains this as a 'psychological' binding betwixt the King and his kingdom, which Campbell [1991:392-4] posits as expressive of Christian theology regarding separation of an earthly paradise, distinct from that heavenly abode of a transcendent God that enjoins immanence within individual questors. Leading to alienation of the soul, it is cast adrift into the wasteland, desolate in a mute and sterile landscape of body and mind. The Fisher King's and Parzival's inability (on his first attempt) to attain to their True Will, renders the world void of purpose and fecundity. Fruitfulness is reciprocated only upon realisation and recognition of the glory and purpose of spirit on all planes in all spheres of being. Fulfilment equals enrichment and abundance - true prosperity of mind, body and soul. It is the jewel and stone of sacred Alchemy, encompassing wisdoms drawn from all sages - the *'Tabula Smaragdina.'* This potency of transmutation is the elixir of Will, enriched and reified by the Gnosis of union. Immortal kingship is won in the 'Castle of Life' [*ibid.,* 567].

Chrétien's Perceval, the holy fool, initially fails, losing the Grail to innocence; he does not recognise connections between the wasteland and his host, the Fisher King's illness. Left unfinished, we are uncertain how Chrétien intended to conclude this legend. In Wolfram's Parzival the Grail platter becomes a stone and the wasteland element is diminished along with its connection to the Fisher King. The Nature of the Grail is simply to heal the king, in which quest, Parzival is eventually successful. In later Grail traditions, Perceval, experienced through life's many trials, finally 'sees' it, but only as it is grasped by Galahad in a completely Christianised version where the Grail is presented as a Eucharistic cup. Religion has replaced philosophy, and hereon in, is attainable only by the perfect, chaste and pure. This implicit celibacy represents the epitome of separation and disassociation with all Divine feminine Mysteries and union of the sacred Godhead through and by his female counterpart, his life and death soul-mate [Jones, 1988]. Perceval is therefore able to heal his host, succeeding him as guardian of the Grail Castle; though empty of it, there-to await its return [Matthews, 1989:163]. Tragically, it disappeared with Galahad's attainment of it, being the only 'perfect' soul, no longer to be saved and offered any other seeker, in continuous succession as before. Its knowledge and lineage is now hidden from us, but not lost to us.

In yet another analogy, Matthews [1996:72] asserts how the 'Celtic' tale of Brons, 'Grandfather' to Perceval and companion to Joseph, could be a probable precursor to the Grail Legends and its relationship with a Fisher King. The premise of Brons' succession is the ability to 'feed' a large group of people from a single fish served upon a 'grail' platter. Brons is also a priest king who serves Mass at a sacred feast within the grail Castle, itself an 'Otherworld' destination. The dish known within the *'Estoire del Saint Graal'* [Campbell, 1991:408] is conferred by Joseph to his successor (as keeper of the Grail) who will henceforth be known by the enigmatic and slightly distinct title: the *'Rich Fisher'*... (*riche pescheur*).

These themes are explored in Jessie Weston's *'From Ritual to Romance'* [1997:110] where she expresses her belief that Robert de Boron was the only writer to make explicit a link between the title of Fisher King and the position of Grail keeper. Furthermore, she dismisses all claims relating to mundane implications of 'fisher', insisting upon its unmitigated allusion to mysticism. The sacred meal of Brons fed only the worthy and in this she seeks a parallel not with the Christian Eucharist but with the purity achieved by baptism of certain (Johannite) Gnostics. Enigmatically, the 'Fisher' of de Boron's tale, though 'healed', 'dies' three days later, linking it firmly with the aforementioned sacramental Orphic bowl of their sacred Mysteries. She proceeds to reveal the fish as an archaic and Divine symbol of all mystics relative to an extensive list of deities from Ea (Enki) to Jesus [1997:120-1].

Certainly the fish is a symbol appropriated by Christianity, and it is known that Christ's apostles were also known as 'fisher's of men' - the papal ring of fishermen, a metaphor of sacred priesthoods since Time immemorial. It symbolises the light of salvation and enlightenment and could logically represent in the distant past a tribal/priestly totem. This view especially supports Weston's perception of these particular (serpent) priests as 'deities who lead men back from the shadows of death to life' [*ibid.*]. Indeed it was also considered to be the holy food of the Gnostics. Pressing further this assertion, she mentions the Jewish custom of eating fish as a sacred and communal meal, eating it in curious anticipation of the 'slaying' and 'consumption' of the mighty Leviathan at the end of Time and partaking of its 'Bliss.'

This is certainly closer to the mark than her proposal of additional links to fertility/vegetation, death and resurrection cults and mythos of the Middle East especially when we consider mythical aspects of maiming throughout the ancient world. Several major and numerous minor deities were known to be lame from Hephaestus to the Devil himself. Many though not all, were smith Gods of metal working and agriculture. Both Aeneas and Jacob fathered great nations: the Romans and Jewish peoples respectively. In all cases, 'lameness' increased their virility, strength and generative power. Though it is equally understood to be a punishment or curse for some lack, or act of perceived 'sin' (hubris). Strangely, deformity disqualified admission into the Jewish priesthood Yet again, if understood metaphorically; these physical abnormalities could be interpreted as indicative of the 'fall', of mortal failings and limitations. Marked by physical defects, these deities are a constant reminder that man no longer dwells in paradise, that perfection does not exist in mortal form. However, their excessive lust and vitality was even commemorated within the limping partridge and Crane fertility dances of the ancient Mediterranean world well into the beginning of the early centuries of the 1st millennium. Surviving as Pagan and folk dances, they are possibly the inspired precursors to specific Morris and circle dances.[1]

Given the extreme absence of these generative and vigorous qualities within the Fisher King, it suggests with greater certainty that the dolorous blow rendered his condition to one of impotence, as mentioned in the opening of this discursive study. What is axiomatic to the acquisition of the Grail in the earlier blending of Oriental and occidental traditions is his role in this purpose. He is without doubt its keeper, and any approach must first be broached through him, the *'Roi Pescheur'*, quite literally Priest King, in the archaic and Gnostic traditions of a true seeker. Moreover, he can be found only within otherworld bastions of initiation, in luminous temples of the starry heavens, above, beyond and within metaphysical planes of being. No other theory presents such a perfect fit, so beautiful a premise or so desirable an attainment.

"In fate and the overcoming of fate, lies the true Grail"
Robert Cochrane

Bibliography:

Campbell, J. 1991 *'Creative Mythology: Masks of God'* Arkana Books. N. Y.
Jones, P. 1988 *'The Path to the Centre'* Wiccan Pub. Pagan Federation. London
Matthews, J. 1996 *'The Grail Tradition'* Element Books. GB
Matthews, J. 1989 *'The Arthurian Tradition'* Element Books. GB
Weston, J. 1997 *'From Ritual to Romance'* Dover pub.inc. US

Ref: [1] http://www.univie.ac.at/cga/art/religion.htm
Previously published in: *Pendragon* # XXXIV no.4 Summer 2007

15. The Divine Duellists

"Myth really possesses its full significance only in those epochs when man believed himself to be living in a Divine world." Jean Seznec

Understanding 'Nature' was a Medieval obsession. Portraying and expressing it was a passion unparalleled in the history of art and literature. The inherent beauty and majesty of the Divine was moulded by the cognisance of artists, visionaries, noblemen and peasants, each contributing vital qualities coloured by religion, folklore, science, but primarily from within the field of *'Hermetics'* as man explored that relationship in a less prosaic manner, through an esoteric veil of sublime Mystery.[1] An aesthetic fusion of iconic Pagan and Christian symbologies elevated spiritual metaphor, replacing harsh and often brutal expression of primeval elemental forces. Philosophical enquiry generated freedoms that bloomed in the European Renaissance throughout which the finest magical minds contemplated alchemy, Neo-Platonism and subversive variant strands of heretical Gnosticism.

No artistic motif was exempt from subtle re-workings of Christian legerdemain, and many ancient fables, once subsumed, became overwritten with the message of the 'New' Covenant and its saviour. Contra to this, the edenic world of Adam and Eve became assigned to the Old Covenant, of hoary, primal Gods, self redemption and iconic enlightenment. This heretical paradise is reserved for those who would walk with the Gods. Allegory therefore became the vehicle of mysticism 'par excellence', punned most effectively in the narrative grandeur of all visual arts and media of the 15th and 16th centuries, most especially distinguished by their unprecedented production of fine tapestries. One set, known enigmatically as the 'Hunt for the Unicorn' embodies a whole corpus of wisdom and alchemical tractates typical of the era in which they were created. Sophia is celestial bride of the Sun/son (who bears the triple-crown) and the Unicorn (vital spirit of transformation). Archaic symbology from a pre-literate age is transformed under complex cryptographica, emerging as a poignant and simultaneously profound revelation of the regeneration of Nature through its perpetual cycle of death and (apparent) re-birth of Divine kings, commonly aspected as twins, and who are frequently portrayed as various mythical beasts of legend.

Complex and beautifully illustrated Medieval collections of fables, legends, cryptozoology, and classical natural history known as 'Bestiaries' were repudiated by pious Christians as heretical accounts of Nature. One of these, the *'Physiologus'* contains many myths surrounding the Unicorn and its capture, most often by the seductive attentions of a 'comely' maid.[2] Within the Medieval obsession for the science of numbers, the mysterious number seven played an exemplary role, relating to the seven days of the week, archangels, musical notes, colour spectrum, seven ages, celestial spheres, planets etc. It is no happy accident then that the number of tapestries in this set should total seven, depicting a dramatic cosmology. As four is the number of matter and three the soul, the destiny of mankind is intrinsically bound to this sacred digit; indeed humanity is held to unfold under its influential auspices - our evolution depends upon egress through the flora and fauna that surrounds us.[3] Revealingly, we discover that within Johannite Gnosticism, there are no less than seven lesser Mysteries.[4]

Related themes within this series of seven exquisite tapestries are explored by John Williamson[5] who concludes their conveyance of the 'Hunt' theme as synonymous with the search, crucifixion and subsequent resurrection of the Christ, Jesus. Of course, this may be true - on one level. However, closer inspection inculcates a deeper resonance with other more mystical philosophies of this complex period, where everything is rarely as simple as it first appears. Grail legends especially, re-interpreted earlier esoteric philosophies that had in fact sought 'Truth' via the demystification of potencies of Nature, not as deities, but as moral qualities or virtues and which subsequently became embodied within anthropomorphic form.

The Medieval ballad of *'Sir Gawain and the Green Knight'*, for example, expresses for many, in esoteric terms, the combatant opposing forces of Summer and Winter, signified by Holly and Oak as respective waxing and waning Solar forces. Both these trees feature significantly in the 'Hunt' series of tapestries. Pertinently, the Green Knight does not die, but regains his head and lives on, his 'Virtue' passed on via his Holly club (sceptre/baton) the herald and fruit of renewal, paralleled in the evergreen thyrsus of Dionysus. Another Medieval ballad, *'Sir Gawain's Marriage,'* [6] focuses upon a central theme of two Knights/Kings exploring through their relationship and duel each Summer, their right to the hand of their Lady (Welsh Goddess 'Creiddylad'). Seated upon a mound, flanked by two sentinel trees - of Oak and Holly, this tale becomes a prime example of the Divine feminine as liminal gate in her pivotal role between waxing and waning or ascending/descending male deific forms. The trees may reasonably be perceived as coterminous with the twin pillars of wisdom, Joachim and Boaz. Mandaean and other heretical Medieval beliefs posit too the alleged reverence of John the Baptist by the Knights Templar and Hospitalliers, in adversarial role, superseding that even of Jesus. The Magdalene, the severed oracular head and the Fisher King as Gnostic priest of enlightenment also feature in this version of events which ultimately establish John and Jesus as dual but equal principles of light and dark.[7] Alchemists also revere the Baptist, and this influence fuses with those relevant elements of Gnosticism,[8] finding mystical expression throughout various Grail legends and poetry of the *'Minnesingers.'* The Johannite tradition was particularly prevalent in southern France, generating themes of sacrifice and sexuality, commonly articulated through alchemical euphemisms.[9] Wisdom is always the prize - the Grail.

It is noteworthy that myth maintains four levels of meaning: literal, moral, allegorical and metaphysical, all subtly interwoven for effect and emphasis. Jesus is known esoterically as a 'Solar' king, therefore if we ignore the distraction that common myth has for convenience, placed his birth at the Winter Solstice, overlaying Pagan and Oriental cultic death and resurrection myths of *Mithras, Attis, Dionysus* and *Adonis* (who has his own not unrelated hunt legend) and through whose death and resurrection in the Spring, we may discern the simple but fundamental premise of opposing tides that wax and wane with the Sun's virtue. Intriguingly, this is also exactly the same position John the Baptist holds in esoteric myth. Common folk practise places his feast day in diametric opposition to that of Jesus - six months each, no more, no less. Plausibly, then, we may conclude there is more here than is immediately evident. As representatives of the waxing and waning Solar powers, we are invited to explore further the purpose and relevance of their deaths by 'beheading' and 'crucifixion' (respectively). Paternal sacrifice perpetuates the alchemical treatise of subsumation.

The Prophet John, conveyor of the 'Word', metaphorically 'loses his head' (the transient ability to prophecie) at the Winter Solstice, and is the significantly older, waning Oak King/Wild Woodwose/Green Knight, to Jesus, who as the waxing, Holly King and more youthful Gawain (as the 'Hawk of May'), takes the mantle until he metaphorically 'concedes' it in turn at the Summer Solstice, irrespective of standard exoteric dogma that shifts these events in order to fulfil a different agenda. [10]

Variant and often contradictory versions of pertinent myths are an inherent phenomenon well known to all mythographers and students of folklore, all serving to enrich resources available to us; obfuscation and confusion are inevitable pre-requisites. Importantly, this reminds us of the need to be open, to seek beyond the immediate and to avoid pitfalls of a blinkered or restricted view. Importantly, the message is of life triumphant, and of the indestructibility of the dual forces of Nature in opposition but which remain in harmony - those of renewal of life from its decay! This cyclical premise is represented in classical myth as the (waning) black Sun of Dionysus (or Osiris-the 'Green One'), birthed anew as the radiant (waxing) Apollo (or Horus) - Tanist twins of the axial 'Mother' or '*Lady Alchymia.*'

Myths surrounding tree-lore unanimously place Oak as significator of age and of wisdom, especially where acquired through oracular prophecy. Verdant and foliate wreathes, worn over or framing the face/head, visually express this theme. In contra-distinction to this, the Holly represents youth, vigour and light. Sacred groves at Nemi and Dodona, once symbolic of the Divine feminine, began to articulate a primary adulation of the Oak as Father of all pantheons, most commonly represented by Zeus (*Dyus Pater*). Tertullian, a 3rd century theologian fittingly intuited the mighty Oak as the 'Tree of Life', the '*Axis Mundi*', whose withering in great age was revived by the vigour of the young Christ.[11]

Saturn too as 'Old Horn King' is an archaic God of vegetation, sterility and barrenness, symbolised by the decaying deciduous Oak tree. He is replaced by the younger and more virile verdant aspect of himself - Holly as 'Young Horn King.' Seasonal Mummers enact this recurrent theme of death and resurrection, which may reflect at some level, the acknowledgment of cyclical renewal, transposed from one representative to a secondary counterpart. Saturnalia was celebrated with clubs and boughs of Holly to accentuate the vigour of new life. There is even a Mediterranean Oak, the *Quercus coccifera* known as the 'kerme' Oak, as an evergreen it is very similar to the true northern Holly.

Interesting contemporary myths reveal Peredur as hero of the bleeding head carried upon a platter, Divine twins who represent the Sun at the Solstices who are slain and revived by a shared Divine spouse, and a series of trials that frequently number seven, forming the basis for many dramatic plays including the theme of St George.[12]

An image begins to materialize more typical of re-generation through a father/son motif than the over simplified Frazerian one of rival suitors, fighting for 'love' of the fair maiden/Goddess where each in turn must literally die as a true 'sacrifice.' Esoterically, the regenerative motif correlates with the alchemical concept of decay and renewal expressed through various stages and for which the conjunction of male and female signifies the highest Mystery. In the 'Royal Art' (alchemy) there exists a tradition of angelic founders of civilization, and of secrets passed from mentor to pupil reflecting this eternal cycle of transfiguration. All opposites are said to co-operate within the 'Great Work'; through this the fall of 'man' into corruption is transmuted, elevating him once again to his former status among the Gods and their heavenly planes. Allegories relate death Mysteries through metaphor, veiling secrets of an eternal unity, of life from the body of the ultimate Creatrix.

Knowing this, we may return now to speculate latent Mysteries within the series of tapestries depicting the 'Hunt for the Unicorn.' The first of the 'set' initiates the seemingly innocuous 'Hunt', searching for that elusive spirit, of wisdom. It depicts several Huntsmen, one of whom is accompanied by four 'Gabriel' hounds symbolising: Truth; Justice; Peace and Mercy - the combined qualities of enlightenment, as discerned through hermetic Gnosis. Central to all seven pieces, we are further presented with the key figure of the Unicorn. Many symbols may initially appear to contradict basic meanings according to their chameleon-like ability which is often dependant upon those accompanying or acting upon them; the Unicorn is no exception. Its morphology depends on purpose: male or female, Lunar or Solar; the single 'horn' confers the fabled 'philosopher's stone' or Panacea.

Equally, the Unicorn embodies the 'Word', through which its manifestation is commonly, though not exclusively, linked to Christ, a view impressed by Williamson in his examination of these images. One of the earliest literary references to the Unicorn can be found in the Old Testament where it is cited as a reem, the *'Ur Reem'* (Sun's Light) indicating the implacable might and sovereignty of Yahweh, the Father-God. [13] Later Christian theologians concluded how Christ inherited this singular power, common to them only, establishing their inseparability - as one! Significantly, original descriptions of the Unicorn reveal its appearance more likened to that of a goat, complete with cloven hooves and a beard, which has linked it to Azazel, Baphomet and the liminal phallic/horned Goat of the Winter Solstice - Capricornus. It did not acquire the more equine and therefore implicitly noble qualities until much later as a development of Romantic Heraldry.

Central to the six main narratives is the primal Tree of Life and

Knowledge. A fantastic fountain waters the four quarters of the garden and the whole Earth by default. A pre-Christian symbol, the Unicorn possesses extraordinary amorphous qualities that link it to the evolution and elevation of the spirit. As the bestial lover of Mary, he is taken and subsequently killed.[14] Yet this spiritual quality does not ascend, in fact it remains earthbound, in his re-emergence within the 'edenic' garden of abundance. This anchoring in the material world suggests the Saturnian qualities of both the Father and those of the son/Sun as Lord of this World. Cogently, the Tree (*arbor vitae & philosophica*) within this finely woven image is fantastical, of unknown genus, yet it clearly bears abundant golden pomegranates, prosaic Underworld symbol of death and renewal (immortality), which are more mystically associated with wisdom, through the rosy dew of its fruit, suggestive of the sexual 'flush' of the (holy) bride, the tree and fruit of life. Roses give honey to the bees, yet another euphemism for sexual bliss, and the 'golden' stage of alchemy.

Water, symbolic perhaps of baptism and purification is present in the form of the fountain alluding to (dual Solar and) Lunar qualities of the Unicorn, and is of course a potency associated with John the Baptist rather than Jesus.[15] The Moon's descent into water could be expressed allegorically in Middle Eastern depictions of the Baptist at the pivotal moment of power shift from waxing to waning Sun. Allegorised in a gesture of supposed humility by Jesus who embodies material aspects of the numinous all 'Father' as he kneels before the Baptist acting as the vehicle of blessing from Father to son. Dominion over water, though not a province of the purely 'Solar' Jesus, was an inclusive attribute of many of his Mesopotamian antecedent 'saviour Gods.' Blood was also an essential ingredient in the archaic baptismal lustrations within many Pagan religious beliefs and practices. And though Jesus' death was allegedly induced by the horrors of crucifixion, it was a vital component in the continuance of archaic myth that he 'shed' his blood, by both lance and crown of thorns. [16] Our modern folkloric celebrations that herald the Feast of the Baptist in June echoes the astrological shift from the airy sign of Gemini (the twins!) to the more materially manifest, albeit, watery (and Lunar) sign of Cancer. It is noteworthy that many of these celebrations involve violent contact and water sports; a purging and purification by this elemental force as coincidence, or some deep resonance of the psyche?

Trees as the *'prima materia'* represent life and Time and the gift of 'Mother' (Earth) providing arboreal clues in the fifth tapestry that suggest the Maiden's significant role: 'Mary' clothed in red as the Goddess of Love and Death - the heavenly Queen of sophianic wisdom. She sits by the apple tree under which the Unicorn is captured, evocative of the Apple groves and nuptial floor of sacred coupling within the *'Hieros Gamos,'* particularly of Eastern myth. Apples also signify immortality, and of all the stages of life, love and death through the Divine feminine that achieve it.

In the next of the set, the Unicorn, now within the sacred (round) enclosure, is placed between two trees, one of Holly, the other of Oak, in liminal suspension as power shifts from one to the other, from Father to Son, from Old King to Young King, in perpetual succession.[17] The accompanying Lion is an agent of Fate and the Stag signifies duality and the point of death. Only through 'death' can renewal be actuated.[18] Nature triumphs: victory is achieved not over, but by living through the vanquished 'foe.' The 'hunter' thrusts his spear deep into the chest of the Unicorn; directly behind him, the iconic Oak alerts us to his true guise, for *"hunter and hunted are but one"!* The abundance of flora and fauna clearly indicate Summer as the season of demise for the Holly King. However, events are somewhat compressed between Spring and Autumn, in order to maintain the impression of continuity rather than absolute decay and renewal.

Jesus, in common with numerous Pagan antecedents, is frequently depicted bound to a (still living) Tau cross,[19] a symbol of (new) life from death, rather than a 'literal' sacrifice. Into this seventh and final piece cloth is subtly woven the unmistakable symbolic tethering or earthing of the Divine, fixed to a 'heavenly' Earth - a true paradise for the transformed and transfigured being, the enlightened aspect acquired through Gnosis, the 'seven' stages of alchemical renewal.[20] Heaven was always envisioned within man's grasp. Bigotry and pious dogma alone removed it to the outer realms. It is Time to reach out and take it back.

Notes and References:

1. *Generic term for human species to avoid clumsy PC use of his/her.*
2. Shepherd, Odell. 1996 *'The Lore of the Unicorn'* Senate pp 48-50
   The Syriac version, erotically dramatizes the Maid as a naked temptress, who suckles the Unicorn in the way of archaic Pagan Goddesses; coupling is suggested before its subsequent capture, death and apparent 'resurrection'. Sexual imagery is of course prevalent within alchemy where the 'Tantric' union of opposites inculcates the highest freedom. Trees feature too as regenerative symbols, often as an extension or substitute for the male phallus.
3. Williamson, John. 1986 *'The Oak King, the Holly King and the Unicorn.'*

Harper Row Pub. (discussed throughout)

4. *Nevertheless, Mary, John and Jesus are all three intrinsic to the role of 'torchbearer' from a long line of hereditary priests, in the continuance of archaic traditions common to the remote Egyptian/Osirian Mystery schools, and to some branches of the modern day Traditional Craft. Again these systems each had separate male and female Mysteries.*

5. Williamson, John. 1986 *'The Oak King, the Holly King and the Unicorn.'* Harper Row Pub. NY pp?

6. [*ibid.*] p63

7. Picknett, L. and Prince, C. 1998 *'The Templar Revelation.'* Corgi Books London. pp103-107

8. [*ibid.*] p150

9. Roob, Alexander. 1997 *'Alchemy & Mysticism'* Taschen Italy p206
   The Rose is the highest symbol of erotic and transformative love, indicative of the Magdalene in the maiden's red gown and in the garden's thorny hedge that constrains (embraces) the unicorn within it. The garden also symbolises subdued consciousness (of the realised soul) amidst the forest of the unconscious.

10. *In order to convey the transience of these themes across Time and geographical space, the Solar and/or Lunar crossover between waxing and waning potencies may now be equally well represented by the seasonal exchange occurring at Spring and Autumn, or as celebrated at May's Eve and All Hallows.*
    Climate and location indicate the relevance; choice the significance. Curiously, the three day period of incubation before 'resurrection' is synonymous with the effectual three day standstill of the Sun around the Equinoxes.

11. Williamson, John. 1986 *'The Oak King, the Holly King and the Unicorn.'* Harper Row Pub. NY p209

12. Baring-Gould, Sabine. 2005 *'Curious Myths of the Middle Ages'* Dover Pub. USA pp346-9

13. Bayley, Harold. 2006 *'The Lost Language of Symbolism'* Dover Pub. USA p100

14. Williamson, John. 1986 *'The Oak King, the Holly King and the Unicorn.'* Harper Row Pub. NY p226
    Esoteric tradition maintains the true virtue of 'Mary' as an embodiment of both the virgin and the Magdalene; for as 'daughter' she becomes jointly synonymous with 'the celestial bride' and 'mother'. Moreover, much of the

flora and fauna throughout the series of tapestries supports the erotic associations of this relationship.

15. Picknett, L and Prince, C. 1998 *'The Templar Revelation.'* Corgi Books London pp288-292.

    The 'Good Shepherd' does in fact oscillate through the Divine feminine. Their union generates the succession of spirit from father to son and the consequent continuity of all life.

16. *It is important here to note only the relevance of the myth; it is neither a Christian pre-requisite nor an article of faith.*

17. *The 'Son' embodies both Lunar and Solar virtues exemplified by the Unicorn. This contrasts with the bold leonine emblem of Christ as a purely Solar attribute denoting lineage within the House of Judah. The prefix 'uni' actually signifies an inclusive state, composed of a secondary element by which it is characterised, the all within the one, a singular collective.*

18. Cooper. J.C. 1998 *'Encyc. Traditional Symbols.'* Thames & Hudson. London.

    In alchemy, the 'Old King' subsumes the 'Young King' in an act of transmutative regeneration.

19. Prince, C. and Picknett, L. 1998 *'The Templar Revelation.'* Corgi Books London p379.

    'Solar' baptismal rites of Osiris and his re generation through Horus provide an archaic precedent for these legends. In fact Osiris is the 'Black Sun', whose symbol of power is the cross. Baptism/purification is also a central component in the alchemical sequence.

20. *The five 'active' stages are approximately: nigredo = 'death's head; albedo = a 'king' drowning; citrinitas = the fertile fields; rubedo = the 'wedding of the 'king and queen' and/or the rose garden. These elements are suggested by the symbology of the five main tapestries, especially in the overtly sexual symbolism of the circle and the horn evident in the final tapestry, indicating conjunction of male and female elements. Sophia as the 'Shekinah' is the celestial Bride of God and supreme agent of transmutation. She is the central 'key' to the king-making transference/absorption process.*

16. Why Cranes? An Exploration into their Mythic Significance in Legend and Lore

For aeons, wings and feathers have symbolised flight, both literally and metaphysically; Jung believed this conferred supernatural aid by default. [1] Naturally, all birds signify aerial mastery and therefore all things connected with Mind. Their flight patterns were studied closely for augury and oracular forecasting. In this latter sense, the faculty of spirit communication was unprecedented.

Effectually, birds represented Divine manifestation as psychopomps of Gods and of 'Fate.' Conversely, as a symbol of the soul, they also embody the principle of absolute transcendence. Larger species of birds are often equated with the Sky, Sun or Moon, becoming totemic representatives - spirit messengers between inherent deities of the heavens and mankind below. Yet abundant legends belie a deeper virtue more intrinsic than this superficial and obvious appellation as messengers between those realms of Gods and men. Folklore and myth abound with tales of collaborations suggesting a natural intelligence of considerable import beyond those of dynamism and freedom of movement, beyond even the invisible principles of flight. Among larger birds, the Chinese merit the Crane (not aggressive like the Goose) with longevity, diligence, fidelity, harmony and prosperity.

Yet according to Nennius,[2] they are also a bird of solitude, of repose, much admired by many early Scottish and Irish Saints. St Columba specifically acquired the appellation of 'Crane-cleric' due to his close association with one of these birds as his 'messenger'. Pure white Cranes are said to inhabit the 'Celtic'[3] 'Isles of the Blest' and these birds retained a reverence consistent throughout histories of these confederates of tribal peoples. It is noteworthy how the Crane's ability to walk on land, swim in water and fly into the heavens deferred upon them a triple state of blessedness. Within Medieval heraldry, the stork/Heron/Crane served as emblems of filial duty, obligation and vigilance. These protective qualities no doubt developed from early Celtic myths involving fealty and vassalage.

Sacred to Apollo, the Crane heralds the light and warmth of Spring as does the Stork, another 'Solar' bird (so named because it lays its catch of fish out in a Sun wheel) whose piety, chastity and prudence earned its favour among Christians. In fact and more generally, all large aquatic birds (Geese, Swans, Cranes, Herons and Storks) represent the Lunar (because they breed in the marshy) waters of creation and therefore the 'womb' of 'Nature' or 'Mother Earth' perceived in all her cultural diversity.[4] These birds attained a popularity and status among the Greeks equalled only by the 'Celts', being sacred to Poseidon, Athena, Hera and Themis, mother of Prometheus, whose particular relevance shall be divulged later.

To Egyptians in particular, the 'Bennu' bird, frequently described as a Heron in its manifest form or Phoenix in metaphysical form, signifies the renewal of life (ergo immortality), transformer of the soul and the rising Sun. Typically this also confers chthonic associations significant among other traditions; 'Pwyll,' (British) Celtic King of the Underworld, was also believed to take the form of a Crane as herald of both death and war. But why Cranes?

The 'Urnfield' culture (so named because of its funerary habits) of Bronze-Age Europe and the Mediterranean (circa 1300BCE) distinguishes the Crane specifically from other aquatic birds; its iconography being clearly sustained even through the later Iron-Age Halstatt period (circa 500BCE) and well into the Romano-Gallic period. The Tiberian Paris Monument of Notre Dame depicts a stone relief of a Bull with three Cranes perched upon its back (*Tarvo strigaranus*). To one side, a bearded figure (Esus?) cuts a branch from a willow (feminine, water tree). Anne Ross believes this is similar to a slightly later relief from (1st century) Treves that also depicts a bull and three Cranes that accompany a 'God', identified as Esus,[5] though it may also represent Mercury, especially as he is accompanied by his consort Rosmerta and a (Solar) cockerel. He is similarly portrayed as a woodcutter. These Romano-Gallic icons thus express a continuation of ideological and synthesized mythology of conquered people struggling to maintain awareness of tribal traditions of totemic significance.

In Romano-Celtic iconography another altar found in Northumberland depicts Mars and Nike with a Goose and a Crane respectively, confirming deific and totemic qualities of a more generalised Nature. Esus is of course coterminous with both Mercury and Mars, especially in the agricultural aspect of the latter, and the psychopompic role of the former. Additionally, he shares with other deities such as Odin and Mercury the gift of protection for all travellers, a watchful quality reinforced artistically by the representation of Cranes upon helmets of warriors. We must remember that Cranes are not aggressive, and will not sensibly be linked to martial aspects of a deity; this precept is erroneous. Intriguingly, the Crane is known to consume large amounts of iron (for life, blood and fertility), strengthening by way of magical correspondence at least, its relativity to Mars.

On a mundane level these reliefs could simply suggest the symbiosis of bird (parasite destroyer) and host - bull. Or they might represent an allegory of the release of life-spirit or renewal of Life in the Mystery of Death. In fact, these obscure monuments have never been convincingly interpreted. Miranda Green tentatively identifies similarities to a third icon, found in Maiden Castle of a Bronze Bull (4th century) with three 'female' figures on its back and asserts possible connections to shape-shifting - transmogrification between Cranes and supernatural women.[6] Finally, this animistic interpretation finally seems to be leading somewhere significant.

In the annals of the *'Book of Leinster'* (1150CE), the deific figure of *'Midhir'* of *'Bri Leith'* (of the *'Tuatha de Danaan'*) assigns three Cranes to guard his sidhe (mound/dwelling) against unwelcome intruders. It was believed these magical birds had the power to drain away a man's will and courage to fight; unsurprisingly, they became birds of ill omen. The Cranes of *'Midhir'* (the beautiful, son of Dagda) *reflected back* to the approaching warriors their own negative intentions, visiting a curse of death or misfortune upon them. In themselves the Cranes are not hostile, they do not attack, neither are they in any way aggressive; rather they act as a harmonising force of justice and retribution - cause and effect or Divine fate. Robert Graves [7] draws a parallel here with the protective mirror of Hera given to Perseus to reflect back the Gorgon's deathly stare willed towards him.

Scottish legends relate how St Columba, the 'Crane cleric' used his own special affinity to these birds to turn a queen and her handmaiden into Cranes for their lack of reverence to him! Insular mythology further denigrated the call of the Crane as analogous to the shrieking of a scold or fish-wife. Gaelic tradition still asserts the appellation of 'corr' (Crane, Stork, Egret or Heron) to scolds and shrews as derisory titles, reminiscent of St Columba's proscriptions against them. Patristic anti-feminine propaganda or a hint of the afore-mentioned animistic principles of shape-shifting? [8]

175

These tales compounded the sinister reputation of these watchful birds, sentinels of rivers and waterways. Naturally, all the positive virtues of these birds became absorbed by churchmen and clerics even as the negative traits became symptomatic of women in general and female society.[9]

In spite of baleful and bizarre associations awarded to the Crane it remained essentially aspected to female metamorphoses. Anne Ross[10] cogently links Crane mythology to archaic agricultural practices, involving otherworldly female deific forms that devolved over Time with increased connotations of ill-fortune and death. As a totem of almost exclusively female deities within 'Celtic' mythology, what process engendered this defamation? Her exhaustive cultic primacy from the pre-historic period into the historical period diminished radically as vernacular tradition increasingly referred to the Crane as a possession of an exclusively male deity. In this aspect she is also his otherworldly 'consort'. Manannan, Esus and Midhir all retain such totemic spouses and their powers of transformation remain subservient to them.

Though much respected, their sinister reputation induced great fear. Eventually, this lead to a superstitious abhorrence of feminine transformative powers, evident within later tales of Saints and Medieval folklore that continued to propagate tales of liberated or sexually permissive women often linked derisively with former Pagan ornithological motifs: Crow = hag; Crane = whore/scold/shrew.[11] Notably, these transformations always occurred on or near water, places of feminine energy. Rivers, wells and springs were of enduring and principal importance to the Celtic peoples who saw fertility in this element inexorably linked to the Divine Mother. In Baltic countries, clay figures of Women-Cranes (dated 5000-7000BCE) are depicted holding out their breasts, suggesting a relationship between the life-giving rain and the life-giving nourishing milk of the Goddess.[12]

Moreover, many legends correlate the fluid and mutable qualities of water, the aerial freedom of birds and the primacy of women to formulate a Shamanic synthesis, sometimes voluntary, but more usually imposed, as in the *'Tale of Manannan'* and *'The Crane Bag.'* In this legend, the Irish sea God, *'Manannan Mac Lir'* possesses a cloak that like the prismic mist associated with him signifies the veil between the worlds, a sword named *'Fragarach'* (the Answerer) that no armour could resist and a 'Crane Bag' full of Treasures (the God 'Lir' is the ruler of Time and Deep Space). Made from the skin of a 'Crane,' formerly a woman transmogrified by enchantment, this bizarre bag contains nine magical implements, reputedly the ancient totems and talismans of Ireland. These included: *'Manannan's"* house, shirt and knife, the belt and smith's hook of *Goibhniu*, the King of *Alba's* shears, the King of *Lochlan's* helmet, the belt of fish skin and the bones of *'Asal's'* pig. Eventually this legendary bag, cognate with the British Hallows of 'Annwyn' passed to several heroes including *'Lugh,' 'Cumhail'* and finally to *'Fionn,'* who all claimed it by hereditary right.[13]

One version of this tale relates how jealousy of her four step-children transformed the Lady Aoife, the second wife of Manannan Mac Lir into a Crane, a bird magically associated in Gaelic mythology with the 'Cailleach,' the dark mother or death hag. 'Aoife' strikes the children with a Druid wand, transforming them into Swans (a common motif in European folklore), a state of enchantment that endures for 900 years. However, they retain all powers of human speech and reason, revealing immediately their oracular abilities and function as messengers.[14] Like Orpheus, they too have the gift of making music so beautiful, all who hear it fall under an enchanted sleep. Aoife is herself punished for this deed, becoming the possession of Manannan in the form of his 'Crane-bag', his treasure house of magic! The four children of Lir remain as Swans until their eventual baptism by a Saint transforms them back into mortal form, whereupon they immediately wither and die.

Clearly, this version of the tale indicates their loss of powers under Christianity as Paganism gave way to its relentless proselytism. An alternative account matches the beautiful Aoife against Iuchra as rivals in love. Aoife becomes bewitched and is placed in service to Manannan. After her death, the legendary Crane-bag is made from her skin.[15] Placed within the seas, it is only revealed at high-tide. Eventually, it passes to Lugh, known for his mastery of the 'Crane-magic', then later by conquest it passes to the sons of Mil, from whom Manannan re-claims it and reveals to no man again until the Time of Conaire.

Both versions remain true to the fundamental premise of a centralised female figure with transformative powers, somehow confined in service to or in possession of a dominant male deity, who considers her powers as hereditary virtues of mankind, dispensed and revealed only to worthy (male) heroes. A similar tale exists of *'Miadhach,'* who is also transformed into a Crane for being a rival in love. She however, lives autonomously in solitude upon an Island expressing the mythic symbolic freedom of Cranes as eternal sentinels till the end of Time, in contrast to Aoife who remains a prized possession of her captor.[16]

In another unusual tale, it is uncommonly the four sons of *'Cailleach an Teampull'* (hag of the temple) who bring death as four Cranes. Only blood from the 'Conra' Bull's skull, owned by another form of this female deity, the *'Cailleach Bheara,'* when sprinkled upon them as a purifying lustration, could transform them back into warriors, whose duty it was to subdue the seven kingdoms.[17]

Giraldus Cambrensis in his *'Expunnatio Hibernica'* I:33 records an important break in superstition regarding a taboo against consumption of eating flesh from the Crane, a remnant from the 'geasa' enforced by fate (usually in the form of a female relative) upon early kings and heroes of Ireland that alludes to both human and deific metamorphosis. *'Conaire the Red'* dies when he breaks his prohibition to hunt the 'birds' from whose ancestral stock he sprang. A book of highland superstitions[18] records similar remnants of this same tradition in which death may be visited upon someone by 'invoking' a desire within them to 'eat' the flesh of a Crane. It is essential not to always associate ominous qualities to shape-shifting, for there are other legends that recall more altruistic qualities of these Crane-women, who (like selkies) were not always perceived as malevolent.

The Irish war hero *'Fion mac Cumhail'* (Finn the fair, circa 283CE) was saved by his grandmother who is recorded in legend as a female Druid/ seer; she transformed herself into a Crane as he fell from a cliff towards certain death on the rocks below. Frequently referenced in fictional literature, these female 'God-mothers' taught the central heroes the 'arts' of hunting, war-craft and incantation in addition to acting as their protective guardian. Fion's lineage through his father, Cumhail the true owner of the Crane-bag (lost to the 'Mil') is recorded in the 'Book of Leinster' whose ancestry is traced back to the legendary *'Tuatha de Danaans.*'[19] Fion slays Liath, avenging his father's death and re-claims the Crane-bag. This confers upon him oracular and divinatory powers; the former warrior then becomes a poet, much acclaimed for his wisdom.

In a parallel tale in British mythology,[20] Gwion acquires wisdom from the salmon pools of Cerridwen, transforming him into the shining browed (enlightened) 'Taliesin', legendary poet and orator whose father the Wood-Wise-One presents an interesting epithet - 'The Tall Crane'. The magical regalia of a poet comprised of a cloak made from skins of aquatic birds and songbirds into which their plumage and long feathers were stitched in. This 'Shamanic' and totemic mantle was known as a *'tuigen.*'[21] Within numerous magical cults, the skins or hides of ancestral, totemic animals were and are often worn by its priesthood to represent, power and authority, but most importantly to facilitate an anthropomorphic spirit connection in the 'Shamanic' sense as we now understand it.

Crane-magic was known to take two forms: *'corrguinech'* - the poet's spell, which by its prefix of Corr immediately reveals appropriation of magical virtues of female seership and sorcery; *'glam dicind'* was a legal oration designed to enforce the Law. Examples in Irish lore of Druids practising these forms in a martial context merits further investigation. Translated bluntly as 'Crane-killing', *'corrguinech'* involved a very specific modus operandi wherein incantations would be performed during a complex sequence of dance steps designed to imitate the Crane's poised stance, standing, then hopping upon one leg with one eye open only, watchful, one hand curled backwards and one outstretched directing the force of the enchantment.

Trance-states would be induced by this highly ritualised drama, the dance and chant of the *'Corr'*, afford the orator access to otherworldly realms from where he/she could draw elemental forces required to effect the spell. Dependant entirely upon movement, rhythm, meter, and vocal skills of the orator, these activate the collective virtue of the *'Crane-bag'*, the knowledge of the *'word'*, the force of the elements and the Egregore of the ancestors, acquired metaphysically through trance and physically via telesmic correspondence of a *'charm-bag'*, both granted by rite of succession and possession. This conforms utterly to hermetic principles of micro-macrocosmic accord. Lunar powers are insinuated by revelation of the Crane-bag only at high-tide. In this way, the aggressive death wish of the enemy was visited back upon them, returned in force, *reflected back*; evidenced succinctly within the tale of the Cranes of Midhir that protected his sidhe and his kingdom from invasion and attack; *reflected back*, just like the stare of Medusa in the mirror of Hera back towards herself!

It is suggested how the meter used could be similar to the formulae given for the 'Celtic' Oath, abjuration of this sacred bond would inculcate universal forces of justice and retribution to fully subsume the foresworn. Those elements invoked by oath would turn against them, overwhelming them in a tide of their own self-destruction – this was *'glam dicind.*[122] It is quite intriguing here to draw attention to the closely paralleling oath-binding faculty of Prometheus, invested by Themis, of Law, Retribution and Fate - Karma in the truest sense of the word.

Of additional value is the quaint mating ritual of the *'Crane-dance'* replicated in the spiral maze dances of Troy, of Solar origin, yet symbolic of the Moon within the labyrinth of Delos (having connection to the bull cult). Timed around the Spring Equinox when migrating Cranes return, they introduce Mysteries of life and death, celebrating fertility and good fortune or fate. These rhythmic dances share fundamental choreography with traditional Irish and Scottish folk dancing sharing further links with dances of the *'threshing-floor'* from the classical world.[23]

As an interesting aside, there is a long held tradition among occultists, Witches, Pagans and Magi for carrying a small bag, commonly referred to as a *'gris gris'* - a totemic talisman whose obscure origins from central Africa as charm or fetish bags were known to contain the image of specific deities or impedimenta associated with them and are identical in principle to those of both Manannan and Perseus. Curiously, the species of common Crane is known as *'Grus grus.*[24] Coincidence? Conjecture? Possibly and certainly difficult to prove; or is it an example of accrued folkloric memory? Never-the-less, we must now continue with another legend of the skin-bag, this Time of one that belonged to Cerridwen. Hers was the coracle in which priestly initiates including Taliesin were cast out to sea, there to discover 'wisdom', the virtue and gift of the sea, borne in the womb-like cocoon of the coracle. Importantly, both Taliesin and Fion attain their wisdom and knowledge from female river/water Goddesses as consorts of the Sea Gods.

Across continents Cranes were also sacred to Cretans and Etruscans; though not necessarily more so than any other aquatic bird. The Ibis, a Crane-like bird in Egypt was said to be the totem of Thoth further correlating water with wisdom. Robert Graves[25] also postulates a complex analysis of the origins for the myth of Perseus and his engagement with Medusa, a frighteningly zoomorphic form encompassing all the powers of the Divine feminine. Herein, the hero is really a proto-type Hermes seeking knowledge of writing from the three graces (or fates) in the form of three Cranes. As Palamedes he gains the treasured gifts of prophetic vision and flight.

Pertinently, he is given a 'bag' in which to carry them - this could in fact be the actual 'head' of Medusa? According to ancient tradition the skull was the seat of oracular knowledge and power. Thus by his possession of her, he acquires these virtues. In the visionary realm of legend, the black-headed Crane with its all white body and dark serpentine head and neck, marked with a dash of scarlet could easily be associated mythopoetically with the 'Gorgon headed' Medusa.

Furthermore, a Gorgon is simply defined as a being that is 'loud-roaring' and 'terrible' and in myth, collectively as a 'nest of serpents'. Gorgons were in fact the three daughters of the 'Old Man of the Sea' (*Phorcys*) and his spouse, (*Ceto*) a sea 'monster.' Medusa is one of a triad of female deities who originated in Libya as personifications of wisdom (long before being adopted into the Greek pantheon); moreover, they were considered muses of poetry and dance. One Greek legend claims enmity between Medusa and Athena (well known for her capricious pique), whose jealousy of her beauty caused Athena to transform Medusa into a terrifying zoomorphic form, complete with bird's claws, beak, feathers/wings and 'serpentine' hair. Her shrill cries invoked great fear and petrifying dread to all who heard it. Athena (Roman Minerva), was of course herself closely linked to a former bird deity from Thrace and endorsed all the qualities similar to those of the female Druids, the God-mothers of heroes, namely those of the arts of war, poetry (incantation) and protection.

Athena, a young Goddess, often accompanied by Nike (deific force representing victory) clearly sought for herself the archaic wisdom of these daughters of the sea and plotted their destruction. She armed Perseus (the hero) with a mirrored shield to *reflect back* the deadly 'stare' of Medusa, instructing him carefully how to defeat the triad's chthonic powers of 'death'. Perseus succeeded and dutifully presented Athena with the talismanic 'bag' containing the 'head' of Medusa, enabling her to appropriate its powers and wisdom for herself. Athena finally placed the 'head' of Medusa upon her shield as a protective totem.[26]

Upon the 'death' of Medusa, Pegasus, the traditional symbol of poetic inspiration, sprang from her body and drops of her blood (life-force) were believed to effect either death or healing! Curiously, Gaelic coins depict horses together with Cranes.[27] Medusa, a cursed beauty and archaic deific form, shares with Prometheus the virtues of freedom, wisdom, the earthly paradise and the gift of inspired and creative enterprise.[28]

Robert Graves, believing the Aegean to be the source of many Irish legends, particularly those involving invasions by the Milesians from Iberian colonies held by Phoenicians, also notes the Crane's popularity relative to several myths of (male) Solar heroes and deities, 'sons' or 'favourites' of Goddesses given as 'Artemis,' 'Athena,' 'Carmenta,' 'Danae,' 'Maia,' and 'Medusa.' According to the *Poetic Astronomy of Hyginus*[29] Apollo was transformed into a Crane (protected by Themis?) in order to flee from Typhon. More notable fables attribute the mythological invention of the many letters of the alphabet to Mercury after watching flying Cranes create chevrons overhead. Of course, we know that it was most probably the Phoenicians who formulated a systematic construction of letters for writing and recording. However, Hyginus claims Mercury gave this knowledge firstly to the Egyptians, from whom Cadmus the Phoenician brought it back to Greece.

Graves therefore deduces intuitively, the true 'treasures of the sea' to be the secret of writing, the alphabet of the Phoenicians, the peoples of the sea - the *'Peleset'*, known in Irish legend as the secret treasure of 'Manannan Mac Lir,' God of the Sea. This may be the speculative origins of the *Ogham* alphabet of later Druids who as a primarily Solar order perceived Cranes as creatures of wisdom and guardians of the secret wealth ascribed to chthonic realms (often associated with the watery depths). Fundamental to countless myths and legends, this is a common motif of the ancient and classical worlds. Fascinatingly, the 'Irish' consider themselves, whether proven or not, as descendents of the Scythians, Spanish (Iberians), Egyptians in addition to Scandinavians.

In drawing together a conclusion, it is especially appropriate to affirm the superlative value of Themis, archaic precursor of Hera and Titanic Goddess of oracular Wisdom, the Earth, the Fates and controller of Justice, Will and Law of all the Gods. These virtues conceptualised the figure of 'Maat' in Egypt, the mother/consort of Thoth/Hermes/Mercury. Cogently, in this later sense she is mother of 'Prometheus,' guardian of oaths, viz. the spoken word. Initially, she presided over the oracle of Delphi as its Divine voice of instruction and prophecy before being usurped by Apollo. It is noteworthy that several Orphic hymns invoke Themis as the 'inspiration' of Apollo.[30] Cranes are her sacred, totemic bird. As an elemental deity, she represents the Earth itself, surrounded (enfolded - held by) the sea, Oceanus; conceptually this correlates completely with the possession of Aoife by Manannan. Themis and all her female counterparts represented the power and authority of the *spoken* word, Prometheus and all his male counterparts came to represent the power and authority of the *written* word, the former subsumed and developed by that of the latter.

Tracing this unequivocal thread regressively across geographical Time and space (the qualities of the God Lir!) from the British Isles of the Romano-Gallic period to the ancient Bronze-Age world of the Mediterranean, we have discovered numerous parallels that feature the Crane similarly and distinctly throughout various indigenous myths and legends that divulge secret wisdom, knowledge, oratory and oracular powers of early deities associated with this peaceful and majestic species of aquatic bird.

Climactically, the invention of writing is traced in myth through the Divine inspiration imparted by these spirit messengers, the deified forms of tribal elders, priests and tutelary leaders revealing a steady transition from female to male; of domination and appropriation of all virtues commensurate with wisdom in all its iconic, zoomorphic and anthropomorphic forms.

Sadly, the beautiful and elegant Crane is no longer native to Britain; the last one was believed shot in 1908 but has since been re-introduced. In myth however, it remains an eternal sentinel upon the shores of the liminal spaces, protecting and guiding the leapers in-between.

Notes and references:

1. J.E. Cirlot. 1971 *'A Dictionary of Symbols'* Routledge & Kegan Paul. London pp26-29

2. Anne Ross. 1974 *'Pagan Celtic Britain'* Sphere Books Ltd. London p359

3. *Being fully aware of all things referring to 'Celtic' as anachronistic, I have nevertheless conformed to the generic titling of that term in its common use within the historic sense for ease of familiarity. Naturally this does not extend beyond its natural disintegration during the Medieval period, thus avoiding the modernistic or romantic inferences.*

4. J.C. Cooper. 1998 *'An Illustrated Ency. of Traditional Symbols'* Thames & Hudson. p161

5. Anne Ross. 1974 *'Pagan Celtic Britain'* Sphere Books Ltd. London p351

6. Miranda J. Green. 1986 *'Gods of the Celts'* Sutton Pub. GB. p191 (please note that the 'French' town - Treves exactly refers to the same 'Germanic' town - Trier, near Luxemburg and often used interchangeably by different authors).

7. Robert Graves. 1999 *'The White Goddess'* Carcanet Press. Manchester. p226

8. Miranda J. Green. 1992 *'Dictionary of Celtic Myth and Legend'* Thames and Hudson. London. p 68

9. Anne Ross. 1974 *'Pagan Celtic Britain'* Sphere Books Ltd. London p369

10. Anne Ross. 1974 *'Pagan Celtic Britain'* Sphere Books Ltd. London p361

11. Anne Ross. 1974 *'Pagan Celtic Britain'* Sphere Books Ltd. London p364-5

12. www.irelandsown.net/Crane.html

13. C & J Mathews. 1995 *'Encyclopaedia of British and Irish Legends'*

Diamond Books Ltd. London. p52-53 *Anyone wishing to explore in greater detail these legends would be well advised to read 'The Welsh Triads' circa1300s - The 'Black Book of Caermarthon,' 'The Red Book of Hengest' and the 'White Book of Rhyderrch'; 'The Book of Leinster'; 'The Leber Gabala Erenn' and 'The Mabinogion'.*

14. Anne Ross. 1974 *'Pagan Celtic Britain'* Sphere Books Ltd. London p309

15. Anne Ross. 1974 *'Pagan Celtic Britain'* Sphere Books Ltd. London p357-8

16. Anne Ross. 1974 *'Pagan Celtic Britain'* Sphere Books Ltd. London p359

17. Anne Ross. 1974 *'Pagan Celtic Britain'* Sphere Books Ltd. London p356

18. Anne Ross. 1974 *'Pagan Celtic Britain'* Sphere Books Ltd. London p355

19. T.W. Rolleston. 1994 *'Celtic Myths and Legends'* Senate Books. London. p164

20. C. Mathews. 1995 *'The Celtic Tradition'* Element Books Ltd. Dorset p66

21. C. Mathews. 1995 *'The Celtic Tradition'* Element Books Ltd. Dorset p51

22. www.clannada.org/culture_crane.php

23. www.univie.ac.at/cga/art/religion.html

24. www.khandro.net/animal_birds.html *(the taxonomy of Linnaeus in 1700s not withstanding)*

25. Robert Graves. 1999 *'The White Goddess'* Carcanet Press. Manchester. p221-5

26. www.arthistory.sbc.edu/imageswomen/papers/kottkegorgon/gorgons.html

27. Miranda J. Green. 1992 *'Dictionary of Celtic Myth and Legend'* Thames and Hudson. London. p 68

28. www.rc.um.edu/editions/shelly/medusa/mcgann.html

29. Robert Graves. 1999 *'The White Goddess'* Carcanet Press. Manchester. p216

30. www.theoi.com/titan/titanisthemis.html

Previously published in: *White Dragon* #52 May 2007

17. The Fruit of Wisdom - Genesis: The Myth of the Fall

"Approach me, all you who desire me, and take my fruits, for memories of me are sweeter than honey, inheriting me is sweeter than the honeycomb. They who eat me will hunger for more, they who drink me will thirst for more." - Sophia (Wisdom) Ecclesiasticus 24:19-22

Within the prevailing culture of the West, we are persuaded to accept the fruit consumed by Eve in woeful disobedience of Yahweh from the Tree of Knowledge somehow imparted wisdom. Some scholars now believe it is quite possible this tree is one and the same as the Tree of Life and Death, a distinction that is extremely relevant to this discourse. We are guided towards the directives in Gen.2:17: *"but of the tree of knowledge of good and evil you shall not eat, for in the day that you eat it you shall die."* Yet in Gen.3:4-5, the serpent offers us a perplexing alternative: *"you will not die. For God knows that when you eat of it your eyes will be opened, and you will be like God, knowing good and evil."* Why has inheriting this knowledge been considered a sin, and a transgression against God?

Gnostic Christians, in contra-distinction to more orthodox followers of their fledgling faith, revered and honoured the serpent as an ancient and universal symbol of wisdom, whose shining light banishes ignorance from whence it falls. However, this altruistic enlightenment was perceived by Tatian the Syrian, an early Christian teacher, as mere carnal knowledge, awakened by the fruit of the tree, commonly accepted as the apple [Pagels, 1989:XXIV]. In fact, for almost two thousand years Art and Literature have continued to persuade us of this, despite the fact that apples never grew in Eden, the climate of Iraq not being suited to their propagation. Why then do we associate the apple with the 'fruit of wisdom'? Certainly the bible provides no clue. In the early *'Massoretic'* texts, the Hebrew word in Gen.3:2 for fruit is *'pri'*, a generic term; and in Gen.2:17, the prohibition merely states not to eat from the tree. Later Greek translations rendered the 'fruit' as *'karpos'*, also generic, an ambiguous term that could mean anything. The 4th century 'Vulgate' offers *'fructus'*, again generic; all further modern translations adhere faithfully to 'fruit'. Who was responsible for the concept of the apple, and more importantly, why; what was the reason for this deceptive elaboration?

Prof. Philip Davies[1] suggested that one of the early Church Fathers was probably responsible. Further research led me to discover this assumption to be correct. The 2nd century Biblical redactor Aquila of Pontus in Asia Minor when translating the Song of Solomon into Greek, misunderstood a text referring to the apple tree [8:5], believing it to allude to the Tree of Knowledge of Good and Evil (Wisdom); from this error grew the myth of the apple as the 'fruit of wisdom' [Pagels, 1989:110]. Later, St. Jerome, when translating the Greek into Latin accepted this misconception. It must be remembered, these writers were more familiar with the myths of Greece and Rome where apples were known cultivars the length and breadth of their ever expanding Empires. Furthermore, sacred to Apollo, apples symbolised health and immortality; when cut, they reveal the 'Star of Venus', primary symbol of abundance and fecundity.

Interestingly, within the Garden of Hesperides, a serpent (child of Typhon), guards the fabled sacred apples, assisted by a triad of radiant beings, the daughters of Nyx/Nox. Wise retainer of Mysteries and secrets, this multi-lingual serpent was able to impart knowledge in rituals where these shining maidens would dispense the golden apples, treasured gifts of immortality and wisdom, timed to coincide with Venus the Evening Star as it rose to the setting of the Sun [George, 1992:129]. These fruits are in all probability, those favoured for their wisdom symbolism – the pomegranate!

Another wisdom Goddess, Athene, aids Perseus to procure apples from this sacred Garden, after which, according to the 2nd century Greek historian, traveller and geographer Pausanias, he was inspired to build Mycenae in honour of the mushroom he found growing there [Graves and Patai, 1964:81]. Graves [*ibid.*] further posits proof of a mushroom cult in ancient Greece within the festival of '*Anthesteria.*' This involved the calling and raising of the dead and tending of departed souls, summoned forth from the hidden waters of knowledge to once again share their wisdom, and which is clearly reminiscent of later spiritualistic rites of necromancy. For Allegro [1970:176] these Bacchanalian rites represent the true '*Love Agape,*' a congress celebrated after the dead God is lamented, risen and consumed, reflecting not an agricultural cult, but an older pastoral link to ancient mushroom cults of the Middle East.

Apples are of course, sacred to other traditions and cultures, particularly of Northern and Western Europe where they also grow freely. Freya dispenses the Golden apples of Idun as treasured gifts of Immortality to the elect, the few worthy to receive this bounty of the Gods in the halls of Valhalla. Avalon too is a paradise full of red-gold fruits that imbue all who consume them with immortality, health and sage wisdom [Purnell, 1970:110].

Even in the New World, a fresco depicting a Mexican paradise shows the God *'Tlaloc'* as a spirit (possessing similar qualities to Dionysus), branch in hand weeping for joy upon entering an orchard of fantastically bright fruit trees and flowers, watered by a river, full of fish, flowing from the mouth of a toad. *'Tlaloc'* rules this ethereal paradise jointly with his sister, *'Chalcioluthlicue'*. Irrigation canals form a cross denoting cardinal points. Behind *'Tlaloc'* rises a spotted serpent, an alternative aspect of both him and his sister. *'Siduri,'* also a wisdom Goddess, originally ruled the jewelled paradise visited by Gilgamesh in Sumer until she made the Sun God, Shamash its guardian. It cannot be mere chance that all early 'gardens of delight' are ruled by Goddesses and feature serpents and fruits of wisdom [Graves and Patai, 1964:80-81].

Nevertheless, other possibilities must now be investigated as plausible fruits in the candidacy for wisdom and/or immortality. Peaches impart these gifts within Chinese mythology, yet Buddhists revere the fig, fruit of the sacred Bodi Tree that sheltered Buddha during his quest for enlightenment. Fundamentally however, none of these fruits offer a viable option. After all, for a myth to have any credibility, it must possess some semblance of logic, and none of these do, at least, not in extant versions of them. Grappling with various theories, a consultation with an eminent mycologist and botanist, offered a possible solution.[2] He enigmatically suggested the careful study of a 12th century fresco in 'Plaincourault,' France. This bewildering fresco is featured in the challenging book by John Allegro - *'The Sacred Mushroom and the Cross.'* All the usual iconography was there, Adam, Eve, the serpent, but the classic apple tree had been replaced by an enormous *'Amanita muscaria'* - the hallucinogenic fly agaric fungi. Historical verification to support this theory, drawn from myth, legend and documented sources, in both written and pictorial forms may be found in abundance; like many things, we only need to look.

Finnish folklore reveals how a Shaman and smith forged the Sun, Moon, Stars and the enigmatic 'Sampo,' a magical object hidden within a mountain. Noticeable by its bright lid, it grinds out wealth and power; linguistically the word 'Sampo' suggests both mushroom and toad [Morgan,

1995:20]. Ironically, both toads and toadstools, long associated with magick and the supernatural, were passionately denounced by Christian teaching as representative of the darker chthonic aspects of Nature, and do indeed stand guilty as charged.

Treasured traditions of countless ethnic tribes and variant cults, including Witches and gypsies using hallucinogenic entheogens, especially fungi, throughout the ancient and modern world are revealed as endemic. Basque Witches are rumoured to have utilised the trance-inducing properties of *'Lycoperdon pyriforme'* (stump puffball) [Morgan, 1995:128]. Indeed the Narmer Palette of 4000BCE depicts a female carrying mushrooms; moreover, *'Amanita muscaria'* (fly agaric) is claimed to have been used in Northern Eurasia for at least 6000 years [Morgan, 1995:48]. Incredibly, according to Church Theologians, this coincides with the creation of Adam.

Myth and legend hail the apple as a potent symbol of fecundity, longevity and abundance, but as a gift of Nature its cultivation is readily understood and propagated by man. Conversely, the sudden appearance and growth of fungi was considered one of the highest Mysteries and related directly to its Divine origins. Priesthoods and tribal peoples' preserve their own truths; history records the frequent and persistent use of hallucinogenic entheogens. However, it is not apples that are painted upon the walls of ancient caves and it is not apples that are carved in stone as foci for worship, nor are they cast in metals as amulets; yet in all cases fungi are. Hittite Royal Seals and idols found at 'Alaca Huyuk' in Turkey depict paired mushroom motifs and hieroglyphs that mean 'great king' [Morgan, 1995:113]. Persian silver plates from the Sassanian period (240-400CE) reveal female consorts of the falcon God feeding him fungi resembling the *'Amanita muscaria'*.

Words stemming from the Arabian root *'ftr'* mean ubiquitously, toadstool, sacrificial bread and Divine ecstasy [Graves and Patai, 1964:81]. Shinto priests in Japan are recorded as having consumed hallucinogenic fungi to induce *'samedhi'*, a state of ultimate awareness. Moving even further afield, we discover how Hindus in India have for thousands of years worshipped the elephant headed deity, Ganesha, whose primary attribute is to connect mankind with the Divine. Again mushroom images known as *'chattras'* are associated with him, the most obvious one being his 'umbrella', a symbol of prajna (the wisdom of the world), which is alludes quite suggestively to the large gilled cap of an amanita mushroom.

In the Hindu Kush (mountains) of central Asia, fly agaric is known as 'Raven's bread', alluding again to its connection to these birds of prey and their association with the dead. Korean frescoes decorate 6th -7th century tombs depicting Taoist Immortals with their 'Jade consorts' who are shown picking mushrooms; they believed the *'Amanita muscaria'* was the Divine mushroom of Immortality and that it held the power of communion with the dead and induced clairvoyance. In a Chinese Buddhist text, *'The Tripitaka'*, there is an account of a sage taking refuge in the mountains to consume mushroom elixir prior to meditation.

Typically, a male initiation rite in New Guinea also involves the use of psychoactive plants during twelve degrees of deepening levels of esoteric revelations [Rudgley, 1999:118-120]. Shamen though, are of course, known to consume hallucinogenic fungi in their vision quests, to aid their ecstatic journeying for healing and for retrieval of knowledge. The *'Tree of Life'*, the Axis Mundi they climb is of course a metaphoric one. Yet these masters of the Old and New Worlds, including the Aegean, Mediterranean and African and even of Oceania all share a reverence for the power of its wisdom. Modern science explains euphoric states of ecstasy as the natural result of hormone secretions, namely serotonins, into the brain; these altered states preserve the greatest Mysteries of life and death.

In the Old Testament, the serpent instructs Eve to partake of the fruit of wisdom that she might be re-awakened to her true state; a state of existence within the body of the Goddess. Adam and Eve's ensuing shame lay in their deviation from subservience to the indomitable Yahweh. His restrictive taboo upon this fruit denied them access to self-awareness, the wisdom and realisation of their own divinity, and personal communication with a sentient deity greater than him, the true creator, in fact. The serpent serves her well.

Hidden within the myth of Genesis and the Garden of Eden, lies the fascinating proposal by Mckenna [1993:76] that Eve was a Mistress of plant-lore, a healer and physician, who initiated her partner into higher realms of consciousness. This Gnosis was facilitated by the ingestion of specific hallucinogenic fungi, posited by Mckenna [*ibid.*] as a species of *'Psilocybe'* rather than *'Amanita,'* although both are known to many ancient cults worldwide, particularly among hunter/gatherers and pastoralists. The settlement of Eden and adoption of farming circa 8000BCE shifted their cognitive responses from the inner world to the outer world, the Cosmos of the microcosm and the macrocosm. Eve endeavoured to remind Adam of a former state of Gnosis, of the Transcendent 'Other', named by

'Pronoia - Arbor Vitae'

Mckenna [1993:96] as the *"Gaian collectivity of organic life…,"* the ultimate female presence within the Cosmos. A Shamanic trinity of Goddess, Cattle and Mushroom is evidenced at sites throughout Anatolia, namely 'Catal Huyuk.'

Deprived access to these visionary inner worlds, and our symbiotic relationship with them, we stand outside creation, apart from its Mysteries, excluded from its secrets. Re-discovery of the Divine plan, of cosmic consciousness is the real reason Yahweh banished Adam & Eve from Eden, not for their disobedience, but because they could see the flaccid emptiness of what he had to offer [Mckenna, 1993:89-93]. Patriarchy, has ever since denied our connection to this source, to the maternal matrix; but truth will out and all feminine forms of wisdom remain stubbornly entrenched throughout 2000 years of andro-centric conditioning. All her guises as the *'Shekinah', 'Sophia,' 'Kali-Ma', 'Purusha'* and the *'Anima Mundi'* allow her to transcend philosophical dogma that attempts to imprison her. The body of the 'Mother' offers us complete immersion through her gifts of Nature as pathways to her Gnosis. Eve, the 'Mother of all Living', finds recognition as a spiritual power in a Gnostic text entitled 'Reality of the Realms'.

In a study of this text by Pagels [1989:66], she suggests that it was Eve's voice Yahweh told Adam to ignore, and so, assuming serpent form (there exists several magnificent paintings of Eve as the serpent, one of which is in the Vatican) she seduces Adam into eating the forbidden fruit. In this form she represents wisdom, she is the source and provider of primal intelligence - *'Pronoia'*, reaching out to Adam to wake from his false existence, to remember, to understand, to know once again the truth. His resistance can be seen as symptomatic of mankind's reluctance to take a leap of faith, into the unknown, into the void. Sometime in the evolution of the mind, some mysterious catalyst initiated the sense of the self as a distinct identity, whereupon it separated itself from the Consciousness of the Creator, this fall into self-consciousness, of an awareness of matter engendered the metaphoric 'Fall'.

Controversial material expounded by John Allegro [1970:XV] in his ground breaking book *'The Sacred Mushroom and the Cross'*, asserts that concepts of religion within the whole of the ancient world have been mythologized from metaphors relating to a conscious reverence of hallucinogenic fungi. This startling proposition is indeed germane to Mystery Cults of the ancient world. Each 'little God' is a perfect embodiment of the essence of male deity. Furthermore, generated from within the womb (Earth) of the Goddess, seeded by rain after storm, accelerating their sudden appearance, their tumescent caps shine in the Moonlight, redolent of spent semen. Spittle is a euphemism for 'semen in the mouth', containing as it does the breath and moisture of God (Shu and Tefnut?). On a mundane level, it was used as a cure for poisonous bites.

The Talmud mentions an eleventh secret 'herb' said to induce intoxication, the growth of which is described as a vertical column spreading outwards at the top. Allegro [1970:58] also believes that the practice of extreme unction is an imitation of the effulgent seed of life, where the body is made to 'shine' like the Gods. Oily mucous resins are smeared upon the body in imitation of the Divine, facilitating re-birth. Could this process more accurately explain the experience of Enoch, whose skin was made to glow as one of 'angels, the Shining Ones'? Embalming shares these esoteric principles and could be a vital precept to mummification and preservation of bodies in the ancient world; Herodotus too, records how Babylonians preserved their dead in honey [Mckenna, 1993:127].

The mushroom's phallic growth from a womb-like sac at the basal tip (known as a volva) clearly reflects the magical-sexual relationship with deity. The legend of 'Phanes,' the shining one, born of the Night, bursting serpent-like from the egg is too close to be ignored. Convoluted arguments prevail throughout this book where Allegro [*ibid.*] argues the origins of such cults to lie in the Middle East, specifically within Sumer. Using etymological methodology, he deduces the Sumerian base form - U (that represents a whole multiplicity of God forms throughout the Middle East as aspects of the ubiquitous storm force deity) to be the single most important phoneme within ancient religions. It emerges from this geographical location, conveying the whole symbiotic synthesis of fecundity and deity together with the powerful and rare elemental force of thunder and storm.

Rain is the heavenly semen; thunder and wind his cries of ecstatic release, forming a cacophony of fecund energy that fertilizes the Earth, wherein embryonic sacs are nurtured, waiting to spring forth into the soft light of dawn from their chthonic wombs, thereto manifest as perfect living effigies of the Gods. Mystical union is facilitated through their 'sacrifice and consumption'. Mind-expanding awareness induces wisdom, as the Nature of the God is truly comprehended. Moreover, these 'little Gods' were perceived as angelic spirit forms, messengers who could traverse the variant realms of matter and air, normally barred to man. Access to these worlds was now possible, indeed encouraged in order to harvest the wisdom of the ages, achieve Gnosis and comprehend one's place within the Universe. Those with an understanding of the use of such plants received high status, enforced by procuring magical names for each plant and fungi. Of course, a name possesses latent power to subdue and manipulate; a powerful praxis germane to variant forms of occult practices [Allegro, 1970:22].

Remarkably, many Semitic and Sumerian words for erect, penis and phallus also refer to mushrooms [Allegro, 170:39]. 'Iskur,' meaning mighty penis becomes the Semitic 'Adad,' meaning 'Big Father', ultimately evolving into the Greek Zeus-Pater (mighty Father), also a storm God. The Semitic form *'Sabaoth'* derived from SIPA-UD (stretched horn or penis) means 'Penis of the Storm', and also refers to Yahweh [Allegro, 1970:55]. Perhaps these terms in relation to a mushroom cult more realistically reflect the concepts behind the much-disputed 'phallic worship'. Links to Egyptian myths concerning the 'lost' phallus of Osiris could be further investigated relative to this tangent. Iconographical depictions of fungi in art, metallurgy, sculpture, carvings and statuary preserve the poetic vision of the seers, priests and Shamans, echoed again within sacred writings of the Rig Veda through to the songs of the Mazatecs shamen of modern-day Mexico.

Among nomadic and ethnic peoples, many classic Russian and Slavonic folk-tales have preserved a long tradition of fungi consumption, becoming typically interwoven with mushroom related magical exploits. The infamous Baba-Yaga is almost always surrounded by various examples of *'Amanita muscaria'* that she notoriously 'feeds' her victims. It is hard to resist the implicit directives within them. Other strange tales relate how couples embark upon a walk into the woods to go 'mushrooming' where strange and wonderful events occur.

These dreamlike qualities are recorded by Maria Gimbutas,[3] a Lithuanian archaeologist. Famous for her challenging work to the established understanding of the role of the Goddess within the Neolithic of Old Europe, she strongly supported the theory of ritual consumption of hallucinogenic fungi and other psychoactive plants such as ergot, to stimulate shifts in conscious awareness, comprehension and experience of deific entities. She also believed this practise was germane to all major religions, finding expression in the elements of fire and water, dualistic principles of life, symbolised within hallucinogenic fungi. Through them the self is re-united with an environment wherein no separation exists, thus is awareness and sensory perception increased and expanded.

A mushroom similar to the false chanterelle is represented on a 20,000-

year-old mammoth ivory Earth mother from 'Lespugue,' suggesting orgiastic and psychedelic Goddess worshiping societies. Similar motifs, replete with mushroom imagery, echoed throughout the ancient world, supporting a history rich in pharmacological and toxicological reverence and use. Folklore, myth and legend conspire to conceal a higher purpose. Robert Graves was so convinced about usage and consumption of fungi within the ancient Greek Mysteries, where one could 'know God', that he used a bas relief of two women (believed to be Demeter and Persephone) holding objects strongly resembling the 'psilocybe' mushroom on his book cover about the Eleusinian Mysteries. Claimed to be the ambrosia and nectar of the Gods (revealer of wisdom and food of immortality), a ritual 'porridge' named *'kykaeon'* containing a species of ergot (*Claviceps purpurea*) was consumed [Morgan, 1995:48].

Graves, in his essay, 'The Two Births of Dionysus' offers us the very intriguing possibility that Demeter's real secret was not the cultivation of the grain harvest. In fact, it is now widely accepted that grain had been cultivated for several thousand years prior to this in Turkey, the Middle East and Egypt. Rather, he asserts, her secret gift was the wild plants that grow within it, namely the *'Papaver somniferum'* (opium poppy) and *'Claviceps purpurea'* (ergot), which could be baked into cakes for ritual consumption without loss of potency. Their juices and extracts could also be added to spike the ritual beverages to further increase their mind-enhancing properties. Wasson confirmed this assumption in 1977, but its highly toxic and deadly side effects lead Mckenna to suggest an alternative ergot species - *'Claviceps paspali'*; containing more active alkaloids than purpurea, it also offers far fewer toxic peptides. Preferring barley to rye, 'paspali' would naturally become directly involved within the brewing process where its psychoactive properties become separated from the toxins, facilitating safer ingestion [Mckenna, 1993:130-6].

Divine Soma

"Soma, storm clouds imbued with life" Rig Veda

Amazingly, it is R.G. Wasson (d1986), a retired banker, whose personal conviction that *'Amanita muscaria'* was the Divine 'Soma' of the Indian scriptures, to whom we really owe a considerable debt. His research alone opened the academic world to these remarkable possibilities. Convinced the evolving language of artistic motifs was linked to references within the Vedic scriptures, Wasson began his earnest studies into the nefarious realms of hallucinogens within religions of the ancient world. The eminent poet and mythographer Robert Graves, was a close friend and correspondent of Wasson, who had also travelled to Oaxaca and consumed hallucinogenic fungi administered by the *'curandera'* Maria Sabina [Morgan, 1995:19]. Mazatec priests are called *co-ta-ci-ne*, meaning 'the one who knows'; healers are either *'curandero'* (male), or *'curandera'* (female). Together, Graves and Wasson explored hidden worlds, alternate realities and the entheogen induced realms of paradise. During the 1950s, Wasson journeyed to Siberia and Mexico to witness and partake in the ritual use of fungi. His research firmly established the role of sacred mushrooms within human culture, especially their use within the sacred Mysteries of Life, Death and Re-birth.

Maria Sabina (d.1985, aged 97), a Mazatec healer of 'Shamanic' tradition, like the ancient seers and oracles of Greece, believed the spirit of wisdom present within the fungi spoke through her - *"It is not I who speaks"* said Heraclitus, *"it is the Logos"* [Munn, 1973:3]. In a fascinating paper entitled 'Mushrooms of Language', Henry Munn [*ibid.*] relates how Mazatec shamen believe their mushrooms 'speak'. Historically, the Aztecs (Sabina's ancestors), regarded the mushrooms as the 'Flesh of God' and since their Christianisation, as the blood of Christ. Ironically, invading Spaniards re-named these fungi, *'Raiz diabolical'*, the Devils root! [Taylor, 1966:85].

In legend, holy mushrooms grew from the spilled blood of Quetzalcoatl; these are, even now, the; *"Spirit food of the luminous one, flesh of the world, flesh of language, in the beginning was the word and the word became flesh. Flesh became linguistic. - The food of intuition-the food of wisdom"* [Morgan 1995:20]. Hence, wisdom is a communicated visionary experience. The renowned anthropologist Claude Levi-Strauss observed how shamen, inspired by poetic language become oracles and healers. Moreover, he records how Maria Sabina, a 20th century Mazatec *'curandera'* called out *"My father, who art Master of this World"* for guidance on her journey. Strong is their belief in his path that offers true happiness; as the origin of 'Light', this Master of the World is beseeched not to abandon them to the blindness of ignorance.

Maria Sabina said of the fungi *"They aren't called mushrooms, they are called prayer.....they are called wisdom. They are here with the Virgin, or Mother or the Nativity - They are the Holy One"* [Munn, 1973:19]. Although modern ceremonies are now saturated with Christian imagery and terminology, the basic rituals are reminiscent of a darker past. Copal, sacred to the old Gods, burns continuously and the mushrooms, taken in pairs, retain the duality and ambiguity of their ancient deities. Consumption is revered as a *'Holy Communion'*, a true Eucharist, where the actual flesh of the God is eaten, and whose spirit guides the seekers to higher truths. Many legends tell of mushrooms as products of semen, blood or urine of deities spilled upon the Earth in sacrifice; as such, they contain their spirit essence [Morgan, 1995:95].

Anthropologist Weston la Barra, deduced that because many Indo-European religions have animal totems, shape-shifters and shamen, and that hallucinogenic fungi are native to all these people, including Northern and Western Europe, the two must be synonymous. Siberia does of course maintain a tradition of hallucinogenic fungi consumption reaching back millennia [Morgan, 1995:95]. However, as fungi are not believed to be native to the Middle East nor to the Indian sub-continent, this would explain the need for substitution where tribal migrations into less temperate climates sought similar, psychotropic plants.

A survey by Flattery and Schwartz [Mckenna, 1993:113] considers *'Peganum harmala'* (Syrian rue) a viable alternative, whose active constituent harmaline, is a beta-carboline of decreased toxicity and increased psychoactivity to that found in a similar relative within the New World plant *'Ayahuasca'* (vine of the dead and vine of the souls), in use by the late Vedic period. Modern researchers have offered Ephedra (a plant found in the remains of a Neolithic burial in a cave in Shanidar, Iraq; its healing and hallucinogenic properties are well-attested). Later, Syrian rue and cannabis are offered as possible substitutes for Soma/Haoma [*ibid.*]. Yet the obvious eludes them.

However, early scriptures describe Divine Soma as *"growing up a mountain;" "the colour of flame;" "possessing the eye of Agni; "with a dress of sheep;"* whose growth habit *"creeps like a serpent out of its old skin."* All these metaphors convincingly describe *'Amanita muscaria,'* - even the yellow juice it yields when crushed. Even more revealing is the phrase. *"In the belly of Indra the inebriating Soma clarifies itself."* It is well known that hallucinogenic properties, processed by the Shaman or seer, having passed through the digestive system and out into the urine, are almost as potent as when first consumed, but minus all toxins, which are indeed 'clarified' in the belly of its first consumer. [4] Wasson steadfastly maintained that Soma (*Amanita muscaria*), in its original form, was brought into the Indus Valley (Northern India, now Pakistan) cultures of 'Harappa' and 'Mohenjo-Daro,' either dried or preserved in honey, by successive waves of invading peoples from the Steppes region of the Black Sea. A discussion on whether these peoples were warring tribesmen or peaceful migrating nomads is a subject beyond the remit of this paper and irrelevant to Wasson's theory; suffice it to say it did eventually arrive from the Black Sea region to Northern India.

A Sanskrit based 'Hindu' culture accompanied this move in which the God Indra was acknowledged as a consumer of the deified 'Soma'. Described as a plant without leaves, it imparted *'amrita,'* which translates as 'not death', or 'immortality' [Morgan, 1995:110]. The flame deity 'Agni,' shares qualities with the Persian God 'Mitra,' who is mentioned in sacred Vedic and Avestan (Persian) texts, where *'Soma'* becomes *'Haoma,'* a holy drink, consumed only by the priesthood - the pre-Zoroastrian Magi. It was a gift of the Gods, brought to Earth by large raptorial birds from heaven where it grew near the mountaintops. Haoma too brings the wisdom of the sages and the gift of eternal life.

A provocative link is suggested between Shamanic cults of Armenia and Kurdistan where *'Amanita muscaria'* grows freely and where raptorial birds of prey, in particular the Vulture and the Raven are indigenous. The raven, a bird known to relish in the delights of this fungi and from whom it derives one of its more popular folk-names - *'ravens bread,'* is also sacred to many Northern and Western European thunder deities including *'Mitra/ Mithra', 'Indra', 'Wodhanaz', 'Zeus'* and *'Bran'*; crucially, they all exhibit oracular powers.[5]

Significantly, they are all connected to *'Amanita'* cults. The *'Holy Vajra,'* or thunderbolt of Indra, is clearly the lightening rod of inspiration suggested by this reverence of sacred fungi! Incidents of this Divine 'fruit' of Wisdom and Immortality, imparting knowledge and rapture to its adherents are richly supported by many early literary texts of the East. Convinced by such provenance, Wasson and Bedrosian [*ibid.*] resolutely concluded *'Amanita muscaria'* to be the original candidate for the bright and shining intoxicant - 'Divine Soma,' itself a deity shrouded in metaphor.

Later descriptions relate to substitutes in India and Iran when supplies ran out; though in Armenia, plentiful growth ensured its use until political and religious tension led to the horrific massacres of 1915-23. Here, priests partaking in secret sacraments believed to contain this most revered of fungi, performed ceremonies themed around eschatological matters. Soma-like ceremonies enacted twice yearly on the Christian Feasts of the Ascension and the Transfiguration allowed the villagers to consume a special pudding containing sacred herbs and plants. Strict rules determined their collection: at dawn, under the light of the Moon and of Venus, maidens drew them one by one from the Earth as they recited ancient hymns of praise; one plant in particular is described as: *"the serpent who lives in his own tail whose knowledge can be drawn out during the night under the gaze of the stars"!* [*ibid*.].

Mckenna [1993:105] believes these connections further strengthen the relationship between pastoralism, cattle and Soma, a connection more relevant later when discussing the Biblical references to *'Manna'*, said to be ground by great millstones in the 3rd heaven *'Shehaqim'* for the righteous. Morgan [1995:130] asserts that no other plant [6] has been so widely used across Time and space for magical healing purposes and for acquisition of knowledge; as an entheogen its consumption is intrinsic to worship. Within the Rig Veda, Soma is referred to as male and Lunar, in stark contrast to earlier Neolithic associations of fungi with possible female deities. Mckenna [1993:115] assumes this later cultural projection is typical of evolving patriarchal societies. In myth, this phallic emblem of Godhood seeds itself under the body of the fecund Earth: *"a child of lightening, lustrous and silvery as the Moon appears under the stars…,"* Through ingestion of this male fruit body, one attains experience of the transcendent 'other', the ineffable 'She' who is the Source of all [*ibid*]. Immediately recognisable within this myth is the sacrificial death and consumption of a male God, son of the mother (Earth) to experience ecstasy and transcendence.

Sadly, in Minoan Crete and Classical Greece, hallucinogenic induced Gnosis failed to excite the many who now sought solace in drink, in fruits of the vine, though their secrets were still preserved for those who still walked the path of the Mysteries at Eleusis. This too was finally suppressed by over zealous Christians in 268. Mckenna [*ibid*.] further laments the modern world as a consequence of this, stifled under moral anaesthesia, slowly choking on its own bile. He bemoans this deliberate act of sabotage by an effusive patriarchy deprives us of our pathways to feminine wisdom. Plants such as Datura, Belladonna, Aconite, Mandrake, Poppy and some species of Fungi, lost their place in the andro-centric societies where mead, beer, wine and ale became the pathways to oblivion - the antithesis of Gnosis.

It is of course notable that the sometimes androgynous 'Dionysus,' the Classical God of Death, Rebirth and Vegetation Mysteries, whose orgiastic rites (in the absolute sense of the word) of intoxication and Divine madness, with the demise of Greek culture, devolved into the rites of 'Bacchus,' God of Wine and Drunken Revelry. Thus were the Mysteries lost in the vats of inebriants [Mckenna, 1993:129]. A variant myth of 'Dionysus' as son of Moon Goddess Semele equates her with *'Ge'*(Thracian form of *'Gai'*). A new level of understanding, inculcated from his subservience to the Mother, rationalises his sacrificial role, where consumption of his 'body' (fruit body of hallucinogenic fungi, born of the Earth) leads to Gnosis, awareness and knowledge of the ineffable, of wisdom, and of the Ultimate Creatrix. Moreover, this again typifies the central role of a 'male' God within a Mystery Cult whose adherents are female followers of an older, wilder form of magic [Mckenna, 1993:130].

Divine adoratresses (cultic prostitutes/priestesses) performed ritual lamentations, seductively chanting to 'raise' the mushrooms from the Earth in a similar way to that practised until the last century by maidens in Armenia. Three elements ensure the gestation of a living foetus within the womb, these are: the creative spirit (God), semen (man) and fertile blood and effluvia (woman). This third and vital element missing from the seeding of sacred fungi was provided by these priestesses, rich purple hues of menstrual blood, symbol of the Sangreal - the Blood Royal is offered to the ground, a perfect alchemy. King of all serpents is the fabulous Basilisk, a truly magical beast, and Allegro [1970:65] suggests the Sumerian form of this: Sh-A-TUR has two linked meanings: 'womb-blood' (menses) and *'Saturn's Blood'*. Intriguing metaphors for those who follow the Ophidian path of the Black Sun. Evidently, both serpent and mushroom are phallic, chthonic, represent wisdom and are connected to the cult of Dionysus.

Snakes emerge from Greek baskets (*cista*) worn by dancers in the rites of Dionysus, strongly resembling wrists bands (*kesatot*) worn by Witches in necromantic rites described by Ezekiel in the Old Testament. Both *'Maenads'* and later *'Bacchae'* were totally possessed by their God, his power transposing a God-like state in which they achieved frantic union, embracing Gnosis in the final throes of ecstasy [Allegro, 1970:86]. Further references are found within the Old Testament by Allegro [*ibid.*] that suggests Amanita consumption. Solomon's lover, the 'Shulamite' is described within the Song of Songs as possessing: *"two breasts like fawns…,"* strongly suggestive of the caps of these particular fungi. Punning was of course a much employed literary device, utilised to great effect throughout the ancient Middle East and Egypt. Garbled reports of cannibalism where *"little children plucked asunder and eaten raw,"* could assume a totally different meaning in the context of a mushroom cult.

Viewed from a more scientific perspective, the deep brooding silences that are recorded as following the maniacal ravings of the *'Bacchae'* and the

'Maenads' can be clinically identified as parallel to those of 'Amanita' consumption. Intense excitement is followed by delirium, hallucinations, animation, and finally a deep introspective depression. One scholar explained this profound moment as the zenith, the flight of spirit, held in rapt concordic silence, wherein one is closest to God. Well known within occult practice, is the pain and sadness experienced as withdrawal from esoteric, transpersonal identity with deity. On a more mundane level, these periods of rest and activity reflect archaic agricultural cycles of the ancient Middle East. Another myth of Lucifer, as Son of the Morning Star explains how his semen is sprinkled upon the ground each morning in the form of dew. The emerging mushrooms, sparkling in the soft light of dawn must be collected before this shining sacred essence evaporates [*ibid.*].

Closer analysis of the Old Testament reveals how such spermal emissions seeding the Earth to produce sacred fungi could logically be sacred 'manna', the bread from heaven. If correct, this premise would indeed provide an interesting alternative to our request for 'daily bread' when reciting the Lord's Prayer. Tumescent pearl-like drops, collected as seminal dew from these fungi contain a chemical called '*Luciferin*', which is part of an efflorescent compound known as '*Luciferase*', so named by modern chemists. Certain larger genera of fungi (i.e. '*Omphalotus olearus,*' '*Armillaria mellea*' and '*Clitocybe illudens*') and other moss-like species that grow on tree branches also contain this chemical [Morgan, 1995:46]. As an interesting aside, this could explain why in folklore, magic wands cut from infected branches 'glow' an unearthly green in the dark.

As a child of Venus, sacred mushrooms belong to two worlds, the heavenly and the terrestrial, whose esoteric powers, the knowledge of good and evil of true wisdom, or the living 'Tao,' bring the ability to become '*Dioscuroi*' - sons of God. As offspring of the Morning Star, they signify the special relationship between this star and fungi, both appearing at dawn. Examining ancient cosmogony Allegro [1970:113] concludes that within ritual consumption of '*Amanita muscaria,*' the illusion of spiritual resurrection, of victory over death mirrors the microcosmic appearance and growth of the mushroom itself. Hence its cultic associations with life and death, perceptions of heaven and Earth as two halves - a volva and a canopy upheld by a sacred pillar or mountain; these concepts underpin many ancient myths. In particular, the Babylonian myth of Marduk splitting the mighty egg of the great serpent Tiamat, the lower half of which then formed the seas and the Earth (the sac and fluid of the mushroom), the upper half the sky and heavens (the spotted cap) leading to higher realms traversed by consumption of the central stem/pillar, the serpent within. Another Orphic connection is here cognate with magical stones, aptly named 'serpent's eggs,' known to and revered by Druids.

Isaiah identified spirits of the dead with giants of old, the '*Rephaim,*' fallen angels whose gift was knowledge to mankind; Allegro [1970:174] interprets this as heavenly dew, fallen from Venus, generating the mushrooms, flesh of the Morning Star. Further references found in Enoch describing the 'Tree of Life' could allude to the growth and habitat of '*Amanita muscaria*':"*the height of a fir, leaves like a carob and fruits like a vine.*" Allegro [1970:155] explains these as metaphors for Pine and Birch trees, and carob is in fact a word that means both mushroom and food for pigs; groups of these fungi do resemble 'clusters' of grapes. Later researchers following Northern traditions where these trees grow in abundance explain the Nature of its deity in terms of mushroom mythology. '*Wodh*' is a Germanic term for ecstatic, inspired mental activity; '*an*' is master of this state, hence '*Wodhanaz/Wotan*' the Master of Inspiration, of mantic states akin to those of '*Dionysus,*' induced here by intoxication of poetic mead.

A charming story relates how '*Wodhanaz*' entered a cave in the form of a snake, and after consuming three vats of mead stored there, morphed into an eagle to fly back to his kingdom. On the way, droplets spilled from his beak to seed the Divine mushrooms. This then is his gift to mankind enjoined upon his vision quests. Once safely home, he expels the mead into three special drinking horns for personal use. Stylised forms of these horns create a symbol, the Triskele sacred to Northern Tribes, Europeans and Indo-Aryans.

References to '*Soma*' relating to Divine inebriation, termed 'be-mushroomed,' contrasts markedly with the form of '*madhu*' within Sanskrit texts, which could imply a mushroom/mead elixir. Eventually, this shift from consumption in this form to honey fermented mead based intoxicants is but a step.[7] Indeed Wasson[8] indignantly attests how intoxication by alcohol is quite literally, a poisoning. Phonetic language development within emerging patriarchal civilizations vanquished cognitive responses to fungi entheogens; despite this, hallucinogenic plants were often added to wine and mead to increase their potency. Ancient Greek Retsina was probably spiked with '*Atropa*' (belladonna) and '*Datura*' (thorn-apple). Interestingly, thorn-apple, a plant found readily in the regions of Mount Sinai is said to induce feelings of intense heat, of 'burning'. The bush from which it grows could be responsible for the visionary experiences of Moses. Research into original Hebrew texts reveals the commonly known phrase 'the burning bush' as 'the bush that burns,' which significantly changes its meaning. If Moses did consume these fruits, the thorn apples, then it would indeed explain much.[9]

Returning to 'manna' as the subject of Steve Kubby's[10] research, we discover his assertion of an entirely different genus - that of the 'Psilocybe.' Analysis of the Old Testament finds a close match in size and growth habit of this particular fungus, more commonly known as the 'magic mushroom'. Contrary to popular opinion, he insists that no prohibition exists within the Old Testament against the use of hallucinogenic plants (sic). Kubby[11] effectively presents his theory by comparing descriptions of preservation techniques before utilization in ground form as flour for their 'daily bread' and also whole within jars of honey. Nomadic lifestyles require light easily preserved transportable food as tribes move around searching for suitable grazing for their livestock. Upon arrival in Canaan, which is technically, in spite of being the fabled 'land of milk and honey,' a dry and arid land, the Old Testament laments the tragic disappearance of 'Manna'. Naturally, this climate would not be conducive for fungi to grow there. Intriguingly, the Ark was said to contain 'Manna', preserved in a Golden Urn that generations may know of its wonder.

Its spiritual significance is now legendary, founded as it was upon personal instruction from 'The Lord', though obviously not the one who banished Adam and Eve from Eden for the same indulgence. May be this old serpent was up to his tricks again? Certainly, it is recorded how these tribes exhibited similar fearsome qualities of the Norse warrior class of Berserkers; suspected of similar hallucinogenic fungi ingestion, they were hailed as virtually invincible. In their case, however, it was more than probable the species consumed was Amanita [Morgan, 1995:114]. Visual acuity, cunning (kenning - knowing), strength and ferocity are much increased through continued consumption of the precious 'bread' from heaven. Is this then how they knew their God? Did he speak to them in trance-induced visions? Through *'Manna'*, God was understood to 'prove' his people, a 'Covenant' of spiritual fulfilment is drawn up that Kubby[12] interprets as a millennial revelation whereby new adherents to ancient mushroom cults will once again find true wisdom and the path to the Ultimate Deity.

The pandemic qualities of *'Stropharia cubensis'* (psilocybe) are sufficiently convincing for Mckenna [1993:34] to submit it as the most likely candidate for ritual consumption by Middle Eastern nomads, including the *'Hapiru'* (later Hebrews of the Exodus). Unlike *'Amanita muscaria,'* it is nausea free and widely available. Beneficially, it is actively more potent, possessing superior alkaloids and hallucinogenic properties to those of *'Amanita'* (*muscarine, atropine and bufotenin*). Its most likely origin was Southwest Asia, developing in further sites where humans and cattle evolved together. Logically speaking *'Amanita muscaria'* is better suited to the more temperate highlands of Iran/Iraq, now accepted by many as probable locations for Eden. Mckenna [1993:110] suspects Wasson's own contempt of hippie (sic) culture of his Time and their non-ritualistic irreverential abuse of the entheogen *'Stropharia cubensis'* (magic mushroom) was a contributing factor in his choice of *'Amanita muscaria'* as the legendary *'Soma'.* Nevertheless, it should also be noted that Wasson (who erroneously understood *'psilocybe'* to be native only within the New World) did not have the benefit of more modern research that has since confirmed prolific growth of psilocybe genera throughout sub-tropical grasslands of Africa, Anatolia, and the Iranian plateau millennia before migrations of the Indo-Aryans across Europe.

Academic opinion supports the possibility that species of *'Stropharia'* could even be the 'UR' plant of legend. Mckenna [*ibid.*] traces its use further back into Palaeolithic Cults of the Horned Goddess: (sic) *"where man as part of a sentient symbiosis, sucked the sap of wisdom through Nature's fruits."* Mankind as a species has subsequently eaten his way to higher consciousness, intrinsically linking cultural development and regression to its consumption and withdrawal. Acting as catalyst to cognitive responses, we became Homo-sapiens sapiens, quite literally, 'thinking man'. Our ability to conceptualise, visualize and transmute these cerebral impulses set us apart from all other life forms with whom we share this amazing planet; from a neurological viewpoint, we become 'switched on'. [Mckenna, 1993:41].

Our waking conscious state forces us to focus on relevant or immediate issues. In effect, safety valves close off continual intrusions to the supra-conscious; these pathways are re-opened by hallucinogenic substances. Rising trends in agriculture provided the nemesis for nomadic cultic practises, especially in their use to access wisdoms of the 'Great Mother,' whose creative feminine qualities, were almost certainly known to all previous Hunter/Gatherer cultures. Contact with this spirit, the voice within, slowly shifted to become the province of an ever-increasing hierarchy of priest/kings [Mckenna, 1993:56].

Wasson's theory that religion (a highly subjective term) developed when hominids encountered hallucinogenic alkaloids, leading to focus, direction and development is strongly supported by Mckenna [*ibid.*]. This conflicts sharply with Eliade's assumption that Shamanic technique and drug induced ecstasy is little more than moral decadence. Clarification is offered only when the effects of these fungi are fully comprehended. Unlike many other mind-altering substances, active chemicals, psilocybin and psilocin, produce psychotomimetic effects similar to those produced by mescaline or LSD, facilitating a sense of completeness, a connection to the source, an awareness of the central core of one's existence and of communication with it; wisdom is received automatically in symbolic form. Our fore-knowledge determines how we interpret this information.

Across the globe, in the New World, Franciscan friars recorded how (in Mexico) natives ate mushrooms with honey in their religious ceremonies; psilocybin mushrooms are still preserved in this way, their active ingredients being hardly affected by this process. Referred to as: *"los ninos"*- *"dear sweet little ones,"* they are thought of as small children. Further investigation is encouraged into the relationship between honey, mushrooms and the Mysteries; in fact, a little known but relevant myth concerning 'Glaukos,' son of 'Minos' and 'Parsiphae' (Moon Goddess), whose 'death' and preservation in a pot of honey strongly suggest the culling and processing of Soma and Manna, both known to have been preserved in this way. A serpent provides the wisdom to a Shamanic figure, 'Polyidos,' how to return 'Glaukos' to life [Mckenna, 1993:127].

Today, shamen in the New World, Siberia and Scandinavia do indeed subscribe to ritual ingestion of hallucinogenic fungi. Maria Sabina and her ancestors, the Aztecs have, for as long as memory serves them, celebrated a very special festival every eight years in honour of Venus, the Morning Star. Moreover, of Sabina's many epithets - Morning Star Woman was her favourite. To the Aztecs, Venus was associated with Quetzalcoatl, the feathered serpent (coatl also means twin), their most revered of all Gods. His primary role was of teacher, the 'holder' of wisdom. This special festival involves a bizarre frog and snake-swallowing contest. Co-incidentally, the Moon also takes eight years to return to its original point in the heavens, another significant zenith of the Meso-American calendar [Morgan, 1995:138]. In her noted biography, Sabina claims to have used fungi for her vision quests since adolescence. She stresses the importance of their consumption in pairs, understood to represent male and female elements of deity, to facilitate a true harmony of vision. Therein is revealed another clue to the science and logic that underpins the mystical concept of deity as androgynous.

D.N.A.: Ladder to the Gods?

"If the name Lucifer were not prejudicial, it would be a suitable one for this Archetype - the self."

Collected works of C.G.Jung. vol. 9 p.567

Several modern researchers, anxious to present proofs for theories relating to drug-induced ecstasy as pathway to Gnosis, have experimented with various fungi and plant alkaloids. R.G.Wasson in 1955 was the first acknowledged westerner to have participated in a nocturnal mushroom ceremony called a *'velada'*, under the supervision of 'curandera' Maria Sabina. Although she freely admitted that psilocybe genera *'stropharia cubensis'* and *'mexicana'* are the most popular fungi used in Mazatec ceremonies, her own preference was for 'others,' not disclosed. It was her belief that as *"flesh of the Gods"* (Teonanactl), they possess special power… calling them: *"little ones who springs forth."* [13] Traditionally, this was consumed as a rich, thick dark chocolate drink sweetened with fungi infused honey. The following quotes clearly express not only her reverence for these sacred fungi, but her understanding of them as revealers of wisdom:

* "The mushrooms give me the power of universal contemplation. I can see the origin. I can arrive where the world is born."
* "I can cure with language…. nothing else."
* "It is the book of God that speaks to me, it counsels me…..it teaches me."
* "I am the daughter of God and elected to be wise. On the altar that I have in my house is the image of our Lady of Guadalupe."

Unsurprisingly, within this primarily Catholic country, we discover Mary as a Saint connected to the acquisition of wisdom *and* as a vehicle towards experience of God. In an interview with Shultes and Hofmann[14] entitled *'Little Flowers of the Gods'* Sabina continues:

"There is a world beyond ours…where God lives…where the dead live…and everything is known. That world talks. It has a language all its own. I report what it says. The sacred mushroom takes me by the hand and brings me to a world where everything is known. It is they, the sacred mushrooms that speak in a way I can understand."

Meso-American pre-history is saturated with incidents of mushroom cults. Mayan dignitaries write in their sacred book the 'Popol Vuh', of nine Lords of 'Xibalba' in forms that are also used to describe both the Underworld and sacred mushrooms. It is noteworthy that the most frequently experienced vision under the influence of hallucinogenic fungi is the serpent. This close correlation of serpent as symbol of wisdom adjunct to its chthonic associations has become increasingly significant.

Wisdom and knowledge is universally represented by the serpent, symbol of spiritual awakening, encompassing rebirth, the cyclic forces of Nature, the dual aspects of Good and Evil (hence its association with the Tree), the light and the dark, matter and spirit, creation and destruction. The author of the 'Gospel of Philip,' tantalizingly determines the many pairs of opposites as inseparable and mutually independent, Pagels [1989:70-1] links these to Eastern concepts of Yin and Yang, and of completion within the Tao. Here it is revered as the cosmic initiator and the ever-flowing primal energy.

Relevant also, is the serpents' role as guardian of the threshold, the rainbow bridge to the supra-conscious [Cooper, 1998:147-8]. Symbolically, the awakenings of the dynamic forces of serpent unleash the 'Anima Mundi' - the World Soul; but Christian iconography separated the serpent's inherent dualism by polarising its qualities. When placed at the axial node of the 'Tree of Life,' this force is considered beneficent, being associated with Christ, but malefic when placed at the axial node of the 'Tree of Knowledge,' being associated with 'Satan' [*ibid*.].

It is rarely refuted that one of the oldest and most primal forms of the Goddess is a snake/serpent, and existence of a pre-deist snake cult upon Crete is suggested by coins depicting a female figure caressing a snake beneath a tree [Cooper, 1998:150]. Thousands of miles away in the Southern Hemisphere, the aboriginal culture of Australia revere the Rainbow Snake that conceptually is not too dissimilar to that of South America, and is often shown as a pair. Within Eastern mythologies the snake/serpent is interchangeable with the dragon, all representing dualistic union of opposed forces/elements (generally the primal potencies of fire and water).

One researcher working in the 'Pichis Valley' of Peru, perplexed by the almost universal image of the twin snakes/serpents, especially in connection to trance-induced states, decided to investigate matters further. After sitting out late one night drinking and smoking tobacco with a group of local men, he was advised that: *"to see things clearly, one must learn to de-*

focalise one's gaze,' and *'to learn to see things three-dimensionally.''* Narby's [1999:83] erudite research soon led him to realise these people believed access to knowledge, understanding and wisdom, was achieved by drinking a brew concocted from *'Ayahuasca,'* a species of tobacco wherein the active ingredient is *'dimethyltryptamine.'* Strict rules determine its complex preparation and consumption, but when asked how this knowledge was acquired, Narby was simply informed that the plants had revealed their secrets in 'visions.' God manifests in the plants, it is God who speaks to them and God is the Serpent! Scientific studies of the brain have confirmed that due to complex mechanisms that interpret images relayed by neural transmitters from the optic nerve, it cannot tell the difference between what is real and what is illusion. To add further confusion, surrogate serotonins introduced via hallucinogenic drugs, block, increase, enhance or change messages conveyed by the authentic serotonins that are produced by the body to bridge synapses of the brain, keying into cerebral receptors. However, it must be added that when non-organic compounds such as L.S.D. are introduced, then the resulting psychodelia is in marked contrast to more realistic visions, no matter how fantastical, induced by natural compounds [Narby, 1999:48].

So convincing are these amazing three-dimensional images of dragons, serpents and bird-headed creatures experienced under the influence of natural drugs, that anthropologist Michael Harner considers them representative of the Primal Gods, locked deep within the reptilian compartment of our supra-conscious. Strange visions of reptilian forms said to inhabit these deep recesses are normally restricted to the dead and the dying. These shiny black-winged beings once dropped from the sky to create life on Earth, hiding within it, on a truly animistic level. Their Divine spark encoded within every living thing instigated their genesis; hence the oft quoted statement throughout the esoteric and occult world, first coined by Crick… *"We are all stars."* Indeed the Celestial Serpent, often twinned, underpins many ancient eschatological and cosmological myths.

Serpent creator Gods are common to Amazonia, Meso-America, Australia, Sumer, Egypt, Persia, India, Crete, Greece, Scandinavia and the Pacific Islands. Primitive rock art, very possibly entoptic, depicting twin-helixes, shapes that resemble chromosomes and D.N.A. strands in their anaphase stages of cellular duplication, drew Narby further into this intriguing area of his research. He studied an Egyptian wall-painting inscribed with hieroglyphs resembling D.N.A. strands adjunct to an image of a two-headed serpent. Translated, their meaning suggests: *"the joined spirit for vital force twists within its house of water and is the key of life"* [Narby, 1999:].

Eventually Narby realised the link between these crude drawings and the metaphoric spiralling journey of the Shaman, ascending and descending the *'Axis Mundi,'* via ladders, twisted ropes and vines, spiral staircases and tunnels; all providing access to what Jung termed - the 'Collective Unconscious.' This connection to the source centre of life provides direct communication with the structure and formation of the Universe, both micro and macro-cosmically. Narby [1999:63-66] confidently then announced his assertion that the spiral helix of D.N.A. strands are the true serpents of wisdom, accessed directly by plant-induced trances. This is how the plants 'speak'; although understanding and interpreting them is something else entirely.

Now we have to ask, what if these binary strips of D.N.A. do hold the key to wisdom, to self-awareness. Do we understand and accept them as the true duality of our androgynous Nature, where full comprehension induces the Tao? Are these twin serpents the dualistic principles of life germane to the Mysteries? Of course Crick's elegant theory of man as a cell of extra-terrestrial origin may not suit everyone, and it must be stated that although D.N.A. can replicate itself, it cannot create itself; this ability remains the province of a higher order.

Once 'plugged-in,' we can freely access these visionary worlds, where all the wisdom of the ages is stored. Sound, integral to this process, provided by chanting, singing and rhythmic drumming of New and Old World Shamen as inheritors of Stone-Age cultural traditions that shake off conscious awareness, offers us a doorway into their world, that is if we choose to walk through it. Meaningless gibberish, now termed *'glossolalia,'* intoned repeatedly, establishes communication. Vibrations and sonics, integrated through music and Mantra are occult media not yet fully explored by many practitioners. Remember, that in the beginning was the Word, the Logos, the primal intelligence - the word of God. In the East *'Bija,'* sacred sounds 'seeded' the Universe with life. Similarly, in South America, in Peru, the world of the *'mannikari'*, the invisible ones who created life, are considered as ancestors of the *'Ashaninka'* peoples. *'Avireri,'* their legendary leader rules jointly with his sister; he created humans by blowing upon the Earth. Later, she tricked him into becoming ensnared within a twisted vine; suspended for all Time, he sustains the knowledge of the ages.

What is very interesting to note within this tale, is that this vine is suspended in water. Scientifically, this neatly correlates to saline filled cells from which the suspended D.N.A. molecules strive to spiral out of, avoiding contact with it [Narby, 1999:106]. Ultimately, D.N.A. is a single chain, united from a pair of interwoven ribbons of self-duplicating strands, perceived metaphorically as single or double-headed master of transformation. These crystalline chains of D.N.A. network to resemble the Cosmic Serpent, conveyor of wisdom and origin of creation that lives in water and spits fire/light, and who is the central tenet of faith within many ancient cosmogonies throughout both sides of the Atlantic. The caduceus of wisdom has long been associated with spiralling D.N.A. patterns that metaphysically join within the Hypothalamus gland of the brain to induce enlightenment.

Shamen make contact with these ancestral spirals, the spirits of the '*mannikari*,' usually through ingestion of hallucinogenic fungi, though there are other entheogens, including all derivatives of coca, '*Ayahuasca*' (active alkaloid - harmaline, also found in Syrian rue) and 'peyotl,' (*Lophophora williamsii*). Due to its cluster like growth of 'buttons' above the ground, peyotl has for a very long Time been confusingly referred to as fungi. Its active substance is mescaline, a firm favourite of Aleister Crowley who hailed it as a revealer of the inner-self. Another exclusive substance is '*ololiuqui*' (*Imopea violacea*) or 'Morning Glory' seeds known as affectionately as "*semilla de la virgin.*" The latter mentioned by Cortez as '*Catlxoxouhqui*' - the green serpent, is said to induce fantastic 'demonic' images, yet paradoxically has many healing properties. [Rudgley, 1999:25 and Hofman[15]].

All these entheogens facilitate access to wisdom through images expressed as, 'serpent beings of light'. When tested, it was discovered that D.N.A. emits photons or electro-magnetic waves that increase the contrast and intensity of colour saturation equal to those effects experienced by Shamen in lucid states; facilitating a lowering of consciousness, they resonate at a molecular level equal to that of D.N.A. Quartz crystals amplify photon emissions and it can immediately be seen how and why our 'enlightened' ancestors made use of Nature's gifts to synergise connections to the bio-sphere. This is also the ethereal realm of all 'spirits of pure light' and other luminescent phenomenon experienced upon these planes [Narby, 1999:117-129].

Amazingly, this global networking adds credence to Francis Crick's animist hypothesis of directed panspermia - where all is God, and we are all stars [Narby, 1999:73]. Of course animism is the oldest understanding of deity, forming the basis of a primal intelligence with whom we are eternally connected. Ultimately, we could speculate it as the kernel of a proto-Buddhist principle of unity, of no separate identity for the self. This elegantly expresses true deity as both immanent and transcendent. True wisdom of course lies in the contemplation of this Mystery, and may be experienced through sound and movement (music and dance), and through visioning (use of hallucinogenic compounds) as filtered through the complexities of our individual psychology (cultural restrictions) to cumulatively reveal purpose within the Divine plan (religious eschatology/philosophy.)

Narby [1999:125-130] scientifically concludes that myths of fiery dragon/serpents are the result of molecules of *'dimethyltryptamine'* (alkaloids) activating various neural receptors, stimulating a cascade of electromagnetic reactions leading to visible photo-emissions of D.N.A.; these glowing messages are imaged by 'Shamanic' trance induced altered states for interpretation. Our intuition is simply the result of an internal consciousness linked inexorably to this external source. Wisdom is therefore free to all who seek it, its spiritual context being vital to its comprehension. Knowledge is nevertheless, usually taught from one generation to the next, but, without the requisite cultural keys, and attendant Mythos, it is as pointless as reading a book written in an alien language.

Rigorous, disciplined tutelage and supervision within Mystery Schools continue in purposeful preparation of each individual towards attainment of true Gnosis. Some archaic methodologies do not sit well with the social niceties of 21st century living, nor with sanitised moralities of the modern Craft; hence the need for extreme secrecy within those Traditions that have attempted to revive these and other controversial praxes. In Hofmann's[16] seminal work 'LSD, My Problem Child', personal motivation is clearly germane to success and cultural conditioning germane to oneiric experience. Vivid, lucid dreams, a sensation of flying and awareness of the transcendent 'other' are often accompanied by an alarming sensation of bein torn in two, of splitting, of separation, then of unity of wholeness, of union; of Gnosis.

Henry Munn [1973:3] profoundly debates how cosmological obsessions derived from drug-induced insights, sourced mainly from within variant mushroom cults, claim that the 'elemental world parallels life.' For Munn, drugs are unequivocal revealers of truth, wisdom, knowledge, communication and enlightenment, and he objects strongly to derogatory descriptions of their effects as illusory, or delusional, preferring instead, the terms 'inspired' and' intuited'. Equally, Pagels [1989:68] suggests we enter into the arena of pure psychodynamics, where interaction between *'pneuma'* (the spiritual element of our Nature) and psyche (the emotional and mental impulses) induces euphoria.

Obviously, they are both right; or are they? This clearly presents the subjective world of the Mysteries as experienced by those who live them, in contra-distinction to other academic 'observers', who simply write about them. Realistically, if we were to re-introduce such praxes into the mainstream, the results would be anarchic; chaos would ensue as people steadily rise to challenge sterile and vacuous cosmogonies offered by dogmatic modern religions. Ultimately, this is why they must remain the preserve of but few active Mystery Schools, where ancestral wisdom is engineered with caution and sensitivity to our fragile egos. The loss of personal identity offered to the Void is the antithesis of modern materialism. Consequently, Gnostic principles of freedom from this realm of flesh to become spirit, become self-perpetuating...

Bibliography:
Morgan. A. 1995 *'Toads and Toadstools'* Celestial Arts. Berkley, California.
Purnell. B. B. 1970 *'Man, Myth and Magic'* [vol.1.] Marshall-Cavendish. New York
George. D. 1992 *'Mysteries of the Dark Moon'* Harper Collins. New York.
Cooper. J.C. 1998 *'An Illus. Enc. of Traditional Symbols'* Thames & Hudson. Eng.
Pagels. E. 1989 *'Adam, Eve and the Serpent'* Ist Vintage Books. U.S.A.
Narby. J. 1999 *'The Cosmic Serpent'* Phoenix pub. London.
Mckenna. T. 1993 *'Food of the Gods'* Bantam Books U.S.A.
Graves. R & Patai. R. 1964 *'Hebrew Myths: Book of Genesis'* Cassel & Co. London
Allegro. J. M. 1970 *'The Sacred Mushroom and the Cross'* Hodder & Stoughton London
Munn. H. 1973 *'Mushrooms of Language'* Ox. Uni. Press. Oxford
Rudgley. R. 1999 *'Enc. of Psychoactive Substances'* Abacus. G.B.
Taylor. N. 1966 *'Narcotics: Nature's Dangerous Gift'* Dell publishing. U.S.A.

References and Internet sources:-
1. Prof. P. Davies - Sheffield Uni. [Oct. 2002] *(private conversation)*
2. Prof. P. Harding - Chesterfield College [Nov.2002] *(private conversation)*
3. www.erowid.org: Erowid Psilocybe Mushroom Vault

4. www.mushroom mythology: Soma among the Armenians - Robert Bedrosian 2000

5. www.mushroom mythology: Soma among the Armenians - Robert Bedrosian 2000

6. *Although often referred to as plants for grammatical ease, Fungi are technically not a plant at all, but belong to a taxonomic category of their own.*

7. www.swastika.com

8. www.erowid.org: Erowid Mescaline Vault 'Little Flowers of the Gods' - Shultes&Hofmann

9. Graham Phillips - Lecture at Questing Con. [Nov. 2002] *At the Questing Conference held in 2002, author Graham Phillips jokingly suggested this and asserted his belief in its viability.*

10. www.cnw.com/~neruo/gaz/: Manna from Heaven - Steve Kubby [Psych Ill.vol.4]

11. www.cnw.com/~neruo/gaz/: Manna from Heaven - Steve Kubby [Psych. Ill.vol.4]

12. www.cnw.com/~neruo/gaz/: Manna from Heaven - Steve Kubby [Psych. Ill.vol.4]

13. www.erowid.org: Erowid Psilocybe Mushroom Vault - Maria Sabina [Healing Quotes]

14. www.erowid.org: Erowid Mescaline Vault 'Little Flowers of the Gods' - Shultes & Hofman

15. www.cnw.com/~neuro/gaz/: The Sacred Mushroom Teonanactl - Albert Hofman [excerpts from L.S.D. My Problem Child]

16. www.cnw.com/~neuro/gaz/: The Sacred Mushroom Teonanactl - Albert Hofman [excerpts from L.S.D. My Problem Child]

Previously published in *The Cauldron* #115 Feb 05; #116 May 07 and #117 Aug 2005

Clan Ethos

18. Musings on the Sacred

'What the superior man seeks, is within himself, What the inferior man seeks, is within others.' Confucius

Many people who know of my involvement within the Craft and yet remain a teacher of Eastern healing, mystical techniques and an Holistic Therapist ask me if this is not a contradiction in terms. Indeed and assuredly it is not. This is principally because there is no obligation upon me to teach or practise commercially, enabling me instead to mentor individuals to review perceptions of reality, and to advance comprehension of the Universal (magical) laws through evolution of spirit in accord with will. Moreover, disciplines appropriate to either modality are not dissimilar and can be drawn upon to aid in concentration, focus and execution of will and intent in full awareness of cause and effect.

Evolved precepts of Eastern healing traditions, find their origin within ancient Hindu, Tantric Buddhist and indigenous (Shamanistic) 'Bon' practices of Tibet. Buddhism was originally iconoclastic, but more accessible forms developed when absorbed by Chinese, Japanese and Tibetan peoples, who were reluctant to give up their extensive pantheons of minor deities as expressions of the eternal and unknowable truth. Cross-cultural disciplines and substitution of one God/Goddess from one pantheon for another 'similar' form in any magical enterprise must generally be discouraged; yet there is virtue in recognising and utilising any magical act of value and relevance to one's purpose. To clarify this apparent contradiction, sharing basic concepts drawn from within the fundamental potentialities of these healing systems should serve as abstract analogies.

To begin, there is the use of Mantra - Sanskrit for 'sacred utterance'. All Hindu and Tantric Buddhist rituals are accompanied by 'Mantras,' whether uttered aloud or silently, ranging in length from a single syllable to a whole hymn. They may be used for secular, magical or religious purposes. Often they are used as a means of addressing deity and/or manipulation of intrinsic Divine powers, specific to the Mantra used. It is noteworthy that many Mantras deal with quite mundane issues ranging from removing the venom from a snake or scorpion bite, curing diseases and fever, for providing health, wealth and sound sleep to long life, knowledge, forgiveness, and reaching the Divine.

Originally, the four 'Vedas' (sacred Hindu texts), comprised of Mantras to illuminate, inspire, educate and elevate aspirants involved in their expression. Unchanging formats emanate eternal truths, imparting a Gnosis of 'God'. Mantras formulate ritual of every category; even objects used in ritual must first be addressed via the requisite 'Mantra' to imbue them with sacred energy from the corresponding deity. Central to every Hindu Initiation is the traditional gift of a sacred Mantra from Master to pupil (only a twice born person may become a priest and thus receive a sacred Mantra); this serves to transform the recipient as ritually efficacious and is subsequently used in all future rituals. All rites of passage contain Mantras and the initiate may then use the given Mantra to sacralize any ordinary act to increase its efficacy (i.e. bathing, the act of sex to render it fruitful, blessing or consecration of food etc).

Tantrism is a system reliant upon combined harmonic union of force and form, of 'Shiva' with 'Shakti', the God's feminine power and active potency. Mantras imbue meditations and physical activities (sexual or otherwise) with occult knowledge designed to facilitate individual salvation. Yantras and Mandalas (geometric designs and symbols relating specifically to divinity, creation, worship or enlightenment) play an integral part of these acts, accessed by specific placement upon various parts of the body identified with deity; this is a very literal act of invocation. Each of the many deities is expressed through two forms: the visual and the sonic. The latter is deemed closer to ultimate reality, therefore more potent, relating to the transcendent matrix of all language and reality. Mantras are manifestations of God's grace, given in compassion for our development. The ultimate Mantra is the 'Gayatri' Mantra, which also begins with the customary hail to deity - Om, the seed sound of creation.

The principal feature of the 'Gayatri' Mantra is its salutation to the Hindu God, 'Prajapati,' the horned deity, and Lord of the Animals, symbolised by the Sun, perceived creator and benefactor of mankind and our Universe. Syllables within this Mantra specifically relate to the creation and formation of the Earth, the atmosphere and the heavens; order is thus given to the world through form and name. Interestingly, the wife/Goddess of Prajapati, an independent deity, takes the active role in creation, becoming the Universe, paralleling the role of 'Shakti' within Tantric tradition. Subtle vibrations generated by their union create seed sounds that are emulated within the Gayatri Mantra, a process that also connects us to all our homo sapien sapien ancestors, Gods and prophets. Mantras are designed as monologues for manifestation, petitions for Divine grace, stimulating transformation of the soul. Moreover, the format/structure for worship or invocation, including praise, offering and petition are encompassed within both Hindu and Tantric traditions, having key Mantras to effect the requisite purpose.

It is here noteworthy that the five elements play a key role both within the use and potency of Mantras, Mandalas and Yantras, having as 'gateways' guardians, Goddesses or bodhisattvas relevant to each one. The creative aspect of Ultimate divinity is visually expressed as a beautiful and youthful pale skinned 'Goddess', the 'Gayatri-Ma', consort of Brahma and mother of the Vedas. When not referred to within this specific context she is also known as the benign form of Sarasvati. Her role is very similar to that of the Qabbalistic 'Shekinah'. Indeed, within the 'Bhagavad-Gita' can be found a commentary by Lord Shiva, who states that the Goddess 'Gayatri Devi' is the incarnation and manifestation of 'Brahma' who resides in all living things. Her additional four faces are coloured cream, red, yellow and black, and her ten arms hold all the symbols of 'Vishnu;' collectively they represent the elements and supreme expression of truth, creation, order, justice as emanations from supreme divinity (it is very tempting here to equate her with Maat).

This is the form that many Hindus hold as focus for their devotions when uttering the 'Gayatri' Mantra (the oldest and most sacred of Mantras). Interestingly however, the hymn actually addresses the 'Lord Sun' as the inner key, the 'hidden self' within, who is acknowledged as the giver of protection and enlightenment. It is said to confer protection and dispel negative influences; in other words, it seals and banishes.

Ultimately, it is a prayer to the 'Supreme Divine Being' that serves to stimulate the intellect so that we may realise the supreme truth of ourselves in relation to it, a prayer to the 'self' to unveil itself and for manifestation of pure wisdom Gnosis. For many therefore, the 'Sun' symbolically represents illumination within all experiences; the Atman; the soul - pure consciousness, thus it is hoped to make the 'self' shine more brilliantly by our relation to it. It connects us to the seven worlds by their association with the seven Chakras relative to the Kundalini (a subject beyond the remit of these simple musings).

Personally though, I favour the Vedic rather than the Qabbalistic system as the former is inclined to raise awareness up through the body and beyond as it seeks enlightenment on the spiritual plane, recognising the interpenetrative 'oneness' of all things, whereas, the latter summons spiritual force, perceived as emanating from above, down into the body as an empowerment for generation on the manifest plane. It is of course a very individual and personal action and people must find their own way to an awareness or experience of deity (however you perceive this force to be).

Unsurprisingly, there are many other things within these systems that can also be seen to parallel much of what we hold dear within Traditional Craft practices. Particularly significant, is the midnight Witching hour that signals 'Yang' Time. Quite naturally, this force is active and progressive during the period of Time when the 'higher self controls the lower self and continues until noon. 'Yin' Time then assumes control, in force until 'Midnight'. Yin incorporates the passive, inactive period when the lower self commands and the higher self obeys. It should now be apparent why a basic awareness of other disciplines can enrich the understanding of our own.

Generally speaking, when conducting a rite, use of Vedic Mantras or discussion of polarity in terms of Yin and Yang would not be advocated, but a more immediate or superior method of self-preparation prior to engagement in any magical work, especially those undertaken in solitary workings is yet to be discovered. Meditations unreservedly employ such methodologies, providing harmony, focus and vital equilibrium. It has long been recognised that many of the Craft's more eclectic traditions originated in the Middle and Far East, serving to enrich and expand both our conscious awareness and experience. However, this should never prevent anyone from exploring more indigenous practices; rather, it should enhance and diversify our options. We should deny nothing that comes to us, for none of it is inherently contrary to our individual argosies, which will be enriched exponentially by such diversification.

Previously published in: *The Cauldron* #109 August 2003

19. The Mystery Tradition

"We have not even to risk the adventure alone. For the heroes of all Time have gone before us. The labyrinth is thoroughly known. We have only to follow the thread of the hero path. And where we thought to find an abomination, we shall find a God. And where we had thought to slay another, we shall slay ourselves. Where we had thought to travel outward, we shall come to the centre of our own existence. Where we had thought to be alone, we shall be with all the World."
Joseph Campbell (*The Hero with a Thousand Faces*).

Robert Cochrane firmly believed that: "*Genuine Witchcraft is not Paganism, though it retains the memory of ancient faiths…it is the last real Mystery Cult alive.*" He taught that Witchcraft and Paganism were not synonymous, each possessing both complementary and more commonly, contradictory elements, especially regarding fundamental issues such as tenets of faith, intrinsic Mythos and working practices. In defence of Cochrane's somewhat divisive opinion, this essay will hopefully generate thought and discussion, with a view to correcting a widely held misunderstanding of this distinction, in terms of both Robert Cochrane's intention and a wider Craft perspective.

Historically of course, boundaries between Pagan and Witch have changed significantly, and the more recent advent of Neo-Paganism and Wicca (not fully developed in Cochrane's Time), has in most cases, extended these still further. Yet others have become blurred, masking distinction, creating a small overlap into which anyone finding themselves, is immediately subject to belonging within both. In reality of course, there is no universal definition of the term Pagan or Witch, each maintaining concepts widely known and accepted by a vast body of disparate people. To further exacerbate this particularly sensitive issue, the terms Wicca and Neo-Paganism are again quite dissimilar in meaning from Folk magic and other Traditional forms of Witchcraft.

Neo-Paganism, typically refers to a broad eclectic movement that invariably finds expression (though not exclusively) as a religion, albeit one that is commonly environmentally based; at its core, it therefore represents a 'return' to Nature, to pantheism. Neo-Pagans (as individuals) generally remain totally independent and autonomous - precepts that are quite at odds with many forms of Folk magic and Traditional forms of Craft still practised today. Within their syncretised celebrations we can easily recognise many ancient Pagan elements and themes, which, despite the Reformation have survived, and are also clearly evident within many of today's 'Christian' festivals. Conversely, with the exception of the (original Gnostic) Mass, how many rites now associated with Witchcraft have been similarly adapted into the Christian Church? With many banned or outlawed my guess is that you would find it very hard, if not impossible to find any. Yet, paradoxically, Pagans rather than Witches have largely rejected Christianity. Surviving within established religion, Witchcraft has acquired significant Christian glosses, and many Witches, though by no means all, consider themselves to be of 'dual-faith'.

Neo-Pagans, Wiccans and Traditionalists, have revived various ancient classical/Hermetic practices. While the first two stress humanitarian aspects where emphasis is placed upon goodness, caring and sharing, the latter tends to concentrate instead upon more magical, alchemical tractates. Cochrane summarised this divergence in his conceptualisation of Paganism as an 'alternative science' in contra-distinction to the 'occult science' of the 'true' (sic) Craft. Many from either modality are often solitary practitioners, treading the path of self-development, promoting spiritual consciousness. Again, both possess diametrically opposed means, often achieving variant ends. Unfortunately, this serves only to further obfuscate disparities between magic and religion. According to the late Sybil Leek, Witches were *"women who have unusual powers of both Good and Evil, who manipulate supernatural forces, including invocation of spirit"* (sorcery); put succinctly - Witches *work* magic.

How then do we differentiate a Pagan from a Witch? Looking in a dictionary is not particularly helpful; the generic term - Pagan (a country dweller/simple rustic), is, according to Hutton[1] a bit of a misnomer. He stresses that many city dwellers, often of high status, practising a variety of religions and philosophies such as Neo-Platonism were also classed as 'Pagans.' In other words, anyone within the Occidental world who remained outside the sophisticated state religion of Christianity was considered a Pagan. Indeed to early 6th -10th century Christians, the term 'Pagan' was used indiscriminately to describe anyone - Monist or Polytheist! Hutton also affirms: *"By assuming that Witchcraft and Paganism were formally the same phenomenon, they are mixing two utterly different concepts and placing themselves in a certain amount of difficulty."*[2] Witchcraft thrived just as readily as a malefic practice within all Pagan and pre-Christian religions as it later did within Christianity. Essentially, in the West at least, it is non-religious and independent of culture. Consultation of the *Russell Hope-Robins*

Encyclopaedia[3] reveals the term Witchcraft described thus: *"Before 1350, Witchcraft primarily meant sorcery, a survival of common superstitions - Pagan only insofar as the beliefs antedated Christianity, never Pagan in the sense of an organized survival of opposition to Christianity or of some pre-Christian religion."* The Encyclopaedia further emphasises that sorcery and magic are archaic, world wide practises, indulged by young and old alike for self-gratification in contra-distinction to the self-development praxes adopted by Neo-Pagans.

The non-Pagan concept of Witchcraft appears rooted in Assyrian, Akkadian and Sumerian belief in the arcane caste of men and women who have requisite skills to perform sorcerous acts. Throughout history, diverse groups of Pagans have shared an observation of Witches as malignant forces; beings who cursed and hexed freely, revelling in malicious torments, worshipping a 'Queen' of the Underworld.

Witches were presented as rulers of darkness whose hags, crones and remote virgins presented the very antithesis of their own worship of a more 'benign' pantheon of Gods and Goddesses. Accompanying this was a very real fear of the Witches' ability to cast the 'evil eye' and to shape-shift in order to execute their capricious whims. Hence, numerous Pagan and folk superstitions relating to protection and warding off such encounters have survived the passage of Time. Modern Pagans in general, view this archetype of 'Witch' as an outmoded stereotype, a caricature of Medieval paranoia; but in reality, is it so far from the truth?

Broadly speaking, modern Pagans, (Neo-Pagans and many Wiccans) are essentially animistic; they worship Nature, see divinity everywhere, possess a healthy respect for the ecology of the planet and enjoy a heightened Goddess awareness. Furthermore, many Pagans increasingly embrace a distinctly metaphysical concept of deity, beyond which is a widely held belief of an unknown and ineffable Godhead - the source that emanates all things. So far so good, in fact many Witches may even share some but not all of these traits, albeit from a differing apprehensive perspective. Within the practices of Neo-Paganism and Wicca, there frequently exist many pantheons, from which some followers adhere exclusively to one dedicated system. Others typically practise an eclectic syncretism, believing in and worshipping appropriate God/dess forms of choice.

This differs markedly from the Traditional Witches' concept of archaic and/or primal Tutelary deities (assigned by mandate) that remains constant, especially within closed hereditary families and practitioners of folk magic. These forms are simply a focal Goddess and (sometimes) horned consort, affectionately referred to as the 'Old Ones', who are often deified concepts of long distant ancestors; exogenous to this, infinite and unknowable phenomena simply exist via a panoply of phantasmagoria. Beyond this, the ineffable forces simply are; no explanation is required or necessary. Of course there are exceptions to all these generalisations. And boundaries between them merge with each generation of seekers and workers of the Mysteries.

Within the traditional workings of Cochrane, these deities are never summoned (though their avatars, spirits, and various aspects, however, may be) called upon to work with or to be over-shadowed by. Ancestors and past Clan members are revered, honoured and invited to share in all celebrations. Once inside the working area, which remains 'open' throughout, yet another departure from Paganism, the Magister and Maid are envisioned as manifest personifications of their Tutelary deities, embodying the cumulative Egregoric Virtue of generations of practitioners gifted to them solely by rite of transmission. The duty that falls to them is therefore absolute. This may seem draconian, but is fundamentally profound, particularly when carried by leaders with integrity, and who are firmly anchored in reality and truth. Egocentrism and delusion implode this grace, essentially destroying its inherent virtue. The primary purpose of Clan Rites is not for personal or group 'development' per se, but to engage in trance work, wherein commune and converse is sought among those revered ancestors, and to re-enforce their place in the hereafter alongside them in the Castle of the Great and Terrible Goddess. The Stang, as portable altar and point of contact, manifestation and sacrifice, placed outside the circle/working area represents the Old Horn King/Horned God, the true 'Father', who is guest of honour and locus of presence.

Importantly, Prof. Hutton[4] postulates the theory that modern Wiccans lack the universal ancient principle of sacrifice, performing rituals for their own pleasure instead of the Gods', no longer propitiating help and benefaction through offerings and sacrifice, choosing instead to work with metaphysical correspondences. Whilst I have to uphold this as an extremely effective and productive method of working it is very different and considerably distinct from the older, more traditional ways of working, where a personal bond is forged between the deity/ancestor and the propitiator. Indeed, so binding is this relationship, that when pressed, our ancestors would cry: *"I worship the Gods that my father's father worshipped,"* asserting that each Clan's 'Gods' are personal to them only; they may in some cases remain nameless, but to each, they are known intimately.

Such vital links to the Clan's ancestors are continuously stressed; 'heritage' and (spiritual) 'bloodlines', maintained by the Egregore, are of paramount importance. Everyone within a particular lineage has access to the 'group soul' (the Egregore) and there is no greater terror or dread than that of being outcast from the protective mentoring of this guiding entity. When associations within Pagan groups end in discord, where one would simply move to another and begin working anew, the aforementioned act of banishment within a Traditional group, effectively alienates those outcast from their guiding deity. All ties are thus severed, both temporal and spiritual.

The enigmatic phrase oft quoted by Cochrane *"the quick and the dead,"* refers to yet another elementary difference between the Witch and the Pagan; which in his belief was expressed thus: the Witch crosses the river to be in the shady realms of the dead, while the Pagan remains with the 'quick', normally taken to imply the living, but it more properly means the life force, as a quickening principle. Evan John Jones however, apparently reverses this rule placing the Pagan with the 'dead' and the Witch reposing with the 'quick'.

We therefore need to analyse briefly the purpose in these seemingly contradictory comments.[5] In fact it is clear they are both articulating the *same* truth, subject as they were to personal obfuscation and grey magic. Cochrane was implying somewhat assertively how the Witch removes to ancestral realms to await rebirth but which E.J. Jones interprets more rationally and quite poetically as reposing with the 'quick', retaining the vital quality of pure essential virtue that is lineage specific for progression in death, through the next life and the life hereafter. By both estimations, this places the 'Pagan' with the nebulous dead, uncertain of their place in the hereafter. The emphasis of both men is clearly upon the return into and continuance of family, within 'Hereditary' traditions.

Cochrane did however accept the Pagan's view of paradise - the 'Summerlands' or 'Tir-Na Gog', that some consider is only reached after many elevating incarnations, while others suppose it to be the place all Pagans go to await re-birth. Either way, he firmly believed this was in no way comparable to the Old Craft's poetic view that Witches, upon death cross the river to the Castle of the Pale Faced Goddess that spins between the worlds, a place peopled and created by distant ancestors and Clan/family members; a place where we shall reside until it is our Time to be reborn through Her 'cauldron' *back into the Clan.* Superficially, at least, both these inter-worlds appear to be romantic projections, reminiscent of non-Christian nostalgia, based probably in either Druidism or the 'Celtic twilight.' There however, the similarity ends.

Our Clan Mythos, like many others, declaims rather positively, that we shall be re-incarnated amongst our own, each vital spark returned to the flame that nurtured it. Robert Cochrane insisted each 'Witch' or student of the Mysteries should accomplish the skills required to remain impervious to the leaching powers of the 'Lethe,' the River of Forgetfulness. This ensures positive re-incarnation, retaining some if not all memory of the true soul self. Until the last decade at least, this certainty contrasted sharply with the many vague and disparate theories shared by modern Wiccans and Neo-Pagans, who often link rebirth to karma - the laws of cause and effect, rendering their next life uncertain and obscure, even where rebirth or transmigration occurs from the heart of the 'Summerlands.' The Clan also assert that we must pay in this life for our actions, effect follows cause swiftly and justly, there is even a specific Clan law to enforce this rule. This is utterly distinct from the general exposition of the much misunderstood law of 'three-fold return'; both laws relate to something intrinsically more profound than the common understanding of them.

Hence, a true Witch dedicates his/her life to this link with the dead, the Castle and the Supreme Creatrix, forging and strengthening the power, energy and wisdom imparted to them by their ancestors. They travel the well-worn path, whose guides are those of myth and legend, the group and family being the focus of importance. Here they become the 'quick.'

Modern Wiccans and Neo-Pagans reject these ancestral links believing them to be restrictive barriers, choosing instead to focus on the self, often following their own intuition and instruction; reliance upon this view of the self is stressed in preference to that of the group. Taking the self as the only guide upon the path; they become the 'dead', having no ancestral 'lamp' before them. Nevertheless, for the genuine seeker on either path, such a quest liberates them from the cycle of re-birth, ultimately achieving enlightenment as a solitary engagement. Cross fertilization over the last few years particularly, has merged these concepts as Pagans and Wiccans have refined and re-defined their eschatologies in line with other traditions.

Traditional Craft maintains such links with the past, along with other darker elements of note. One of the darkest of these is the 'Poisoned Chalice Rite,' wherein trauma is voluntarily induced in order to reveal genetic memories; this is one of the Cauldron Mysteries linked with the old Iberian Cult of the Dead that seeks to emphasize the role of the Divine King. Through this extended worship of the Horned God of whom Bacchus is one of the oldest traceable and recorded contenders, it is recognised that the ultimate source generates all powers of magic and fertility.

For the Witch, these Pagan rites are far removed from the numerous (modern) misconceptions regarding the frolics and revels erroneously associated with historic celebration. The transmutation of Solar and Lunar flux within them is considered one of the greatest ancient alchemical Mysteries. From this belief developed the practice of sexual initiation for the continuation of both spiritual and physical 'bloodlines.' Ripe with secrets and memories (preserved by numerous hereditary families advanced through the Spirit of the 'Egregore') both forces are generated by sexual stimulus, where the activated bio-electrical current facilitates 'the passing of absolute Virtue' much advocated by Cochrane as the only authentic and productive method of Transmission.

As to the Mysteries, these are revealed in ritual, often during trance from the sacred liturgies of an extant and vibrant, living faith, whose secrets are yielded via experience of them, not discussion of them. Witches seek to employ spirits primarily via the evocatory 'artes,' whereas the Pagan seeks to avoid these often difficult energies, preferring instead the use of invocation, which is undertaken as a connection to the higher aspects of the self only. Again, this is one of the primary reasons why the Witch prefers to work outdoors. The Pagan generally reposes within a sheltered temple. Of course there are exceptions in either case and both are equally valid. Neither is superior, just different. They must however, be understood as requisite of very different *'genii loci.'* Polarity is another tenet fundamental to the concept of Wicca and Neo-Paganism, absent from the Traditional Craft, especially that of Robert Cochrane. When executing the Houzle sacrament, the female holds the chalice and the male the knife, juxtaposing a direct sexual symbolism enhanced by the very real physical bio-magnetic contact between Magister and Maid.

Deity is also perceived very differently, according to Adler, Paganism consists of pantheism, polytheism and animism. This is quite distinct from a Witch's often monist perception of deity, where the duality of good and evil, mind and matter as sovereign principles is denied. Of all the world religions, most, posit a wholly Divine monist principle which maintains a moral ambivalence, of which the Vedic God Shiva (often synonymous with Kali), is a prime example; another, from the New World is Quetzalcoatl, the Mexican God of Love and Destruction, Life and Death; another, Sekhmet, the Egyptian Goddess of War and Destruction is also the Goddess of Healing. They are neither distinct nor in conflict with each other, but present a universal harmony of Truth, the cosmic law of Maat. Such principles are profoundly beautiful. Moreover, it has to be remembered that dualism is not a concept rooted in Old Europe, but is a concept founded within the East, from within the ancient Zoroastrian and Manichean (circa 600BCE - a contested date , which may be pushed back to around 1200BCE) religions whose extreme dualistic beliefs subsequently influenced Judeo/Christian and some Gnostic theology. However, Cochrane's Gnostic principles adhere to this holism; spirit and matter are merely transformative stages in our magical egress; they are not and should not be perceived as conditions of enmity... *'En-aat-em-a-shu-t-em-neter'* (there is no part of me that is not of God's essence).

This particularly disparity in concept has over the last forty or so years become less evident due to the increased overlap of Wiccans and Neo-Pagans who now also believe in a totally sentient, ultimate deity who is paradoxically both immanent and transcendent. Parallel to this is the shared belief in the Tri-form Goddess, whom Witches elevate as Hekate 'Mother' of the Fates, worshiping Her triune aspects as Time, Life and Death. Her triple Mysteries of past, present and future are however, shared by the Neo-Pagans and Wiccans who correlate these instead with the more naturistic Maid, Mother and Crone. In general, concepts derived from Eastern Mysticism can be found within the rituals of many Neo-Pagans and Wiccans which have overlaid earlier Old European concepts; this is largely evident in the 'quarter' guardians - elementals of the four cardinal points which were once stellar, but later attributed to the four winds.

Though we must accept that some traditional practices also incorporate many Eastern principles, their cognitive and cogitative perceptions and modus operandi remain quite distinct from those of their Pagan and Wiccan counterparts. Moreover, Witches make appeals and acts of propitiation through the 'Old Ones', utilizing a direct ancestral link to perform magickal deeds, rather than simply the 'adopting of' or the 'affinity to' certain inherent characteristics.

Until the 'Witch-craze', the English word Wicca (Witch), meant sorcerer, it was then transformed to mean heretical diabolist, the emphasis shifting from acts of malevolence to worship of the Devil and practise of his black arts. Thus, throughout Western history, Witchcraft was seen as a syncretism of Christian ideas based upon Pagan religious concepts - they were indeed heretical diabolists, and in practise, despite the shedding of Christian overtones, many traditional Witches still are; exploiting a dark heritage and repertoire of cursing, hexing and evocation, often of long dead family members or ancestors. Few Wiccans and Neo-Pagans would ever consider such activities, believing them to be the province of the magician (sorcerer), preferring instead, creative visualization, or path-working.

Pacts with the Devil, associated with Witchcraft and folk magic, especially during its alleged apogee (16-17th centuries) have remained symptomatic of the Christian faith and yet like Paganism have no place within the ancient, classical world. Even then, while Pagans were calling upon Bacchus, Witches evoked Medea, Ariadne and Herodias; later, Diana and Hekate. Ironically, it is Witchcraft and not Paganism that has maintained the esoteric truths of the Bacchanalian Mysteries, now lost and abandoned by a generally exoteric and much sanitised Wiccan community.

Of course, it cannot be overstated here that Cochrane distanced himself and his Clan from this title - Witch, believing its form corrupt, debased and self-limiting. His understanding (and my own) is one of preservation of belief systems originating in the ancient past, evolving in accord with the eternal teachings of the Mysteries as we strive for Truth. Above all, he believed its modern practitioners are fulfilling their sacred duty as priests of that faith. It is irrelevant whether or not these practices are continuous or have been revived; for despite the vast cultural and temporal gulf, the Mysteries are perceived as our heritage and we honour highly that duty.

Mysteries are by definition, initiatory traditions, unlike many now associated with Neo-Paganism, who often reject this primary act as unnecessary; another major tenet that separates 'Witches' from Pagans. Intrinsically, they are experiential gateways to at-one-ment; elitist and secretive, they withhold sacred liturgies from prying eyes of a public at worst unwilling and incapable of extreme devotion and commitment, and at best simply disinterested. Once initiation has taken place, a 'Covenanted' bond engenders an intimate relationship with the presiding Tutelary deity. Thereafter, this deity alone will be upheld in a monolatrous relationship. Paganism, conversely, is not so God specific.

Within the Clan of Tubal Cain, magical abilities linked through transmission of the Egregore, namely the 'Four Arts', are gifted ('seeded') from Maid to Magister to Maid in continual succession, whose arbitrary use determines the Witch by intention, not just belief. Sadly, there is a very obvious predilection among the swelling numbers of Modern Craft practitioners to gloss over the realities of history. In denouncing the archetypal Witch, many choose to deny or reject this diminishing facet of their heritage, severing vital links that preserve ancestral truths intrinsic to belief and practice. Disconnection obfuscates evolution. Every path must have a beginning and an end. But more importantly, of those who desire to preserve this contentious heritage, will they yet continue the Time honoured traditions, to teach and practise the true and aspirative arts of the 'Mystery Traditions' borne within them?

Bibliography:
1. Hutton, R. 1999 *'Triumph of the Moon'* Ox. Uni Press p4
2. [*ibid.*]
3. Hope-Robins, Russell 1964 *'Encyclopaedia of Witchcraft and Daemonology'* Peter Neville London. p547
4. Hutton, R. 1997 *'Pagan Religions of the Ancient British Isles'* Blackwell UK p335
5. Jones, E.J. 2001 *'Roebuck in the Thicket'* Capall Bann Pub.UK p166

Further Reading:
'The Wiccan Mysteries' by Raven Grimassi
'A History of Witchcraft, Sorcerers, Heretics, and Pagans' by Jeffrey B. Russell
Additional material extrapolated from various original letters and Manuscripts written by the late Robert Cochrane and the late Evan John Jones.

Previously published in: *The New Wiccan* #Vol.7, issue 1 Beltane 2000 (under the nom-de-plume of Agnes Toadflax).
The Cauldron #122 November 2006

20. A Man for all Seasons

"All mystical thought is based upon one major premise; the realisation of Truth as opposed to illusion. The student of the Mysteries is essentially a searcher after Truth, or as the ancient traditions described it, Wisdom. Magic is only a by-product of the search for Truth and holds an inferior position to Truth. Magic, that is the development of total Will, is a product of the soul in its search for ultimate knowledge. It is an afterthought..."

Robert Cochrane - *Pentagram* 1964.

True to his airy birth-sign, Robert Cochrane was mercurial, philosophical and possessed of an insatiable appetite for knowledge that led him ultimately to absorb material from diverse and eclectic sources. No idealist, his realism grounded his feet firmly upon 'terra firma', imbuing him with a zealous passion for life. Yet fire and water were tempestuous forces in the chart of this enigmatic figure. Emotional, aloof, temperamental and energetic, all forces combined within the heart to generate spiritual mysticism, the driving passion of his short life. Such a combination marked him for a true avatar; typically caught in the lure, he was burned out by the chase.

Like any true craftsman, he was able to mold raw material into a magical synthesis, creating a marvellous working system, at once instinctively true and intrinsically beautiful. It has even been claimed that he attended meetings in the early 1960s with an Hereditary Craft group in Cheshire for ritual instruction. Yet by his own admission, Cochrane was more than willing to play the fool, feigning ignorance to acquire knowledge from others, where a real egotist would have wasted Time proclaiming their own rather than listen to others! Languishing for thirteen wasted years in the wilderness wounded him so deeply that his despair thereafter coloured all his work and philosophy, leaving him with a voracious appetite for Truth and Wisdom, allowing him to shed the superficialities of those less desperate than himself.

Ardently in favour of growth and evolution, his mutable genius lay in his adaptability, wherein he retained sacred core concepts, transmuted via any and all available media. Adverse to dogma, perceived by him as the yolk of inspiration, his truths are as free as the wind, yet remain as puzzling as the origin of the Universe. Ultimately, it becomes about where you place yourself in that spectrum, how you choose to discern and define truth, how you choose to be in this ever expanding Universe that draws us ever onwards towards Gnosis; for the world is not flat, the world does spin, man can fly - fact or heresy? It is simply a matter of perspective and 'time'; that of course is relative. So where does that leave us?

Claiming much, he enjoyed histories within Hereditary, and Traditional Craft, describing his faith in terms of: *"It is a religion, mystical in approach and puritanical in attitudes. It is the last real Mystery Cult to survive..."* Yet like Abulafia, another radical (Medieval) mystic, neither prophet was acknowledged within their own Time. Abulafia believed that human beings, as vehicles for change resulting from their own spiritual experience, could and should vitalize old traditions to render them worthy of transmission. Most prophets turn against temporal power, the employment of magics, and manipulation of 'fate.' In reality, abhorring the simplistic rusticity of *"dancing peasants,"* Cochrane proclaimed that the forces of Nature were but a means, not an end. Such a dichotomy presented him with a crisis of conscience. As a member of the 'People', he was obliged to teach the 'five arts' (the four gifted magical skills to each named heir and the fifth, was of the 'blood'), yet as a mystic, upon the path of Gnosis, his soul yearned only for the bliss of union and release.

Moreover, he posited higher truths for the Mysteries in which nothing was as it seemed. The quaint gloss of arcadia merely obfuscated all pervading truth. Writing to Bill Gray, he mentions that the 'old pellars' are far from simple, retaining a deep and complex philosophy as spiritual heirs to the original Mysteries. Cochrane also believed that *"Nothing about Witchcraft is ever stated definitely. It is always left to inference and your (my emphasis) judgement."* He later added: *"Witchcraft is not primarily concerned with messages or morality gained from the dead. It is concerned with the action of God and God upon man and man's position spiritually."*

Nonetheless, I disagree with Cochrane's opinion that divinity and spirituality remain products of the '5th art' - a 'blood' heritage, explained by him thus:

"I cannot die until I have passed my virtue on. I carry within my physical (my emphasis) body the totality of all the Witches that have been in my family for many centuries. If I call upon my ancestors, I call upon forces that are within myself and exterior. Now you know what I mean when I speak of the burden of Time."

This cherished belief, refers more to personal prowess and skills within Hereditary families, being distinct from the 'Clan Egregore' assigned cumulatively through generations of devotion and dedication to the higher spiritual Mysteries, by a physically diverse family drawn as one in spirit; the blood family being but a small cog in the greater spiritual cog of humanity and therefore ultimately of God. Blood is thicker than water, but spirit is more potent than matter. Cochrane's early adherence to the 'blood' principle owes more to his anguish from his 'wilderness' years, later reclaimed but never securely felt, than it does his underlying, instinctive mystical and religious beliefs, never properly defined, at least, not publicly. Rather, I believe our true legacy to be a spiritual one, and thus we are created 'spiritual' heirs. Another heresy?

Moving backwards quickly in 'time' (which is of course a subjective and relative phenomena) now to cull another sacred cow - Pharaoh didn't marry his sisters and daughters to acquire a 'blood' inherited power, but to maintain political control of his empire. Once this practice ceased, his power base crumbled and the rise of the Priests contracted a grip that even the 'heresy' of Akhenaten and his revisionist reforms could not eradicate. Furthermore, not until Pharaoh and his (chosen) Chief wife have undergone certain rituals and proclaimed specific oaths, been anointed by the (King-making) Priests is the spirit of Horus (God) believed to reside within him. Contrary to popular opinion, he is not born with this divinity inherent, but must acquire it by rite and priestly sanction. He is *awarded* this office and sacred duty. So many diverse dynasties ruled Egypt, with no unbroken 'holy' bloodline reaching down through the ages. One Pharaoh simply 'inherits' the title along with the Divine spirit of Horus from his predecessor as a spiritual heritage. This is the true 'Divine' right of Kings, not blood. Joshua became the spiritual heir of Moses (in preference to his own sons) in this way.

The practice of the Tibetan ascension of the Dalai Lama may be similarly viewed. His spirit may re-incarnate anywhere in any person, of low or high birth. Again this is not a heritage of the blood, but one of spirit. It appears that people have become obsessed with the wrong things, sidetracked by the controversial drama of sensation and hype. Atrophied beliefs sound the death knell for Truth, lost in the skirmish for fame and fortune. Simple objective observance reveals otherwise. Inspiration shines forth its yielding light - Gnosis. Truth springs only from an open, progressive mind, not closed within the dogmatic confines of an unyielding status quo. Each of us must discover such truths as these along the path towards

The Truth, and retain the wit not to confuse one with the other.

Moreover, perceived differences between Hereditary and Traditional Craft are invariably petty or superficial and do little to elucidate the real points of departure. It is my belief, and some, though perhaps not all will agree that the Hereditary Craft is generally a tradition that affords the continuation of folk magic, the secret traditions of which are handed down from one generation to the next, concerning for the most part family versions of the One Truth that underpins them all. Autocratic and hierarchical, each family will have its own way of doing things and generally remains closed to outsiders. Their Gods are Tutelary and/or specific ancestral deities having known names.

Traditional Craft on the other hand is often more flexible and eclectic, absorbing current trends by adaptation in order to survive. It has loose associations and affiliations, but is often though by no means always, autonomous. Deities are amorphous, largely unnamed syntheses, referred to vaguely as - 'the Old Uns,' or other quaint colloquialisms. On the other hand, Mystery Schools are about particular initiates, drawn from disparate sources, re-incarnated souls seeking advancement and ultimately, enlightenment. Each will be initiates of differing levels, yet all sharing the same focus, bound by the same spiritual heritage bestowed by angelic forces that designated this sacred Gnosis to mankind aeons ago. The Clan of Tubal Cain is a synthesis of these three principles.

Of course, these are of necessity, broad generalizations, and no discrepancy or offence is to be found in either. Every person must decide for themselves the veracity of each principle; the point is to discern the purpose and function of these often misrepresented and misunderstood distinct schools of thought. Seek and ye shall find, that is the legacy of Cain. That being so I will continue to cull and dispense my herbs into unguents and aromatics, offer healing to those who come to me, teach what knowledge has been imparted to me, but not as 'ye olde wylde wytche', but as an alchemist, a philosopher - an eternal seeker and child of the Mysteries.

And so isn't it Time all this nonsense was laid to rest? My sentiments will regrettably cause offence to some and to those I offer the caveat that each of us is entitled to express our opinions, and so on that premise, I offer my own small voice in a sterile wilderness. Hopefully not all of my words will fall on deaf ears. They are my own, though they clearly reflect those of my spiritual ancestor, Robert Cochrane. As seer, poet, mystic and Gnostic founder of 'The Clan of Tubal Cain', created from within his 'family line,' referred to by him somewhat enigmatically as 'The People of Goda', Cochrane said: *"The genuine Witch is a mystic at heart. Much of the teaching of Witchcraft is subtle and bound within poetical concept rather than hard logic."* There are two things that we as human beings encompass; one is a material body and the other is a spirit, the spark of divinity that animates it. The body dies, decays and ceases to be, whilst the spirit alone lives on. Generation continues to perpetuate the species and provide further vehicles for this spark to incarnate and fulfil its purpose, to find its way home.

Science has proven that everyone is not only related to one another, but to the first humans. This means that, short of inbreeding to the point of extinction, all of us somewhere possess 'Witch-blood' from some ancestor however many genera back. Therefore by Cochrane's reckoning this affords them all *"the ear of the Gods."* Yet we know this simply isn't so. Many children born into 'Witch' families heed not the call of blood, while other, apparent outsiders rise from Divine inspiration to become teachers, prophets and mystics in their own right. Sadly, the need to conform to this fiction also inspires contrived 'bloodlines' as proof of worthiness. Another heresy?

Following the Gnostic line of thought, what is really important is the spiritual heritage alone, for that spark of divinity within us all lays inactive and dormant awaiting development and fruition. There is no elite, chosen race, no privileged minority. This is not a vocation. We have no choice. It is not something we can put down because we don't feel like it. It burns the soul, not the blood. The 'blood' we speak of is metaphoric and refers to that of the Divine son, shed that we might live. Each of us is summoned and that call cannot be ignored. This is exactly why initiation is so vital, so intrinsic to that awakening, of anamnesis that engenders the needs of a seeker asleep upon his path. Sadly, some of us die seeking while others are born knowing. These are the teachers, the avatars who guide and lead us along that path taking an errant humanity by its hand towards the ultimate light. Surrender is a pre-requisite (of self-will to Divine/true will).

Initiation duplicates the first magics, when 'Gods loved Man,' but the golden spark has become corrupted by the dross of a material existence, each disillusioned soul sinking deeper and deeper into the mire. Faith alone can restore this. The great God Pan (Cain, the All-Father) is not dead, how could he be?, for in a truly pantheistic way, the virtue of grace is everywhere, in everything, in everyone; we have only to open our eyes, our hearts and minds to see Truth, Love and Beauty - the absolute Trinity. From the uniquely naïve (in the sense of being open and unsophisticated) perspective of a child, pantheism is simply Monism. "All is One and One is All, and ever more will be so."

Within absolute reality there can be no secrets, the Mystery revealed is one earned via one's own unfailing dedication. It is not spoon-fed, nor is it to be imparted by anyone other than yourself: *"you are your own teacher, as seen through a mirror darkly."* You are your own saviour. In redeeming ourselves we redeem the World Soul, and that is why Robert Cochrane said: *"All Ritual must be Prayer."*

The 'Word' is the vehicle for such transmission and Robert Cochrane used this to great effect, capitalising upon any literature that came his way in which he could overlay his message. Yet sadly, the message was not always well received. Never-the-less, he firmly believed that it was useless to *"cast pearls before swine,"* that gems of knowledge, though artfully concealed within metaphor and innuendo, must reflect the needs and moods of its Time, as eloquently phrased by Baha'u'llah of the Baha'i faith:

> "Follow the way of thy Lord, and say not that which the ears cannot bear to hear, for such speech is like luscious food given to small children. However palatable, rare and rich the food may be, it cannot be assimilated by the digestive organs of a suckling child."

In other words, faith, religion, devotion eschatology, cosmogony must be clearly understood, needed, required, relevant and above all, subject to the times and culture in which they are to be practised. The 'Word' must conform to meet the needs of its recipients or they may not heed it, may not want it, may not recognise it and may not know it. This is why the message must evolve, must never stagnate or become turgid dogma. Thus may the luminosity of the Pearl of Wisdom shine through its simple guises, a truffle worthy of the humblest of creatures.

Previously published in: *The Cauldron* #123 February 2007
The Hedgewytch #40 November 2007

21. The Triune Compass (The Three Rings/Rites)

"...all that can be said about the Mysteries has already been written into folklore, myth and legends. What is not forthcoming is the explanation. It was recognised that these legends, rituals and myths were the roads through the many layers of consciousness to the area of the mind where the soul can exist in its totality. These and their surrounding disciplines and teachings became what the West describe as the Mysteries." Robert Cochrane

Robert Cochrane, atavistic spirit, former (late) Magister and founder of 'The Clan of Tubal Cain' believed there to be few genuine cuveens extant throughout the British Isles, wherein few 'real' Crafters generated actual power via the flux of polarised gender imbued with genera of virtue culminating in a co-hesive fusion, or magical harmonic. Moreover, he insisted this 'natural' state could not be acquired but was a 'blood' gift in the full and traditional sense. Even so, as an avid reader of Leland, Graves and Murray, it is unsurprising that he was influenced by ideas promulgated throughout their pages. One book in particular, mentioned by Cochrane in one of his letters - *'Etruscan Roman Remains in Popular Tradition'*[1] mentions the strongly held principle among Etruscans that a Witch/Wizard [sic] could not die until his/her 'power' had been transferred to another, ceded somewhat possessively within 'bloodlines'. In its original context this simply meant that the soul was irredeemable until it had 'passed on' its accrued 'karma', or measure of 'sin' embodied within the transient authority bestowed cumulatively from one generation to the next.

Moreover, Cochrane's phrase that a Witch loses his/her power when 'blooded' by an outsider is also reflected later in this book where Leland [*ibid.*] relates folklore of the Northern Italians who remained convinced that if a Witch loses one drop of blood whilst engaging in a supernatural act against anyone not of their Clan, family or tribe, their power would drain away with it, the daemonic 'spirit' within now freed, from its venal prison. Contra to this, I would also like to assert that true genius is in fact a Divine gift, a spiritual gift that cannot be inherited on a cellular level. Bearing this in mind I should like to introduce the reader to just a few of the bewildering works of this enigmatic figure, through a beguiling a maze of metaphor in order to reveal something of his uniquely poetic acumen whereby it is hoped a greater understanding of his spiritual legacy may be achieved.

Convinced he was the repository of almost three centuries of hereditary Gnosis, he proselytised a surprisingly 'modern' perspective of Traditional Craft practices. His idiosyncratic expositions accentuated his innovative flair for evolutionary and militant interpretation. As a radical reformer of his religion he aspired to integrate disparate views, to consolidate them en masse in opposition to the then newly emerging and popular 'Wica' [sic].Naturally, working methodologies differed considerably, in accord with their inherent philosophies, creeds, Mythos et cetera; yet some basic similarities prevailed, affording common ground, recognised and appreciated by all traditional practitioners of their arte. Even so he expounded his belief that instinctive and intuitive modus operandi were infinitely superior to dogmatic working by rote, asserting that form (Purusha - black, passive) that is, the structure and symbolism of the ritual was secondary to force (Prakriti - white, active) invoked, or how this virtue is won, maintained and assimilated. In this he recognised three basic ritual forms fundamental to all those of the 'True Faith'; named 'The Three Rites,' they refer to each of three rings that inculcate the following formulae of the Compass:

1. Divination - retrieval of information from the Akasha;
2. Spell-casting and other acts of Magic - invocation of heavenly force applied through will and intent;
3. Communion - evocation of mystical energy, experienced and shared by the whole group.

Cochrane defines the rings (working areas) as 'a map of the other worlds' but emphasises how all tools and words spoken are relevant only within the actual rites, beyond this demarcation, their intrinsic value devolves into mere fantasy and delusion. This is an important point, often overlooked in common magical practise. Furthermore, any ritual involving all three forms embraces the Qabbalistic principles of the Three Primary Mothers of Creation - Fire, Water and Air (Shin, Mem and Aleph) and the resurrection of the Father through the Son as the Horn Child, a core Mystery of archaic provenance. This antique Trinity of Truth, Love and Beauty are reflected within the tripartite Nature of mankind, i.e. spirit (pneuma), matter (hyle) and soul (psyche) respectively and are alchemical principles that feature as basic tenets of mysticism.

The Three Mothers also represent Fate, Destiny and Eternity and their primal qualities formulate elemental virtues evoked as Air within the First Rite - the medium of transmission, inspiration, extrapolated from the winds, auguries and omens. In the Second Rite, Fire manifests in the kinetic energy of metal, the forged material of the knife, sword and stang and thus the innovator of power. Finally, the Third Rite utilizes Water as an emotional quality acquiescent within the womb matrix, the memory and nerve centre of life and the Universe itself; embodies the timeless virtues of patience and omniscience.

In addition, the Three Rings/Rites conceal the Mysteries of the Triune form of the Hunter, Tubal Cain and the Roebuck in the Thicket. Yet, they must not be considered as hierarchical nor confused with stages of Initiatory development, rather, they should be understood as pertaining to the modes of ingress, congress and egress. Psychologically and in Jungian terms, these transmute as Intra-psychic, Inter-psychic and Extra-psychic forces, having natural compatibilities with the three celestial stases exhibited through the stellar/Lunar, Lunar/Earth and Earth/Solar currents. Each of these Rites is 'opened' differently, using tools appropriate to the 'Ring' or theme of the Mask (discussed later, under 'tools').

It is noteworthy that unlike Wicca or Neo-Pagan circle casting, the 'ring' denotes the separation of sacred space only, from surrounding mundanity; it does not delineate protected space, neither does it conserve energy raised within it precincts. This important distinction highlights a conceptual gulf between these uncompromising factions. The 'ring' may also encompass a complete ritual arena, comprising of more than one circle, dancing grounds, areas of preparation e.t.c. It is in fact a temporal boundary in no way affording a liminal shift between the realms. For devotional and Solar rites, the charges are delivered sunwise/deosil, but for acts of magic and divination they are delivered widdershins, making full use of the geomantic forces of the Earth's motion.

In the First Rite, the Cuveen stang is placed centrally (see diagram) emulating the axial pole and geomantic omphalos of the Universe where the Paracelsion character of chthonic theory or forces of the 'Stang and Serpent' are employed to open this 'ring.' When placed to the South (Earth), squaring the circle with the staves of the elements, the 'Broom and Lamp' form the bridge that fords the magical tides of manifest causes. When placed in the North, it becomes the central pillar, flanked by those of the horn (severity) and knife (mercy). North is the draconian gate of power, perceived as the sacred Gate of Heaven. Typically the Stang resides here, as primary altar. It is Daath upon the Tree and as such it represents the Time/space continuum of ascent. Purists would argue how the Qabbalah has no place in the Traditional Craft, yet many qabbalists readily discern concepts cognate with that system. Moreover, Cochrane's own work reflects clear Qabbalistic influence, noted by the eminent (late) Magus William Gray with whom he worked and shared much correspondence.

The schematic serves to reveal the fluid mobility of the secondary altar (commonly a chest or reliquary housing Clan totems, fetishes and other impedimenta), the cauldron and other wands and staffs pertinent to the season, Nature of rite and relevance to the first, second or third 'ring.' For workings of the First Rite, a skull, fiery symbol of (the Alder God) Bran as the oracular head is placed (west), asserting the emphasis on the Lord of the Mound. This is juxtaposed with the watery cauldron of rebirth (east). A caithir rod (north) rests upon the secondary altar placed to draw directly from the stellar regions of the Hyperborea. This opposes a Horned Crown mounted upon the Summoner's staff (south). This format focuses a power zone from east and west into the northern quadrant of the ring (air - divination). △

Looking at the 'ring' of the Second Rite, it exposes another conceptual shift: the secondary altar has moved to the centre, the fire and cauldron stand in the east (fire) opposing the Summoner's staff in the west (water). A riding pole in the north (air) supports a lamp that radiates the flow of creative energy. This opposes the broom in the south (Earth).The cuveen stang, 'masked' and garlanded is also placed in the south. Charges, chants and prayers evoke the aspect appropriate to the Sabbat upon the Stang as supreme representative of the Horned God, 'Divil' or Master. This format focuses the power zone that 'squares' the circle from all cardinal points into the centre of the ring (fire - invocation of 'heavenly forces'). △

Finally, for the Third Rite, the masked and garlanded stang becomes the Master of Ceremonies in the north (named by Cochrane as the 'farmer' - Cain, the Father of all) accompanying the Magister's hand staff. In the opposite quarter the secondary altar holds the mirror and the pentacle, or whetstone, balancing the horn in the west partnered by the knife on the east. Central to all of this a fire burns beneath the 'charged pot.' This Rite only, maintains the true correspondences of the tools symbolic of their elements invoking the archaic and alchemical cross of power. These four magical tools are also coterminous with the Grail weapons having associations with ancient rites of Kingship and the 'Hieros Gamos.' This format focuses a power zone from the east and west into the southern quadrant of the ring (water - evocation/manifestation). ▽

Austin spare believed that: *"will is our medium; belief is the vehicle and desire the force for raising of magickal energy."* Such perennial truisms are in accord with the 'Law of Seven' which states that four qualities are imperative to the success of any one of these Three Rites: emotion, symbolism, direction, and aspiration, which when combined with unity (of purpose), leadership (including a balanced and harmonic Egregore) will conclude in the seventh that of a manifest and comprehendible Godhead. This is one way in which the 'seven become one'; thus all alchemy is fused in the completion and communion of all magicks and bliss achieved in the climactic act of this final stage of the sacrament.

Eight Watchers comprised of four pairs, (of opposite gender), one incarnate, one discarnate hold the first level – the corporeal Compass, together with Magister, Maid, Summoner, Seer and Scribe form the minimum pre-requisite of 13, though generally these (ideal) roles are not so easily accommodated. A quaternary of power is engendered from the twin masculine forces of Apollonian (air) and Dionysian (fire) magics harmonised with the female primal watery Hekate in her manifest (Earth) and un-manifest forms (water, or primal abyss) and all symbols used must represent the aspect of Godhead synonymous with purpose.

On a mythological level the thirteen tools can be said to relate directly to the Thirteen Treasures of Britain for which Arthur traversed the Hollow Hills of the Underworld - 'Caer Annwyn'. This is the telling of the 'Mound and the Raven'. Each tool/weapon/treasure plays a significant role in the rings empowered by them. A cursory study impresses their import as symbolic on all four planes:

Skull - pharmacopoeia of dew-filled manna; Bran, oracular Alder God; Q'ayin, God of smith craft and agriculture, Baal, fertility God of fire, prophecy, craft, and death, of magic, alchemy: *"all things of this world belong to him, the star-crossed serpent."*

Horned Crown - animal totem, a symbol of the anointed, chosen or blessed, emblem of supreme right to assume Divine authority, tool of office, vinculum of bestial morphology.

Mirror - mirrored doorway into the astral realms, and macro-cosmic

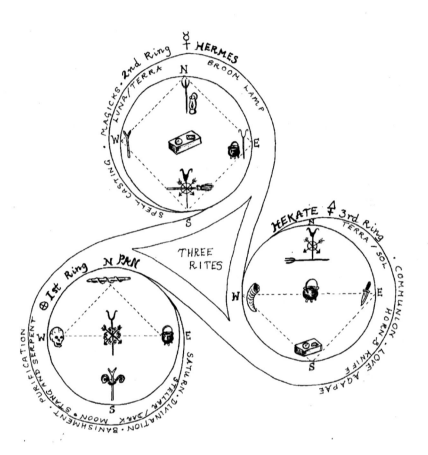

'Triune Compass Rosa'

reflector of virtue. Gateway of ingress and egress.

Pentacle/whetstone - elemental symbol of protection and kingship. Grail - *'lapsit exhillis'* *(Earth)*

Horn/cup - Cornucopia of abundance, female (receptive) genitalia *(water)*. Feminine Mysteries of Creation and Destruction.

Knife/sickle - experience, knowledge, victory, conflict, courage, choice, sacrifice, physical love, intuition, inspiration, supreme tool of balance, without which it cannot be used. Small knives may be substituted for three nails in acts of cursing. Its wielder holds the powers of life or death, justice or mercy….therefore it is temperance. *(fire)* Masculine Mysteries incorporating the 'Order of the Sun' and the Grail Mysteries.

Staff/stang - conveying more than authority, it is ancient totemic power, invested by might. It represents the supreme 'right' in continuity and perpetuity from inception of absolute awareness of status. It is the manifold symbol of Tutelary spirit, indicating the presence of manifest deity. Thus it becomes the altar of sacrifice – the Rose of the Hearth. It is the nightmare and middle pillar of Yggdrasil *(air)* stang: Godhead, unity & point of union/sacrifice and at-one-ment. Old and Young Horn King. Manifestation, absolute power. Supreme altar. Love. Truth and Beauty. Representing the hermaphrodite it embodies male and female virtue, wisdom and the third Mystery. The term 'masking' relates to specific symbols placed upon the stang relative to the rite performed in the form of tools and garlands, and to the actual totem animal mask or skull. These may also be mirrored upon the Magister. In its most basic form the 'Mask' represents the four worlds of the Qabbalah, described elsewhere upon the original basic sketch allegedly drawn by Robert Cochrane. At its base rests the gateway of Malkut (Assiah), seen as the serpent, the geomantic force of the Earth. Next, crossed arrows (Yetzirah) delineate the two opposing triangles of fire/air-male and water/Earth-female. When conjoined they superimpose to produce the hexagram (Briah), the graphic representation of the archaic 'yab-yum' in which the active female mounts the passive male. A crescent Moon cradles a circle of stars, the eight stations of the Sun (Atziluth) - the Horns of Venus, the Master's crown mirrored by the stars of the Zodiacal mantle, of Nuit herself. Beyond Her lies the primal abyss. This simplistic analysis offers the merest glimpse of its eternal Mysteries. The diagram central to the original sketches conclusively parallels a philosophy correlate with Qabbalistic metaphysics.

Cloak - beyond humility, concealment and protection, this encompasses the 'true' self - the shadow, the absolute self, the ego we are required to fully integrate as the magical 'self', the mind evolves in accord with True Will. i.e. -Divine Will.

Rods/wands/spear - Caithir rod: ancestral authority etymologically linked to seat/throne, it also means 'big' and is commonly used as a blasting or cursing weapon, also for 'charming'. Generally carved from antler, bone or crystal, but occasionally wood, in which case alder is preferred. Pointed at one end, it is suggestive of the spear. Keppen rod: a measuring tool (synonymous with a 'ruler,' ergo a symbol of authority/kingship/lineage), it also symbolises spirit, illumination and eternity, seen by many as the equivalent to the Egyptian ankh. This is often forked at one end, sharpened and indicates a weapon of sacrifice similar to the hand staff carried by the Magister. Spear: pierces the cauldron with its metal (iron) tipped point (Khronos) as an act of love in which the principle of life draws down the Moon into the flux of the Mother (Hekate) to generate the *'Aqua Vitae'* - the red blood of life…spirit brought to manifestation.

Besom - paradoxically a male phallic tool as symbol of civilization and domestication, therefore despised by Italian Witches (who 'rode goats or wolves to the Sabbaths'). Used in stamping dances, it is 'worn' over the shoulders (like a weapon). Female tool as instrument by which the 'family' *"turn without motion between three elements"* (earth, air and water - hazel, ash and willow). The fourth is fire - the flying ointment allegedly applied to its shaft. Thus like the riding pole it is the mount of flight, the instrument of ascent and pathway to the Mysteries. The riding pole in another sense is the night-mare of hypnogogic dreamscapes.

Cauldron - abyss, void, flux, wisdom, generation, creation. Remember the true meaning of the cauldron *"…bring forth the star son, and you have Dionysus, the Horn Child and Jesus Christ in one…"* (Son of the Father, prophet and sacrificial king).

Cords/girdles/garters - symbol of sacrifice and subjugation, birth, death, a Witches' ladder or rosary, a spellbinder. In folk magic it is used for spellcraft. It is our own personal strand of fate, ours to hold and weave, guided by will into the great web, the ultimate matrix and key to our destiny. Synonymous with the scourge it also represents submission, stimulation, surrender, discipline, fealty, ascent and descent. As substitutes of the Tephillin and phylacteries (Jewish bindings embodying the power of prayer and the 'word' for use in the Merkavah Mysteries) they generate the virtue of sacred charms and chants, protecting and purifying.

Arrows - Two arrows, one black, one white (the archaic colours of Fate) form a cross upon the stang suggestive of the 'Lunar cross' of Bride, although conversely, it also represents the holy cross of the Gnostics and Mithraic initiates. They also suggest the twin pillars of Joachim and Boaz. Within Tubal Cain, this cross essentially represents the arrows of Neith, the primal Mother, who protects, creates and destroys us. As a Universal and primal deity, Neith has other 'weapons'- a sceptre (symbol of rule and power) and the ankh (symbol of life). Also known as the 'Cow of Heaven,' this Sky-Goddess is cognate with Nuit giving birth to the Sun daily and creates both primeval Time and cyclical Time. Formed from two v's, one upward and one downward, they are in fact the chalice/womb and the blade/phallus, depicting the conjoined virtues of both to manifest Charis, or Grace. Therefore *Solar, Lunar* and *stellar* fluxes combine in this one simple symbol.

The 'ring' itself can be aspected as the 'threshing floor,' where such rites were known and recorded up to 1873 (In fact the Regency revived a ritual exemplifying this concept). During Harvest-Time, a 'bride' performed the anointing amidst family members who danced and paid homage to a table and a throne made from planks drawn from the threshing fields. A significant magical precedent for this is known in Biblical times when David purchased threshing fields as an arena to house a sacred (high) altar in Jerusalem, in thanks for its continued abundance during plagues and pestilence that had decimated surrounding areas. The site is believed by many to have been Mount Moriah.

In a letter sent to Norman Gills ascribed to Cochrane, is an enigmatic list that outlines the 'Basic Structure of the Craft;' its content incorporates principles and symbolisms of 'The Three Rings/Rites,' the thirteen ritual tools and many coterminous praxes taught to us by E. J. Jones. More than anything Robert Cochrane ardently asserted that the Craft preserved no great secrets, that everything could be won for those brave and true enough to traverse the many realms of existence. Yet he also recognised in the Mysteries a premise that can never be taught - only full experiential and initiatory immersion can induce their apprehension. Indeed a Sufi parable succinctly concludes this Truth:

"Even though a donkey be laden with books, it is still only a donkey."

Notes and References:

1. Leland, C, G. *'Etruscan Roman Remains in Popular Tradition'* 1892 T. Fisher Unwin Pub.
   All other material relative to this brief exposition may be found liberally dispersed throughout: *'The Roebuck in the Thicket'* 2001 and *'The Robert Cochrane Letters'* 2002 both written by E.J. Jones and edited by Michael Howard. Capall Bann Pub. UK.

Previously published in: The Cauldron #124 May 2007

23. Traditional Enigma

Many though by no means all practitioners within the Craft today be they Neo-Pagan or modern revivalists, wittingly or unwittingly, generally follow distinct precepts as promulgated by Gerald B. Gardner. These praxes have until recently, dominated all Craft media such that alternatives seemed almost unimaginable. Two articles were penned in response to widespread interest in non-Wiccan Craft: 'The Three Rings'/ Rites(The Triune Compass) and its companion piece, 'The Alchemy of the Compass,' that subsequently generated several enquiries. Some questions raised within these correspondences, concerned general points of divergence between material presented in these articles and those typical of 'Wicca' (though naturally, not all questions raised were discussed); others ranged from authenticity of the rites to who and how many groups practise them today. For those interested parties who declined to make contact, the following may be of interest. Regarding authenticity, they are indeed and have precedents that will shortly be revealed. As to who and how many, may not be stated, suffice, however, to highlight the divers and autonomous clans and families who abide by their own lore and custom relative to each tradition. So, while there are many similarities throughout the Traditional Craft in general, the following authoritative statements apply only to my own: that of 'The Clan of Tubal Cain'.

My mentor and former Magister, the late Evan John Jones brought a good deal of traditional lore to 'Clan Tubal Cain' (then under the Magisterial auspices of the late Robert Cochrane), when he became a member in the 1960s, as in fact did several others, whose former knowledge and experience substantially enriched the locus of 'Clan Tubal Cain'. These things were frequently discussed as part of a direct one-to-one mentoring process, a pattern no doubt repeated between later students of other Clan members when it splintered in the wake of Robert Cochrane's untimely death in 1966, forming several groups with related practises. These teachings have over subsequent decades been widely disseminated, existing in many recognizable or similar formats throughout the Traditional Craft, and which continue to enrich and inspire more recent Craft innovators. In fact I have been privy to considerable examples of such material, which, despite claims to be innovative or ground-breaking, are actually sourced from Clan lore and its praxes. Yet still other workers, in particular, the late Andrew D Chumbley, made profound use in his 'Azoetia' of the basic magical and psychological principles of the three fundamental pedagogical occult modes that are intrinsically linked to the three rites as expounded by Robert Cochrane himself, who said: *"there are three basic rituals common to all members of the true faith."*[1] One rite Cochrane describes in terms relative to divination, the second in terms of thaumaturgy, and the third is pure theurgy.

Enigmatically, in another letter to Joe Wilson,[2] Robert Cochrane refers again to the three parts of the 'Faith', of which he says he knows only two - that of the masculine and the feminine Mysteries, one Solar, apprehending the conscious, civilising force; one Lunar, being concerned with the intuitive unconsciousness. In typical fashion, he goes on to explain to Joe, how the 'third' Mystery is lost, a certain tease, because later in the same letter, he breaks down the Solar and Lunar Mysteries by analogy with symbols on a French Menhir, one line devoted to each of these Mysteries. He concludes by almost throwing away the fact that the last line relates to the third part of the 'Mysteries' - that of the earthly priest/magician adding a clear directive that understanding the whole thing will divulge the complete basis of the 'Faith'. There is so much more to this than is immediately apparent, especially in light of the aforementioned information above.

Similarly, emotive mysticism and magical potential articulated within Robert Cochrane's own short but succinct description of this break down of the three rites into conceptual modalities intrigued me sufficiently to explore these matters in greater depth with Evan John Jones over several years. Evan John Jones also makes a guarded and considered reference to three aspects of setting the ring, somewhat modified for public consumption, which also require separate sites, relative again to purpose.[3] Over Time, the Mysteries within Robert Cochrane's teachings have sustained the interest of many students whose own research, summaries, teaching/lecture notes bear witness to this enigmatic source.

Moreover, despite being introduced to (Evan) John (Jones) and the Traditional Craft before ever I entered 'Wicca,' I became a Wiccan initiate prior to my eventual elevation within the Clan, having no expectations for it beyond hope. Once inducted into the Clan I discovered its concepts to be a fascinating window into other worlds, previously unexplored, including most particularly the three related Druidic rings/realms and those of Faerie. I was however, familiar with some intriguing illustrations and material regarding a 15th century French miniature, mentioned and discussed speculatively in varying degrees of interpretation by Liddell,[4] whose placement of geometric power zones is quite thought provoking (a variant is herein depicted within my own illustrations, alluding to the triune Mysteries), a concept he believes is echoed in 'Celtic' Druidism. This proffers significant links to the Masonic placement of officers, though Valiente[5] asserts this as a source of much later Witch lore; Prof. Hutton,[6] considers this and a similar illustration within the critical context of Craft historiography as widely published images since 1952.[7]

What these two early illustrations clearly reveal is the accepted premise of a ritual space, in fact or conjecture, demarked by four (commonly wooden) agricultural implements, one to each Compass point; a clear precursor for subsequent development. North is presented as the location ascribed to deity, and male and female oppose each other at the cardinal points, forming the familiar 'cross' quarters. Modern Craft practises range from this deceptively simple formulae to considerably more sophisticated ones. The crude illustration of the three basic rings offered within my own article falls somewhere in the middle and is sourced entirely from the variant and dispersed teachings of Robert Cochrane, enriched and supplemented by Evan John Jones' own wide personal repertoire.

With the exception of the referenced appendages to Robert Cochrane's schematics, the auxiliary graphics, again, are devised by myself, based upon Clan material discussed with Evan John Jones. They will undoubtedly and unavoidably share certain superficial similarities to several that may be found elsewhere, particularly those influenced by the teachings of Robert Cochrane, or that can trace their source to them, each set pertinent to each group's own interpretation and practice of the three basic rings. Obviously, to a point only, do these diagrams reflect an impression of these concepts.

Although much of the material explored had already been available to the public for some Time, specifically within both Robert Cochrane's and Evan John Jones' own published works, this summative correlation places it within a wider craft perspective, suggesting a more encompassing context for those workers inspired by cumulative teachings. Liddell further articulates other pertinent issues raised by this enigmatic miniature with regard to some known and some more speculative traditions of the Craft. Some of these, particularly in respect to levels of induction, Clanship structure, including the fealty of kindred groups, placement and role of officers, totemism, the devotional use of cords/halters, the allegiance to Lucifer as the indwelling mechanism of evolution and the sole transfer of

Virtue to a chosen successor and spiritual heir are quite illuminating and serve again to stress imperatives that distinguish Traditional Craft practises from those of Wicca.

With regard to both Evan John Jones's and Robert Cochrane's own writings, much too has been made of the purpose and use of the Stang both within 'The Cauldron'[8] and within various letters to Bill Gray[9] and one letter to Norman Gills,[10] specifically. The latter, in particular refers obliquely to the way the Stang as a sacred altar is 'masked' according to the rite being performed. The appropriate tools placed before it, garlands upon it and the Clan animal totem affixed to it, have of necessity been omitted, though Evan John Jones had previously made some discreet references to these placements in 'Sacred Mask, Sacred Dance,'[11] and the 'Mask' diagrams have long been accessible to perhaps the more curious seeker of their mystique. Therefore, those who work this stream with integrity and intuition will find much of satisfaction and interest.

Within my own article, the 'Stang' is described and depicted in relation to other implements placed around the ring itself. However, two illustrations were added to Robert Cochrane's schematic, thus revealing graphically how the Qabbalistic Tree of Life and the Druidic realms share similar associations within the Craft, which again increases their application across wider perspectives of modern Craft modalities. Within the 'Alchemy of the Compass' these mystical precepts are given greater depth for seasoned Crafters, again in accord with several known works already explored by Evan John Jones in his books and many articles for 'The Cauldron'.

It was his earnest wish that these rites be fully developed and put into firm and devotional practise fulfilling both his and Robert Cochrane's magical argosies. We worked together to that end - and this was my closure on that promise, a culmination of knowledge and experiential Gnosis, from inception at the source through to fruition via confirmed and attested spiritual inheritance. My objective in this was ever to revitalise these disparate themes with the breath of continuity, drawn directly from the Egregoric spirit imparted to me, to engage all the streams Robert Cochrane's legacy may have inspired, both private and public.

All written sources used are published and widely available; they are herein noted for interested parties to pursue, and anyone who is already an ardent student will readily discern those teachings within both my afore mentioned articles; for those who are unfamiliar with Robert Cochrane's filtered legacy, these two companion pieces will hopefully invite that study.

This brief addendum will be closed with rather a lengthy but extremely relevant quotation from the work of Robert Cochrane. Again, typical of his philosophy, it merits deep and contemplative analysis to bear true fruit.

"The real Mystery is only uncovered by the individual, and cannot be told, but only pointed to. Any occultist who claims to have secrets is a fake - the only secret is that which man does not understand - otherwise all wisdom is an open book to those who would read it. One is discreet about certain things because of blank incomprehension or misunderstanding, but wisdom comes only to those who are ready (my emphasis) to receive it - therefore much of the nonsense believed by Gardnerians and hereditary groups alike is concerned with secrecy. There is no secret in the world that cannot be discovered, if the recipient is ready (my emphasis) to listen to it - since the very air itself carries memory and knowledge. Those men that speak of secrets and secrecy and not of discretion or wisdom are those who have not discovered truth. I personally distrust those who would make secrets - since I suspect their knowledge to be small. I was taught by an old woman who remembered the great meetings - and she took no terrible oath from me, but just an understanding that I would be discreet. She did not require silence, only a description of what I had seen and what I had heard and said when I was admitted. The Gods are truly wise - they know the future as well as the past and they admit not those who would abuse knowledge or wisdom."

Robert Cochrane

Notes and References:

1. Jones, E.J. 2002 *'The Robert Cochrane Letters'* M. Howard [Ed]. Capall Bann UK (letter 8 to fellow Crafter and cunning man Norman Gills), pp 170-1

2. [*ibid.*] p51-53

3. Jones, E.J. & Clifton, C. 1997 *'Sacred Mask Sacred Dance'* Llewellyn Pub USA pp 161-2

4. Liddell, W.E. 1994 *'The Pickingill Papers'* [ed] Howard, M. Capall Bann UK pp48-63

5. Valiente, D. 1984 *'The ABC of Witchcraft'* Robert Hale London p266

6. Hutton, R. 1999 *'Triumph of the Moon'* Ox. Uni Press. UK p294

7. Hope-Robins, Russell 1964 *'Encyclopaedia of Witchcraft and*

Daemonology' Peter Neville London. p31

8. TC#76 1995
9. Jones, E.J. 2002 *'The Robert Cochrane Letters'* [ed] Howard, M. Capall Bann UK p74
10. Jones, E.J. 2002 *'The Robert Cochrane Letters'* [ed] Howard, M. Capall Bann UK p166
11. Jones, E.J. & Clifton, C. 1997 *'Sacred Mask Sacred Dance'* Llewellyn Pub USA pp 160-1

Previously published in: *The Cauldron* #129 August 2008

23. The Alchemy of the Compass

"Human beings are alchemical metals - and we change from dross to gold slowly… it is the work of Godhead on that person, and the gold increases according to how it is cherished... it is the gold of spirit, sometimes dulled by foolishness - other times shining bright. It is only bought by our personal search for the Grail, the Holy Cauldron."
Robert Cochrane

Within the traditions of the Horse-whisperers is preserved the secret nay-word of Cain, first smith and Master of the Horse. Pico della Mirandola, a Renaissance Hermeticist profoundly expresses this underlying concept as: *"The Work of Magic is nothing more than marrying the Universe."* Both fraternities seek to achieve Divine communion via manipulation and mastery of the four elements within the fifth - the Quintessence. This reification affirms the Golden Chain of cosmic synthemata of the Hermetic macro-microcosm between man (matter) and God (spirit).

The Upanishads speak of four states of the soul: waking; dreaming (hypnogogic); deep-sleep (oneiric) and spirit waking (astral/lucid venturing). In this last state the unsleeping spirit seeks ecstasy bound within infinite vision (*Turiya*). Beyond the order of the other three, the astral form becomes both seer and creator of his/her own absolution. Robert Cochrane, poet and mystic, devised (though never completed them himself) a set of four rites embodying Traditional Craft elements that were syncretised within a greater body of mystic corpus.

Unusually, these rituals are conducted for the most part in silence and stillness, consecutive periods of action and in-action, poise and motion, that separate and refine the focus of the aspirant to the zero-still point where *"man transcends Time to become One with God."* Ceremonial invocations are simply meditational aids, mere commands to the supra-conscious, as are the chants, calls and use of sigils; real transformation as an induction towards illumination is engendered by the action of subjugation, of total surrender to the forces invoked.

Cochrane opined that the keys to understanding truth lay with the guardians of each Tradition, discarnate ancestors and deific forms who benefit the next generation of spiritual heirs. *"Prayer is the ladder that binds the body to the Earth whilst the soul ascends into the dizzying heights of the heavens."* Magical subtlety is about inference rather than obfuscation, in a world where things are not always as they seem. This 'Grail quest' correlates with the fulfilment of Gnosis under the 'Order of the Sun', the life's work of a true mystic. Importantly, in one of his letters to Bill Gray, Cochrane discusses the 'Invocation of Fire,' utilised as either an elemental or angelic force; in another letter, he stresses the twin forces of Air and Fire, both masculine, draconian energies of completion.

Cochrane understood the cyclic Nature of wisdom asserting how its discovery *"creates the alchemy that brings forth an answer."* Among his many teachings the controversial and enigmatic '1734' numbers have generated profuse and diverse speculation.[1] Often complex, they all reveal something of the poetic and individual Nature of his work. And yet, fundamentally, within Clan practise, the reality is deceptively simple: One 'Will' to open the seven gates to the triune (three) God of the four square garden. The Solar cross of 'The Clan of Tubal Cain's compass essentially formulates the celestial substance of the central Monad, where four qualities cross-polarize in perfect balance. This central core or neutral zone is where one may achieve enlightenment - 'Unio Mystica'. Exogenous to the traditional nine knots of the Witches ladder (four Solar rites, four Lunar rites, plus one other at Twelfth Night) are four additional rites that facilitate unfolding mystical pathways exemplified within 'The Clan of Tubal Cain' as a seasonal quaternary. Alchemy is the science of God, our gift of transmutation from matter into spirit or the body of light and bliss - Premdeha.

Three philosophical principles of hyle (body), psyche (soul) and spirit (mind) fuse with those of the trinity to render the body subject to an alchemical transmutation paralleling the cumulative allegory of the quaternary of rites. Known in the outer as the 'Rose Beyond the Grave', 'The Cave of the Cauldron', 'The Stone Stile' and 'The Castle of the Four Winds', this crucial tetrad can be further demonstrated to reflect the four worlds of the Qabbalah, moving from Assiah to Atziluth. Beginning with the 'Stone Stile,' the aspirant delineates physical boundaries, defining the ritual landscape, preparing the bridge and consecrating all tools required for the work. Next, they will engage the 'Castle of the Four Winds', the repository of all power and knowledge for those tools of the mind needed to forge the journey ahead. After this, the nebulous and fluid qualities of the Fates are sought in 'The Cave of the Cauldron' for insights and confirmations of possible outcomes and pathways to bring the work to fruition.[2] Finally, in the 'Rose Beyond the Grave', each aspirant is finally prepared to conjoin knowledge generated by the previous three workings into a highly experiential rite wherein one realises the Ultimate Truth of all things *'Khabs em Pekt'* (light in extension). A Mystery beyond comprehension: shhh, silence - the riddle of the sphinx.

The cross of elements that form Malkut can be seen to express the baptismal cross of both Gnostic and Mithraic initiatic traditions. Spirit and matter intersect dead centre, the zero-point of equilibrium or trans-liminal phase of Maat. This womb of Nuit, astral gateway to the numinous deep of the duat or daath, is entered by trance induced states acquired by conscious engagement of liturgical faculties expressed by each of the four rites, singularly and cumulatively. Here the veil is ruptured and the essence of the Grail partaken.

It is said that cyclical rites of transmutation within the 'Great Work' are undertaken in no less than three years, and this tetrad is no exception. Beginning in the Spring of the first year, under the astrological auspices of the Taurean Bull, the first rite of the 'Stone Stile' is executed; then, some nine months later when brought to fruition, the second rite 'Castle of the Four Winds' is undertaken in the following Winter under the angelic aegis of Aquarius. Similarly, with two more intervals of nine months, the final two rites are performed in Autumn, 'Cave of the Cauldron' and the following Summer, 'Rose Beyond the Grave', under Scorpio and Leo respectively.

Nine final months conclude the cycle, returning the aspirant to the point of origin, where the process may be repeated, until thus annealed, the tempered soul acquires the adamantine body of enlightenment. Thus the ring is traversed in 36 months, a full circumambulation of 360 degrees. Each quarter section equal to one of the four faces of Brahma represents the four stages of mind to which the aspirant must focus his will during each successive period of repose and activity. Again, we have individuation 1 achieved in seven stages 7, in three years 3, through four rites 4. A table of correspondences indicates specific points of reference pertinent to each rite including the curious association of the Four Horsemen of the Apocalypse. These are of course relevant to the stages of the journey and the theme of each rite.

Compass point	SOUTH	NORTH	WEST	EAST
Colour/horse	Black	White	Grey/pale	Red
Element	Earth	Air	Water	Fire
Alchemical stage	Blackening	Whitening	Yellowing	Reddening
Physical state	Body	Mind	Heart	Will
Sensory quality	Sensing	Thinking	Feeling	Intuition
Magickal phrase	Tascere	Noscere	Audere	Velle
Virtue	Fortitude	Prudence	Temperance	Justice
Manifest quality	Flesh	Humours	Bones	Spirit
Apocalyptic weapon	Balance	Bow & crown	Death/ scythe	Sword
Apocalyptic beast	Bull	Angel	Eagle	Lion
Quaternary of Rites	Stone stile	Castle of the 4 Winds	Cave of the Cauldron	Rose Beyond the grave
Nature of rite	Boundaries	Power	Divination/ prophecy	Death /rebirth – union.
Conscious state	Conscious	Sub-conscious	Un-conscious	Supra-conscious
Qabbalistic plane	Assiah	Yetzirah	Briah	Atziluth
Season	Spring	Winter	Autumn	Summer
Principle of change	Solidifying	Movement	Meta-morphosis	Quickening /dis-integration
Astrological sign	Taurus	Aquarius	Scorpio	Leo
Tetragrammaton	He	Vau	Heh	Yod

In addition, four archangels and four princes of daemon are invoked as custodians and executors of these rites. Of enormous esoteric significance, the no. 40 represents perfection and the 'perfect prayer'; each quarter segment of the circle of rites is given the value of 10 (reflecting again the male/female harmonic) in order that the rites accrue this figure symbolising the expiation and penitence essential for disintegration of negative karma, purification and individuation.

Co-terminous to transmutation of the fool within the Grail legends, the soul seeks illumination via the 'Holy Paraclete,' also perceived as the One; On, the mythical fiery Phoenix, primal fire and supreme God of light is Eros/ Phanes Protogenus - *"Love in all forms is the one and same force, the mark of divinity upon man."* Such an undertaking requires the release, resolution and perfection of the three philosophic principles of hyle (body), psyche (soul) and pneuma (spirit). In the Merkavah Mysteries of the Qabbalah, the ten emanations by the supernals become seven qualities, which by the four elements become the three Divine hypostases, which by the polarity of two become One, viz: philosophical Mercury or the Hermetic Dragon-the crowned hermaphrodite or perfected one.

Medieval Qabbalists based their glyph of the tree on an earlier Chaldean model which illustrated eight rings, spheres/levels. Ascension occurs on the 8th rung of the *'Scala Philosophorum'* (ladder), uniting the virtues of heart and intellect, soul and mind, Sun and Moon-sulphur and mercury. Yet since nothing is truly supernatural in the sense that nothing exits outside Nature (except God, who remains a part of yet distant from creation), our mystical perception is based on the premise that we aspire towards God; our transmutation is therefore a deepening of cogitative illumination. In this way Robert Cochrane used invocations as protean catalysts, primed by the inherited wisdom of spiritual antecedents akin to Hebraic and Sufi traditions. (pupils and students within esoteric Mystery traditions 'inherit' their virtue as a spiritual legacy; remember, Joshua became the spiritual heir of Moses above his own sons, likewise, many Sufi masters, deed their Gnosis to an elected aspirant). Thus the circle (in this case, the ring of 36 months) is closed when the seven have become one!

Above all it must be understood that the manifest compass is but a reflection of its celestial counterpart. Each virtue, colour and deific force has its own reversed quality. But this is the true Mystery of the Absolute that cannot be explained or taught; only through full immersion and experience of its arcana will true Gnosis be achieved.

"The Faith is finally concerned with Truth, total Truth. It is one of the oldest of religions, and also one of the most potent, bringing as it does, Man into contact with Gods, and Man into contact with Self."

Robert Cochrane

Notes and References:

1. Valiente, D. 1989 '*The Rebirth of Witchcraft*' Phoenix Pub. Inc. USA p122
    (*Both John and Doreen made light of the grey magic expounded by Robert Cochrane concerning the actual significance of these numbers and their relation or relevance to others of note within the Clan.*)
2. Jones, E. J. 2001 '*The Roebuck in the Thicket*' [ed] M. Howard. Capall Bann UK pp68-85 (*These four Rites are discussed in greater depth within this book*)

Previously published in: *The Cauldron* #125 August 2007

24. What is an Initiation, really?

"Initiatory death is necessary for the beginning of spiritual life; it lays the foundation for rebirth to a higher level of being."
- Mircea Eliade.

The act of Initiation is an archaic and vital practice that has been much criticized and rarely understood, despite the resurgence and popularity of Craft and other magical fraternities in recent years. This essay seeks to present the reader with a summative view of its true purpose by some of its chief exponents, both ancient and modern, avoiding generalisations and devolutions into arguments both for and against it laboured elsewhere. It does not seek to argue reasons either way, for it is hoped the information herein may allow each individual to determine such causes and provide judgement on subjective merit accordingly and to their own satisfaction. Of course it is impossible to be objective about so deeply personal a matter, the higher self having accepted its true will in such an undertaking. Thereafter, the only obstacle that remains is the ego, the self, or mundane, lesser will. The raison d'être explicit throughout this exposition should ease the shift of this most problematic of impedances to individual spiritual growth and progression.

Contentious opinions assert that 'initiation' into Mithraic, Eleusinian, Osirian, Bacchanalian, Orphic, Craft, Lodge or Cuveen does not a priest, Witch nor magi make, and some would add that these things are ordained from a higher, less human force. This vocation, or calling comes from within, a deep recognition of spirit to spirit, of like to like.[1] We are often told that initiation 'instigates purpose, focus and direction' into 'spiritual awakening,' of 'expanding consciousnesses, or 'It opens the door.' Jargoness terms for what exactly? Of course the exoteric acceptance of the meaning of initiation is merely a rite of admission (into a group, lodge, cuveen etc), where we are offered a reciprocal relationship with our peers; conversely, the esoteric meaning implies a binding, a conforming to an awakened spiritual patterning. This now begins to sound more promising.

Jung believed that the need to join a secret society was merely an intermediate step along the path of individuation. Moreover, he suggested that becoming party to its secrets would eventually wean the individual once again onto the lonely road of Gnosis. Trust in the group is reciprocated by the confidence to paradoxically, ultimately reject that group in order to effect his/her individuation in the natural progression of spiritual evolution.[2] This solitary path is one that all aspirants eventually 'realise'. It is not enforced, nor imposed; it is never a lack of choice. Destiny must be embraced via interaction and mastery of one's own fate. The aspirant will only recognise the prize offered when individual will harmonizes with that of the Egregore. Patricia Crowther, well-known teacher and High Priestess of the Craft of G.B. Gardner teaches how *"a way will be shown, and knowledge imparted, yet the journey is always alone and the true will tested to the very brink of breaking point."*[3]

However, to pursue this further, we must first understand the general exoteric (mis)understanding, of 'initiation,' as admittance into a group. Irrespective of whatever form this takes (ranging from a simple introduction to a highly formalized induction ritual), it is in fact, in truly anthropological terms, a 'Rite of Passage'. This 'behavioural rite' acknowledges, welcomes and recognises a new member into an existing group, clan or societal form and may involve sacrifice, tests, ordeals, taboos and even the swearing of oaths (Oath: words expressed constitute a binding in law between all persons present, and witnessed by a *Divine* entity - ergo, a sacred act). Importantly, it must be stressed how such labours show allegiance to the other members of that group as do these initial oaths, and not to the Gods, spirits or deities who act as witnesses to that body of people. It is a commitment to the path of his/her initiator bound by the sacrament of the word, the law or covenant of that group. This announces to their spiritual ancestors, or inner-plane contacts the presence of a new member (as recognised by them) to be protected and guided by the Egregore (or group mind/spirit). Occurring at a conjunction of dream and reality, all former ties are normally severed, imparting emancipation from former allegiances where sought. Such abjurations allow the psyche unimpeded progress on their path.

In the Sangraal rites,[4] William Gray unequivocally affirms sacrifice as an integral and esoteric part of any true initiation - that of the self, given to man and God in abject humility. Followed by a 'Grail' sacrament, a myth enactment of association to the Fisher-King, a blood kinship is evoked, forging a sacred and inviolate bond of service. This covenanted rite requires consumption of bodily fluids as a shared life-force, a pre-requisite for attainment into the 'Mysteries.' This parallels completely the *'bloedisan,'* the old English blessing, a consecration with blood offered in sacrifice. Flesh is the body, offered as an agent for the Divine, a genesis of a higher undertaking. Although both are indisputably sacred and covenanted acts, they do not involve the mechanics of transmission or individuation therefore should not be classed as 'initiatory' rites in the strictest sense. They may be performed as a prelude or even post ritual as *'agapae.'* On their own, these acts do not properly induce 'initiation'!

Looking at the Sanskrit word for initiation - *'dīkṣa,'* which translates as transmission, it describes a link to the greater and purifying process, a combination of the light of spiritual Gnosis and purification. Now it becomes apparent that true initiation engenders something else altogether. Mantras and other magical techniques expand conceptual cognition, increasing sensitivity and awareness of our 'sixth sense'. Acting as a mental 'douche' that aggressively forces mental impurities to the surfaces, in order to effectively purge and disseminate them. Then, under instruction and guidance from both physical and spiritual teachers (assigned during the Induction processes), the 'self' is carefully attuned towards individuation. The culmination of this long and arduous process is the 'initiation 'proper.' Transmission requires both giver and receiver; this invalidates the anachronistic term -'self-initiation'. Vivienne Crowley in accord with this view expresses it more properly as self-dedication.[5] Oneiric transmission is possible, though genuine cases are exceptional and exceedingly rare. Similarly, within certain organizations, 'grades' awarded infer recognition of hierarchy and/or rational categorization of process of technical development and can in no way reflect personal and spiritual maturation nor experience of Gnosis. These further inductions should not be perceived as 'initiations'.

An excellent explanation of the intrinsic meaning of the term 'esoteric' is -'hidden, sacred doctrine of teaching'. Referring to the Mystery Traditions of Pythagoras it also means - 'an initiated disciple', viz, by the mind! This is significantly different from 'occult', which is given as - 'more than hidden, beyond the range of ordinary knowledge, and symbolism not understood by the conscious mind.'[6] These terms are applied to aspects where interaction with 'mysterious' forces of Nature is achieved through imparted or inspired knowledge. Looking deeper into this, we discover the Greek term - *'Mysteria,'* (the root of Mystery) actually translates as 'initiation'! Thus are we introduced by a master, leader, or teacher into the

Mysteries, through the actual 'initiatory' rites of specific deific powers (relevant and pertinent to that group). Mircea Eliade[7] proposed that initiation was an existential key that 'opens' the way.

Confusion regarding appropriate comprehensions may arise when we realise that some induction rites do enjoin active invocations to spirit upon the neophyte. Further investigation reveals these examples to express a supreme lack of subtlety on the part of the officiating 'priest' who in his/her zeal to pass on the 'keys' feels inclined to 'overload' their neophyte. This is not common, but does display a lack of understanding with regard to what a 'true' initiation should entail. What should be 'passed' between them at this stage is not a psychic haemorrhage, but the right of access to ancestral memory, lineage, egregore etc. That is not to preclude experiential or emotive response, but to elucidate a distinction between it and a true initiation, which is the eventual confluence of the student's faith and a teacher's grace within the primacy of the Divine. It is a specific term for a specific act, often confused in common parlance, resulting in its erroneous misuse.

The oneiric world of occultism does of course exist in a parallel realm where proofs of myth and magic remain adjunct to science. Poets, seers, artists and philosophers, driven by their muses all traverse these dark planes in search of the light of Truth, of illumination. Often symbolic, it is revealed most often by analogy - inspired tuition fords the state of knowing with that of the unknown. Our cultural legacies are often initiatory in the sense that they are transposed in traditions, dispersed within attendant Mythos', whose commonalities of core philosophies reserve a cultic elitism not prevalent within more societal fraternities such as the Freemasons and the Rosicrucians. Initiation is then the experience as spirit of entry into the invisible, the noumenal, free of matter; the deathless state of ultimate Gnosis, of apprehension of the Divine, both immanent and transcendent; the source of all being is identified, into which we are assimilated.

Our yearning passion for such a union must be tempered first by the purification of all possessive, negative traits that subvert True Will into acts of selfish goal centred actions. Each individual must be whole and healed in order to undertake his/her journey into the Mysteries. This process begins with Introduction, then Induction into a group, cult, cuveen etc, where training and instruction lead the aspirant towards their own realisation, their own conclusion - The revelation of the 'Mystery' itself, where they finally experience their true 'Initiation'. Such illumination is not an intellectual exercise and is a completely individual sanctification, a reification of the 'self', offered in true sacrifice to the greater being. Alchemically, the dross of the soul has become the gold of spirit. Initiation is an individualistic form of existentionalism, in which Gnosticism is its collective manifestation. However, it is curious here to note how the Gnostic wishes to become the 'son of God'; the mystic remains one of a group within a community of believers and the alchemist wishes to become the 'son of his own work'![8]

Goethe perceived this as 'becoming of oneself', in the true Gnostic sense of 'knowing thyself and being thus blessed' viz, a beatific state of Gnosis. This first stage of self-knowledge evinces a panentheistic awareness, of man the micro unit in the macrocosmic form of being. Reborn anew, each aspirant is baptised in the light of such Gnosis, forming the prism of ascent, his *'Scala Philosophorum.'* What it does not and cannot do is confer extraordinary powers. Never-the-less, cerebral stimulation, generated by this catalyst increases cogitative and cognitive faculties that manifest as a syncopated resonance with the inner harmonic of a Hermetic Universe. Understanding this Mystery becomes the burning quest of Truth. Each aspirant momentarily returns to the moment of conception in order to re-align their fate in accord with his/her chosen destiny; regression to this point removes the spiritual errors, committed in ignorance, accrued up to that point. Henceforth, absolute responsibility is born singularly by that re-aligned soul, for its redemption and salvation.

Initiation elevates the aspirant to the liminal horizon of ingress/egress between micro/macro cosmic realms where they learn to function in both planes simultaneously, yet belonging in neither. They are the 'leapers between', existing in the shadows, perched between repose and action. From this point of equilibrium, the initiate may choose at will to enter each realm. Ritual *'modus operandi'* are tools that take one outwards and upwards; fornication and feasting bring one back down and in. Sexual forms of Tantra for blissful sublimation are exogenous to this discourse and will therefore remain extraneous to it. Such increased sensitivity to the noetic world induces empathic trance states, whose complete mastery inculcates absorption of information synergistically from both realms.

Between Introduction and Induction there may pass a period of Time normatively set at one year, but which may arbitrarily be longer and is commonly offered to suitable candidates. Between Induction and Initiation, many, many years may pass before the aspirant has acquired the necessary proficiency to accede such a transition and by contrast, should be asked for when the aspirant feels 'ready'. From within the Jungian embryonic state, one faces down one's daemons (the spirits within that reside in the dark shades of our inner being), to experience the disintegration of despair, to emerge, chrysalis-like, an individuated, holistic being. Magically, it is the putrefaction and corruption of dark matter, its sloughing off, that allows the body to receive the ultimate light body, an epiphanic revelation of self, aligned to the primal still-point of creation of pure existence wherein the mystic achieves apotheosis - at:one:ment. It is a physical, emotional and spiritual commitment signalling new life, of renewed hope after the symbolic death of the soul that rises invigorated and empowered, purposeful on its singular path. Theatrical simulation of death allows the aspirant to participate in their own drama, the penultimate step in the realisation of their own true destiny, leaving the hungry soul forever smitten for the final, ultimate union wherein death stalks it as a lover, or a hunter its prey. Primarily, initiation opens the heart to the passion of the soul.

Initiation is actualised via symbolic elements and ritual dynamics that exert alchemical processing of the aspirant through four psychophysical elements; these manifest as kinaesthetic sensations, ranging from: nausea (water); anguish (air); inspiration (fire), and imbalance (Earth), after which the body experiences a rush of sheer exhilaration.[9] The impressionable psyche has been actively manipulated into a mythological reality culminating in one existential moment of exultation. Occultism propounds the principle of self-revelation via transcendence, a state of grace conferred by sacred acts within initiatory rites that must remain secret in order to preserve the Hermetic principles of virtue axiomatic to it. Secrecy is therefore incumbent upon the aspirant as an act of self-discipline, obedience (to the higher-self), fealty (to his/her teacher/master), honour and the preservation of the 'Mysteria' itself. About the aspirant, this secret becomes a shield against outer forces of corruption, a sentient force that separates and protects him/her from profane influence. Withdrawal from the outer societal mores induces self-reliance and spiritual integrity.

Regarding the meaning of the word - 'sacred,' again it must be stressed as entirely distinct from religious connotations, which is only a mere humanistic corruption of the true sanctity of its actuality. Sacred, represents a pure stasis of Divine manifestation, of blessed completeness, of total unity, a harmony, of utter equilibrium in 'Maat'. An initiation takes the religious virtue (of the aspirant) and transmutes it into the sacred (the aspirant's realisation or atonement).[10] As realised individual seeds of divinity, the nurture of our growth will determine the fruition of labour.

An initiate is the repository of the sacred flame, lighting the way down the chain of being to the eternal present, lifted from our singular bi-polar axial root into the immortal flux, the supernal collective.

The body of the initiate (perceived as the Father), houses the descent and union of the spirit (the son) into the seeking soul (Shekinah/world soul) of the aspirant. It becomes the altar, the sacrificial place of assimilation and transformation. Jung expressed these three as the shadow, the anima/animus and the wise old man/woman.[11] Absolutely nothing else can be substituted for this sublime act. One undergoes this extreme rite or one does not. Unlike rites of introduction and induction this rite is not compulsory. One can remain upon a path, within a group, cuveen or lodge and never aspire to this level. Furthermore, when one does, the sacraments of Baptism and the Eucharist are finally confirmed. From the Latin - sacramentum, meaning oath, an act of appeal to a Divine witness, the sacraments are defined as an outward sign of grace, derived from Covenanted rituals. A 'Covenant' is an agreed exchange that confers a sense of belonging, a binding, a mutual magical relationship that is as eternal as it is supernal.

Covenants assign people to specific deities, to Tutelary God forms, named and personal to the group/cuveen/lodge etc to which one is inducted whose name may even be presented as a password into that Clan/Tradition, or Magical Lodge. Invocation of this name during a Covenanted ritual gives access to its power. This is an archaic practise originating in a Time when the Gods were thought to have conferred their power directly to mankind. Sacraments are therefore Covenanted actions, invoking this ancient premise. Tradition must retain its causal purpose in step with evolutionary Gnosis; ignorance of this stifles ascent wherein the bonds of stagnation perpetuate the suffocating pressure of outmoded doctrine. Analogy must remain adjunct to context, failure to be relative leaves the traveller stranded in a stark landscape, unfulfilled and alienated.

There is nothing more profound or deeply mystical than the acceptance of spirit, the lifting of the veil that shrouds the conscious homeostasis - the sentience that simply is. Thus the eye of the beholder is illuminated into a baptism of light; the beloved becomes the lover, a guide to the ultimate reality of true existence. A true initiation comprises of at least two active parts and a third of repose. The first of Earth and water (female qualities, i.e. birthing and baptism) relates to the psychic descent of the soul: the transformation - kenoma; the second of air and fire (male qualities of spirit and vigour) relates to the pneumatic ascent of spirit: the transcendence - pleroma. Pneumatic initiation inculcates the understanding of our true self as surviving the process of disintegration of the illusory physical body. The third and final part, of repose, is the passive acceptance of this Truth, and the acquisition of all Gnosis from within the Divine androgyne.

Thus the purpose of initiation is to propel the psyche into the experiential and numinous world of pneuma to achieve a realisation of divinity. Maturation engenders comprehension beyond universal archetypes, of cultural images in sublime context and the apprehension of the synchronicities of kairos (perfect or Divine Time). Initiation is a catalyst for the comprehension of True Will, which is no less than Divine will. Through initiation we understand our true (Divine) Nature, negating all conflict between ego and superego. Thereafter, all acts of magic become an act of will, specifically of true will. Complete surrender evokes complete absorption of the lesser will, allowing us to act freely and spontaneously without fear of confliction. Gnosis is not a rejection of the world but an awareness of the dual gifts of our humanity and divinity, their harmony and symbiosis. Successful symbience is reliant upon this premise. Complete detachment defeats the purpose of life and the enlightening principle of Luciferian evolution.

Notes and references:

1. Andre Nataf [ed]. 1994 *Wordsworth Dictionary of the Occult* Herts. UK. p1
2 . ditto, p17
3. ditto, p 37
4. ditto, p45
5. ditto, p80
6. ditto, p210
7. Patricia Crowther 1992 *Lid off the Cauldron* Weiser. USA. p36
8. S&J Farrar 1984 *The Witches Bible* Magical Childe. USA. p9
9. Vivienne Crowley 1996 *Wicca* G.B. Thorsons. UK. p92
10. ditto, p224
11. William G. Gray 1986 *Sangraal Rites and Ceremonies* Vol.4 Weiser. USA.

My sincere and especial thanks to Aneta, whose consultation provided confirmation and support of many of my own views expressed herein.

Previously published in: *The Hedgewytch* #37 February 2007

Bibliography

Alexander. M, 2002 *'A Companion to the Folklore, Myths and Customs of Britain'* Sutton Pub. UK

Allegro. J. M, 1970 *'The Sacred Mushroom and the Cross'* Hodder & Stoughton London

Ann. M. & Myers-Imel. D. 1993 *'Goddesses in World Mythology'* Oxford Uni. Press

Baring-Gould Sabine, 2005 *'Curious myths of the Middle Ages'* Dover Pub. USA

Basford, K. 1998 *'The Green Man'* G.B. Whitstable Litho Printers Ltd.

Bayley. Harold, 2006 *'The Lost Language of Symbolism'* Dover Pub. USA

Bisson. L. M, 1999 *'Chaucer and the Late Medieval World.'* N.Y., Macmillan Press.

Black. J. & Green. A, 2003 *'Gods, Demons and Symbols of Ancient Mesopotamia'* British Museum Press. London.

Boase. R, 1977 *'The Origin and Meaning of Courtly Love.'* Manchester Uni Press. Manchester

Branston. B, 1974 *'The Lost Gods of England'* BCA London

Brien. O, C, & B, J. *'The Shining Ones'* Dianthus Pub Ltd. UK

Burnley. D, 1998 *'Courtliness in Medieval Literature.'* Longman Press. England

Burrow. J. A. & Turville-Petre. T, [Ed] 1996 *'A Book of Middle English.'* England, Blackwell Pub.

Burne. Charlotte, S, 1996 *'The Handbook of Folklore'* Senate UK

Campbell. Joseph, 1973 *'Hero with a 1000 Faces.'* Princeton Uni. Press.

Campbell. J, 1991 *'Masks of God - Creative Mythology'* Arkana Books. U.S.A.

Campbell. J, 1991. *'Masks of God: Occidental Mythology'* Arkana Books. USA.

Campbell. Joseph, 1991 *'Creative Mythology: Masks of God'* Arkana Books. N. Y.

Cass. E. & Roud. S, 2002 *'An Intro to the English Mummers Play'* English Folklore Society. UK

Cirlot. J.E, 1983 *'A Dictionary of Symbols'* Routledge & Kegan Paul. London

Cooper. J.C, [Ed] 1998. *'An Illustrated Encyl. of Traditional Symbols'* Thames & Hudson. London

Crowley. Vivienne, 1996 *'Wicca'* G.B. Thorsons. UK.

Crowther. Patricia, 1992 *'Lid off the Cauldron'* Weiser. USA.

Denomy. A. J, 1947 *'The Heresy of Courtly Love.'* U.S.A. The Declan & McMullen Com. Inc.

Doel. Geof & Fran, 1992 *'Mumming, Howling and Hoodening: Midwinter Rituals in Sussex, Kent and Surrey'* Headly Bros Ltd. Kent. UK

Duncan. T.G, [Ed] 1995 *'Medieval English Lyrics 1200-1400.'* Penguin Books Ltd. London

Farrar. Stuart & Janet 1984 *'The Witches Bible'* Magical Childe. USA.

Frawley. Dr. David, 1997 *'Tantric Yoga and the Wisdom Goddesses'* Motilal Banarsidass Pub. Delhi

Ferrante. J, 1975 *'Woman as Image in Medieval Literature.'* Columbia Press. U.S.A.

Freke. T & Gandy. P, 2001 *'Jesus and the Goddess.'* Thorsons. Great Britain

Gardner. G.B, 2004 *'The Meaning of Witchcraft'.* Weiser Books. New York

Gardner. L, 2000 *'Genesis of the Grail Kings'* Bantam Books GB

George. D, 1992 *'Mysteries of the Dark Moon'* 1992 Harper Collins. NY

Grant. K, 1996 *'Nightside of Eden'* Skoob Pub. London

Grant. S. & Kay. S, [Ed] 1999 *'The Troubadours.'* Cambridge Uni Press. Cambridge

Gray. William G, 1986 *'Sangraal Rites and Ceremonies'* Vol.4 Weiser. USA

Graves. Robert, 1999 [Ed] Grevel Lindop *'The White Goddess'* Carcanet Press. Manchester

Green. Miranda J, 1986 *'Gods of the Celts'* Sutton Pub. GB.

Green. Miranda J, 1992 *'Dictionary of Celtic Myth and Legend'* Thames and Hudson. London

Harte. Jeremy, 2004 *'Explore Fairy Traditions'* Heart of Albion Press. England

Heer. F, 1993 *'The Medieval World: Europe 1100-1350.'* Butler & Tanner Ltd Federation Press. G.B.

Hole. Christina, 1976 *'British Folk Customs'* 1976. Hutchinson & Co. Pub. Ltd. UK

Hope-Robins, Russell 1964 'Encyclopaedia of Witchcraft and Daemonology' Peter Neville London

Hutton, Prof. R, 1996 *'Stations of the Sun'* Ox. Uni. Press. Oxford

Hutton. Prof. R, 1997 *'Pagan Religions of the Ancient British Isles'* Blackwell. Oxford

Hutton. Prof. R, 1999 *'Triumph of the Moon'* Ox. Uni Press. Oxford

Jackson. N, 1994 *'The Horned Piper'* Capall Bann Pub. Berks.

Jackson. N, 1996 *'Masks of Misrule'* Capall Bann Pub. Berks

Jansen. E.R, 2004 *'The Book of Hindu Imagery'* Netherlands. Binkey Kok Publications.

Jones. B, Trans. 1964 *'Sir Gawain and the Green Knight'* U.K. Hazell, Watson & Viney Ltd.

Jones. Evan John, & Clifton. Chas 1997 *'Sacred Mask Sacred Dance'* Llewellyn. USA.

Jones. E, J, & Valiente. D, 1999 *'Witchcraft, A Tradition Renewed'* Robert Hale. USA

Jones. E, J, & Howard. M, 2002 *'The Robert Cochrane Letters'* Capall Bann. UK

Jones. E, J, & Howard. M, [Ed] 2001 *'Roebuck in the Thicket'* Capall Bann UK

Jones. Prudence, 1988 *'The Path to the Centre'* Wiccan Pub. Pagan Fed. London

Kieckhefer. Richard, 2000 *'Magic in the Middle Ages.'* Cambridge Uni. Press. UK

Leland. C. G, 1892 *'Etruscan Roman Remains in Popular Tradition'* T. Fisher Unwin. London

Levy. G.R, 1948 *'The Gate of Horn'* Faber & Faber Ltd. London

Lewis. C.S, 1979 *'The Allegory of Love: A Study in Medieval Tradition.'* Oxford Uni. Press. Oxford

Liddell. W, E, & [Ed] Howard M. 1994 *'The Pickingill Papers'* Capall Bann. UK

MacGregor Mathers. S. L, Trans. 1997 *'Goetia - Lesser Key of Solomon'* Maine. Samuel Weiser

Matthews. John, 1989 *'The Arthurian Tradition'* Element Books. GB

Matthews. J, 1993 *'The Arthurian Tradition'* Element Books. GB

Matthews. J, & C, 1995 *'British and Irish Mythology'* Aquarian Press. GB

Mathews. C, 1995 *'The Celtic Tradition'* Element Books. Dorset

Matthews. C & J, 1995 *'Encyclopaedia of British and Irish Legends'* Diamond Books Ltd. London.

Matthews. J, 1996 *'The Grail Tradition'* Element Books. GB

Morgan. A, 1995 *'Toads and Toadstools'* Celestial Arts. Berkley, California.

Narby. J, 1999 *'The Cosmic Serpent'* Phoenix Pub. London

Mckenna. T, 1993 *'Food of the Gods'* Bantam Books U.S.A.

Graves. R & Patai. R, 1964 *'Hebrew Myths: Book of Genesis'* Cassel & Co. London

Munn. H, 1973 *'Mushrooms of Language'* Ox. Uni. Press. Oxford

Taylor. N, 1966 *'Narcotics: Nature's Dangerous Gift'* Dell publishing. U.S.A.

Miller. Mary & Taube. Karl, 1993 *'The Gods and Symbols of Ancient Mexico and The Maya'* Thames & Hudson, London.

Nataf [Ed]. 1994 *'Wordsworth Dictionary of the Occult'* Herts. UK

Newman. F, [Ed] 1968 *'The Meaning of Courtly Love.'* N.Y. Press. Albany

Nicholson. Irene, 1967 *'Mexican and Central American Mythology'* Newness Book, Yugoslavia.

Olfield-Harvey. M, 2002 *'The Horse in Myth and Legend'* Dover Pub. New York

Pagels. E, 1989 *'Adam, Eve and the Serpent'* Ist Vintage Books. U.S.A.

Palmer. Roy, 1995 *'Britain's Living Folklore'* Llanerch Pub. UK

Peter. Thurstan, 1997 *'The Cornish Obby Oss'* Oakmagic Pub. UK

Picknett. L & Prince. C, 1998 *'The Templar Revelation'* Corgi Books GB

Pinch. Geraldine, 1994 *'Magic in Ancient Egypt'* British Museum Press. London

Porteous. Alexander, 1996 *'The Lore of the Forest'* Senate Books. London

Redgrove. P, 1989 *'The Black Goddess and the Sixth Sense'* Palladin. London

Regardie. Israel, 1970 *'The Garden of Pomegranates'* Llewellyn Pub.USA

Rolleston. T.W, 1994 *'Celtic Myths and Legends'* Senate Books. London

Roob. Alexander, 1997 *'Alchemy & Mysticism'* Taschen. Italy

Ross. Anne 1974 *'Pagan Celtic Britain'* Sphere Books Ltd. London

Rudgley. R, 1999 *'Enc. of Psychoactive Substances'* Abacus. G.B.

Scott. G.R, 1996 *'Phallic Worship: A History of Sex and Sexual Rites.* Senate London

Seligman. K, 1997 *'The History of Magic'* Pantheon Books. NY

Shepherd. Odell, 1996 *'The Lore of the Unicorn'* Senate Books. London

Shipman. E.R, 1996 *'A History of Abbots Bromley'* Benhill Press Ltd. GB.

Valiente. D, 1984 *'ABC of Witchcraft'* Robert Hale London

Valiente. D, 1989 *'The Rebirth of Witchcraft'* Robert Hale London

Walker. B.G, 1983. *'The Woman's Encyl. of Myths and Secrets.'* Harper & Row Pub. San Francisco

Wallis-Budge. E.A, 1971 *'Egyptian Magic'* Dover Publications. NY

Warner. M, 2000 *'Alone of Her Sex; The Myth & Cult of The Virgin Mary.'* Vintage Press. GB.

Watterson. B, 1999 *'Gods of Ancient Egypt'* Bramley Books. Surrey

Wehr. G, 1990 *'The Mystical Marriage'* Aquarian Press. UK

Weston. J, 1997 *'From Ritual to Romance'* Dover Pub.Inc. US

Westwood. Jennifer, 1985 *'Albion, A Guide to Legendary Britain'* Book Club Ass. GB

Westwood. J, 1986 *'Albion: A Guide to Legendary Britain'* BCA. London

Westwood. J & Simpson. J, 2005 *'The Lore of the Land'* Penguin Books. England

Williamson. John, 1986 *'The Oak King, the Holly King and the Unicorn.'* Harper Row Pub. NY

Articles and Magazines:

Macculloch. Canon J. A, 1921 *'The Mingling of Fairy and Witch Beliefs in the 16th and 17th century Scotland'* Folklore, vol. xxxii [December - Folklore Society]

Oates. Shani, 2005 'Summer and Winter Solstice Customs' *The Wytches' Standard* #2 Summer Solstice 2005

Blackman. James, 2003 'Halloween Raises its Ugly Head.' *Oaxaca Times.* Oaxaca. October Issue no. 157.

Hutchinson. Alice, 2003 'Dead Heads.' *Oaxaca Times.* Oaxaca. October Issue no. 157.

Martinez. Carlos, 2003 *'Cloaked Lady Death'* Oaxaca Times. Oaxaca. October Issue no. 157.

Purnell. B. B, 1970 *'Man, Myth and Magic'* [vol.1.] Marshall-Cavendish. New York

Websites:

www.azcentral.com

www.peoplesguidetomexico.com

www.salon.com/news/feature/1999/09/03/columbine/index.html

http://www.hinduism.co.za/kaabaa.html

www.hecate.org.uk/history.html

www.inanna.virtualave.net/hekate.html

www.islandnet.com/~hornowl/library/Hekate.html

www.theoi.com/Protogenos/Tartaros.html

www.gnosis.org/naghamm/trimorph.html

http://www.bandia.net/sheela/SheelaFront.html

http://en.wikipedia.org/wiki/Sheela_na_Gig

http://www.whitedragon.org.uk/articles/sheela.htm

www.home.earthlink.net/~wodensharrow/yule.html

www.vinland.org/heathen/mt/wildhunt.html

www.members.tripod.com/GeoffBoxell/hunt.html

www.uidaho.edu/student_orgs/arthurian_legend/hunt/ragnall.html

www.spritpassages.com

www.wikipedia.org/wiki/viridios

www.ancientworlds.net/aw/Post/171007

www.absoluteastronomy.com

www.ancientworlds.net

www.avatarmeherbaba.org/erics/glossh-j-html

www.biblicalholidays.com/shavuot.htm_&

www.biblicalholidays.com/pentecost.htm

www.absoluteastronomy.com/encyclopaedia/f/fa/fata_morgana.htm

www.mysticalplanet.com/lib/pentagram.html_&

www.absoluteastronomy.com/encylopedia/p/pe/pentagram.htm

http://www.univie.ac.at/cga/art/religion

www.irelandsown.net/crane.html

www.theoi.com/titan/titanisthemis.html

www.clannada.org/culture_crane.php

www.univie.ac.at/cga/art/religion.html

www.khandro.net/animal_birds.html

www.arthistory.sbc.edu/imageswomen/papers/kottkegorgon/gorgons.html

www.rc.um.edu/editions/shelly/medusa/mcgann.html

www.erowid.org

www.swastika.com

www.cnw.com/~neruo/gaz

www.mushroommythology

Index

Pan's Daughter - the magical world of Rosaleen Norton by Nevill Drury

£8.99/$14.99, ISBN 978-1-869928-31-8 pbk, 168pp, 48 illustrations

'...an extremely important document detailing the public and private prices this courageous unsung woman-hero paid for unapologetically 'dealing with life on other planes of being.' E.I.D.O.S.

Ithell Colquhoun :
pioneer surrealist artist, occultist, writer, and poet by Eric Ratcliffe

£19.99/$40 ISBN 978-1869928-98-8 - 314pp - 90 ills (25 in colour)

The skills of Ithell Colquhoun in her main practice, that of artist and pioneer in this country of surrealistic art, have been long recognised. Additionally, other interests - alchemy, Earth-magic, active occultism, poetry, druidism, the pre-Christian Pagan calendar, the history and membership of the Golden Dawn - and writing of and involvement in these interests by book publication and in a widely scattered field of correspondence, have created a miscellany of truly gargantuan proportion. Eric Ratcliffe considered it was time to get together some of these pieces, to add something of what is known of Colquhoun's early life and family history and to take the opportunity of listing a comprehensive calendar of her work and exhibitions. The result is neither strictly biographical nor a treatise on any one subject, but it is a first gathering of the roots, passions and multi-directions of this artist.

The Journal for the Academic Study of Magic (JSM)

A multidisciplinary, peer-reviewed print publication, covering all areas of magic, witchcraft, paganism etc; geographical regions and historical periods.]

ISBN 9781906958015, £19.99/$40, 320pp

Flavius Josephus' Terminology of Magic: accommodating Jewish Magic to a Roman Audience: Philip Jewell / The Role of Grimoires in the Conjure Tradition; Dan Harms /Hermetic/Cabalistic Ritual in Christopher Marlowe's Doctor Faustus ; Dana Winters / Italian Cunning Craft: Some Preliminary Observations ; Sabina Magliocco / Walking The Tightrope: A Study Of Secret Astrologers In Mainstream Professions ; J.A. Silver Frost B.A., M.A., Solicitor. / Martyrs, Magic, and Christian Conversion ; Patrick Maille /"Worshiping the Devil in the Name of God"Anti-Semitism, Theosophy and Christianity in the Occult Doctrines of Pekka Siitoin ; Kennet Granholm / "The Witching Hour: Sex Magic in 1950s Australia" ; Marguerite Johnson / Reviews / Obituaries

Order direct from
Mandrake of Oxford
PO Box 250, Oxford, OX1 1AP (UK)
Phone: 01865 243671
(for credit card sales)
Prices include economy postage
online at - www.mandrake.uk.net
Email: mandrake@mandrake.uk.net

Lightning Source UK Ltd.
Milton Keynes UK
21 April 2010

9 781906 958077

Frontispiece 'Lux Mundi' - © Liza Miskievicz